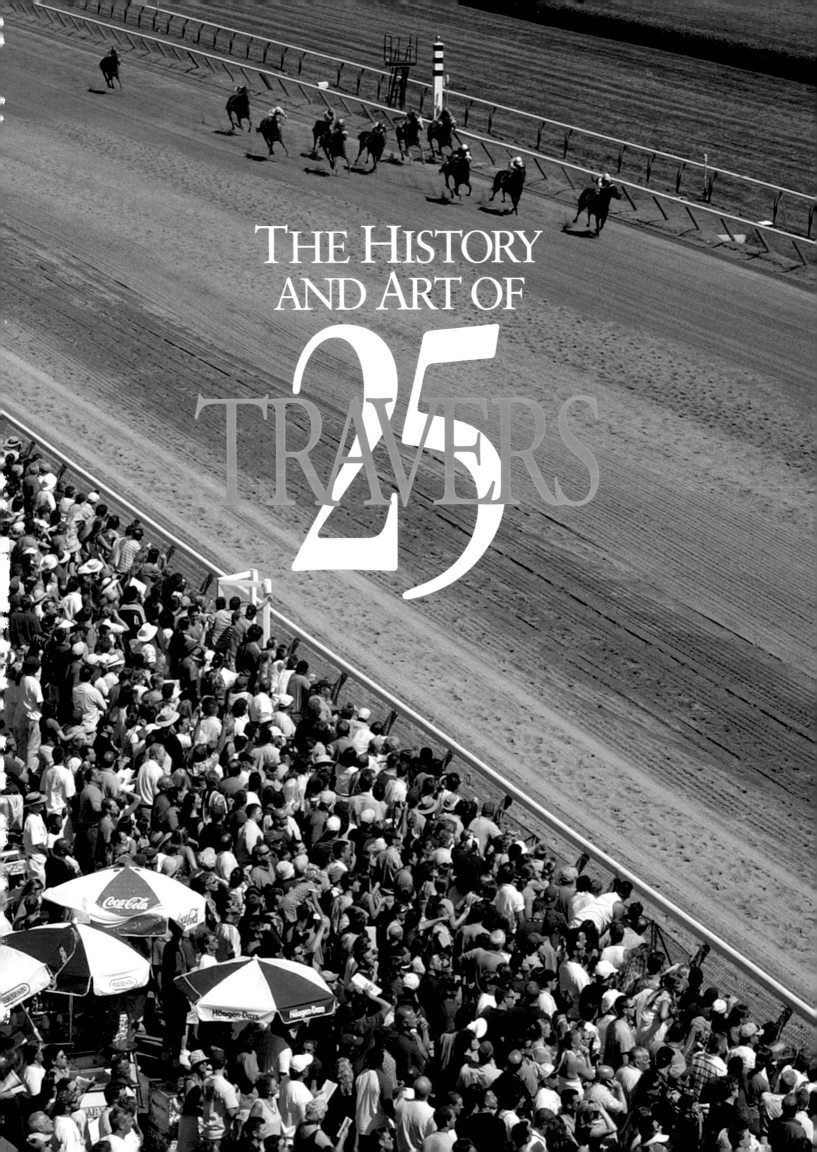

THE HISTORY
AND ART OF
TRAVERS

Design: Nancy Did It! Blossvale, NY 13308

Printed in USA: Brodock Press, 502 Court Street, Utica, NY 13502
                   800-765-3536 • www.brodock.com

BRODOCK

Published by North Country Books, Inc.
220 Lafayette Street • Utica, NY 13502
(315) 735-4877 • Orders: (800) 342-7409
www.northcountrybooks.com

Library of Congress Cataloging-in-Publication Data

Zast, Vic.
 The history and art of 25 Travers / text by Vic Zast ; artwork by Greg
Montgomery.
    p. cm.
 ISBN 978-1-59531-023-1 (alk. paper)
 1. Travers Stakes (Race)--History. 2. Horse racing--New York
(State)--Saratoga Springs--History. 3. Travers States (Race)--Posters. 4.
Horse racing--New York (State)--Saratoga Springs--Posters. I. Title.
 SF335.U6N699 2008
 798.4009747'48--dc22
                        2008011689

Opposite: **A warming sun lights the dawn like a globe and takes the chill off the early morning, as a runner is escorted to the Oklahoma training track adjacent to the Saratoga Race Course.** Albany (NY) *Times Union* photograph by Skip Dickstein

DEDICATIONS

FROM VIC ZAST

*To my horsewidow wife, Maureen, and our horseplayer children—
Jon the handicapper, Annie the longshot player, and Biz the hard luck kid.
So glad to have you along for the ride.*

FROM GREG MONTGOMERY

*To Eileen Donovan, the mother of my children Andrew,
Ian, and Katharine. Without her encouragement and steadfast
support there would not be a series of posters.*

*To Paula Rosenberg, my business partner
and muse. No advocate was ever more vigilant,
courageous, or intuitively creative than she.*

Opposite: **Hot walker Paul Rutherford and Street Sense enjoy some down time after the horse's final speed work at Saratoga Race Course before the 2007 Travers Stakes.** Albany (NY) *Times Union* photograph by Skip Dickstein

CONTENTS

By Carl Nafzger

Top: **Trainer Carl Nafzger, smiling pretty, after Street Sense held off Grasshopper at the wire to win the 2007 Travers Stakes at Saratoga.** Photo by Vic Zast

Bottom: **The cowboy from Texas aboard a Brahma Bull at the 1964 Cheyenne, Wyoming Frontier Days.** Photograph from Carl Nafzger's personal collection

Opposite: **Street Sense is a magnificent ambassador for all the victorious horses of the Midsummer Derby—the Travers Stakes. The spark in the eye, the alert ears ready for the bell, the powerful muscles that twitch, then explode, are characteristics common of each previous winner.** Albany (NY) *Times Union* photo by Skip Dickstein

After Street Sense lost in the Preakness, I decided that we would set our sights on Saratoga and point to the Travers Stakes. It was early June when Jim Tafel and I knew where we wanted to be come August.

Mr. Tafel wanted to win the Triple Crown badly, but once his colt got beat in Baltimore, we were convinced that the Travers Stakes, not the Belmont Stakes, would be a better route to the Breeders' Cup Classic, our ultimate goal.

I'm sure that if Street Sense hadn't lost by a head to Curlin, we'd have run in the Belmont. But as it turned out, we did pretty well with the route that we followed.

Tradition is the key to being remembered in racing, and when it comes to history, Saratoga is an incomparable place, and the Travers is one of the top races in the world.

Through the years, I have had tremendous success running horses in the Travers. With Street Sense, my record is two wins from five starters. That's in comparison to the Kentucky Derby with two winners from three starters. Thirty-five years as a trainer and only eight starters shows how difficult it is to train a thoroughbred that meets the criteria to perform and win these two races while maintaining a win percentage worthy of them.

Street Sense was the first Kentucky Derby winner to win the Travers in a dozen years. The Kentucky Derby, of course, is the one race that everyone knows about. When you're a horse trainer and you meet someone new, he always asks if you've won the Derby. That's just the way it is—it's the one race that everyone follows and watches.

The Derby has gotten this way because it's been promoted as a great event—and it is. The Travers, on the other hand, is one of the most important races of the summer because great horses have won it.

Outside of Saratoga, I don't think that anyone you meet for the first time will ask you if you've won the Travers. But that doesn't mean it isn't the summertime Derby to me. For people who know racing, the Travers is a very significant race.

I came to training horses later in my life than other trainers. Remember, I was a professional cowboy. Then I realized that age was a detriment to a bull riding athlete. I was ranked third in the world in 1963 and qualified from 1963 to 1965 for the National Rodeo Finals. It was 1968 when I took out my first thoroughbred-quarter horse trainer's license.

That was the same year I married Wanda. Together, Wanda and I began in the thoroughbred business when I went to work breaking and training for Polo Ranch in Cheyenne, Wyoming.

Wanda, my family, and I bought the first horses we raced ourselves at the Keeneland September Sales in 1970. We did all the work that the horses required—grooming, exercising, and shoeing them. I guess you could say that it was the love of the horse that made us who we are today.

I first heard of the Travers in the late 1970s, when I was still very new to the sport. But it was always a race that made a lot of sense to me. It gave everyone time to develop a horse as a three-year-old. It is a great back-up for the Kentucky Derby, because by the time that the Travers comes around, the three-year-olds are no longer boys—they've grown up to be men.

To win the Travers, you have to have a horse that has matured mentally and physically and has proven his ability to get the distance. By 1981, I had my first Travers starter—Fairway Phantom. That summer was my first trip to Saratoga.

Over the years, I started four more horses in the Travers, each with what I

thought had a good chance. Besides Fairway Phantom, my Travers starters were Par Flight (1984), Hold Old Blue (1992), Unshaded (2000), and Street Sense (2007). I won with Unshaded and Street Sense. There was no horse that I was more sure could win than Street Sense.

It was fun being at the barn with the Travers favorite, talking to writers and photographers every morning. Believe me, the pressure to win and the attention you get with the favorite is nothing compared to the backstretch of Churchill Downs during the week before the Derby. The only time I don't like the press is when they're not there on Sunday morning.

Street Sense was an exceptional horse and had won the Jim Dandy in such a way that I was sure he'd get better from it. When he crossed that Travers finish line, Mr. Tafel shook my hand, and I realized then that we had been together a long time and had enjoyed some extraordinary moments.

Standing in the winner's circle, I said "thank you" to the fans of New York. We had a wonderful time in Saratoga that summer. It's a shame that more people don't think of the Travers the same way they think of the Derby. Maybe it's because the race is in New York and the people there take what they have in stride.

"How good are you?" is the question that's answered when you win at Saratoga. It's the greatest race meet going. Saratoga is one of those places you don't go to just to be seen. When you win at Saratoga, it's the most unbelievable feeling in the world, because you've beaten the best trainers, the greatest jockeys, the fastest horses that come from all over—from New York, Kentucky, the Midwest, Florida, California, and Maryland.

Maybe a book like this will give the Travers some promotion that will make it an international event. I want everyone to know about the Travers the way I do. And when I get my next Kentucky Derby winner, I'll try to bring him back to Saratoga.

Nafzger, a native of Plainview, Texas, was elected to horse racing's Hall of Fame in 2008. He is the trainer of two Travers winners, including the 2007 winner Street Sense—the only horse to win the Breeders' Cup Juvenile and the Kentucky Derby.

By Vic Zast

Practically every visitor to Saratoga Springs who can link a subject with a predicate writes about this horse-loving city and its spellbinding racecourse in idyllic prose.

The message now is no different than on postcards the track used to mail free of charge in the 1960s. Fans who took a minute to drop one in the handy no-postage-required mailbox would write, "Wish you were here. Having a great time. Hoping to get lucky. Dinner at the Wishing Well tonight."

Unfortunately, dear reader, I have nothing significant to add to that. Despite the unending ways in which the Spa City has evolved, a timeless consistency in everything that describes it remains, rendering further exposition superfluous.

The Saratoga phenomenon, as we know it, all started because a man—make that William R. Travers—built a simple, wooden grandstand in 1864 on a patch of dusty ground a mile east of downtown on the north side of Union Avenue. In his dreams, he believed that racing thoroughbreds could provide an enjoyable alternative to taking in the therapeutic waters.

I don't know what Travers was drinking when this reckless idea came to him. But I do know that there is a flow of bubbly in this charming Victorian burg in addition to the stream to be found beneath its streets. Dream big enough dreams and spectacular results will follow, Travers figured. His faith in an idea is an incomparable experience today.

In truth, Travers was fronting the dreams of other men. A year earlier, John "Old Smoke" Morrissey, a gaming house operator, conducted a four-day race meet in a field, in what is now the Horse Haven stable area. A third man, John R. Hunter, was equally intrigued. Could it be that this trio of rascals really knew what it was doing? Or, does gambling in every form require a flight of fancy that the boring can't fathom?

By the way, Saratoga Springs then and now can cause even a teetotaler to be light-headed. When mixed with two fingers of nostalgia, what happens on the most ordinary day in this superlative environment often turns to lore. Countless explanations of history can be accurate in myriad forms. Perception takes precedence over substance in a place where intuition creates fortunes.

Many cities have neighborhoods preserved in their splendor and a noticeable devotion to culture and the arts. In Saratoga, one's enjoyment of people doesn't quickly evaporate when they die. Few zip codes give tradition as compelling a reason to carry on as 12866. For a lover of horse racing, a summer without Saratoga might as well be a year in a coma.

"Health, History, and Horses" decorates the signs at several of the city's borders. But in my part of town—the racetrack—these overarching themes commingle in the presentation of a sport that has captured my attention for nearly fifty years.

It was the "Black Stallion" novels by the late Walter Farley that introduced me to the wonderment of thoroughbreds. Later, my uncle, Stan Severyn, taught me to wager. Stan was the owner of a grocery store in Buffalo, New York, and at age twelve, I was ripe for the temptations he laid before me.

Working as a stock boy for my uncle, I would run his bets down the street to his bookie so his wife, Ann, wouldn't know about his gambling. "Two, two, if come, four, four, in reverse, four dollar place parlay" was my mantra each noon at the Jefferson Grill, spoken deliberately and cautiously to a bookie named "Bo," a king-sized Kool bobbing up and down in his purple lips, the silver smoke licking

When **William R. Travers built simple wooden bleachers in 1864, he dreamed it was the start of something grand. Today, the Travers Stakes, held each August at the racecourse he founded, bears his name.** Photo from the George S. Bolster Collection, Saratoga History Museum, Saratoga Springs, NY

Colorful hats and bonnets adorn the lovely ladies who frequent Saratoga in summer. Albany (NY) *Times Union* photo by Skip Dickstein

the space above his bowling-ball head in bursts like an Indian's signals. How exotic and addictively sinful the experience was.

Once those lessons were learned, I began going to the racetrack in person. After several years of learning the ropes at Fort Erie and Woodbine, I made my first trip to Saratoga and have since somehow managed to find myself there each August. You can start chicken-scratching some numbers and doing your calculus, but I believe it's been forty-five years straight that I've been at Saratoga Race Course at least a day—usually for the Travers—each summer.

My commitment, in the beginning, was affordable. For one thing, the racing was held Monday through Saturday, only four weeks each summer. The crowds weren't as large as they are now, and a crafty kid with a few bucks in his wallet could manage. I'd bunk in with a friend who tended bar at the Hall of Springs restaurant, then ride free through the gates of the racecourse lying flat on my back in the rear of the track ambulance he drove for his day job.

It was a seersucker suit that draped my skinny frame, as I lay prone beneath the squeaky-clean sheets on the stretcher in the flat-bed. Of course, saddle shoes, like golfers and clowns wear, completed the outfit. Mike Fitzgerald, who contributed his memory of what happened when Jaipur met Ridan for an upcoming chapter, beat the system some other way. But, in his case, it was the pursuit of a day's wages that enabled his passion, not a damned outright scam, and, therein, is a difference.

Once married, my wife Maureen and I sought lodging at Mrs. Steele's cabins—you know the place, or at least you can picture it. Mrs. Steele's was a row of screened-in, single-room, roadside bungalows—each with a yellow lamp to light the doorway and a metal chair, only one, on the stoop. There in my honey's embrace, the sound of creaking bedsprings was overwhelmed by a parade of passing semis, or, if after the rush hour ended, by the chirping of crickets in the fragrant pines that surrounded the property.

Alas, those precious summer evenings have passed—lost to life's ever-changing challenges. Was our procession through time a complication? First, the step up to air-conditioned South Broadway motels with heated swimming pools and cars of aerodynamic design in the parking lot; then the Holiday Inn and Sheraton-Saratoga Hotel with fancy rates but walls so thin we could hear the kids in the room next door playing Pac-Man; then a rental house remodeled from a barn with basement game rooms; and finally our own cozy abode on Fifth Avenue, so close to the yearling grounds that the sound of horses whinnying, instead of an alarm clock, wakes us up.

Greg Montgomery's Saratoga streak isn't as long as mine, but it's more impressive. Montgomery settled in the area in 1980 and promptly recognized the importance of racing, even though his knowledge of the sport before his arrival was minimal. In the convening years, he created a collection of twenty-three Travers posters. Over the span of this time, I've collected about a dozen. Don't ask me why I have missed some.

In the end, I suppose it's a lucky thing, because when I learned that some are out of print and that all have never been presented in one collection, the thought of writing this book suddenly came to me.

You, too, have probably collected a few of the posters on your own—it's unavoidable. They are timeless in their fashion and relate to many scenes that make Saratoga racing a unique pastime. Why, you'd be foolish not to.

I dare say that in Saratoga County, you can find a Montgomery poster on every block. On my street alone, you will see one in each house but two. But, then, of course, the owners of those homes haven't invited me in to take a look.

Greg Montgomery's posters define Saratoga uniquely. If any racecourse has earned the right to have its own special "style," Saratoga Race Course, in all its transcendent glory, is the one that has. The irony is that no other "look" but one which is classy and consistent would suit it. Consequently, no other look but Montgomery's is now *de rigueur*.

The Travers Stakes is the apotheosis of Saratoga horse racing. It represents the history, traditions, and quality of its resplendent surroundings. Although the old racecourse hosts other races that occasionally may surpass the Travers in effect, there is none that's the equal in anticipation.

Racegoers are serious enough about the sport to learn all they can about each horse before heading to the betting window. Albany (NY) *Times Union* photograph by Skip Dickstein

I suppose that at this point I should provide at least a partial list of the famous Travers champions to support my contentions. You can begin well into the race's history with the 1920 winner, the mighty Man O' War. Add the names of Twenty Grand, Whirlaway, Native Dancer, Gallant Man, Sword Dancer, Buckpasser, and Damascus, and you need not look to the last fifty runnings to establish a provenance nonpareil with other races'.

Nevertheless, my purpose is to tell you about the winners from 1986 to 2007. It's a period that includes a few horses that history would otherwise forget, except for the lucky day they won the Travers. On the other hand, these last twenty-two editions include horses, and races, for the ages.

Time and space do not permit me the luxury to report all the preparations, events and conclusions surrounding this study. Much of what is written has been written before. But no chapter is strictly the facelift of one account, but dozens. The point of view regarding what happened is personal. If opinions differ on what actually took place, blame the occasional discrepancy on perspective. We all see the world differently.

There was a conscious effort to provide more than what took place on the racetrack. But, with maybe one or two exceptions, a replay of each race was included. For those with greater interest in understanding the details, the *Daily Racing Form* has graciously provided the charts for an Appendix. But note the words of William Faulkner—"Facts and truth really don't have much to do with each other."

Three chapters go back further than 1986, the year in which Montgomery began his series. In 2008, Montgomery created a commemorative poster for a one-man show at the Saratoga Arts Center Gallery, and his interesting triptych (on page 116) portrays three races that stand above the other one hundred thirty-six Travers.

Each of these Travers, on its own, could have been the subject of a poster or a book. To say that researching and writing the exploits of Jim Dandy (1930), Jaipur and Ridan (1962), and Alydar and Affirmed (1978) was not as enjoyable as recalling the circumstances of Travers Stakes that I actually saw, wouldn't be forthright.

It's not difficult to recall twenty-two Travers, if you've been to them. Although not all these Travers became the "Midsummer Derby" they were advertised to be, each was a classic for one reason or another. So rich is the tapestry of horse racing that stories abound in even the least lasting details.

Anyone deeply involved in a race will tell you that the few minutes in which it is run are merely the denouement of a play with a beginning, a middle, and an end. Not long into the writing, I noticed that the same people played different roles in different Travers. There's an ad hoc Travers community that links chapter to chapter. D. Wayne Lukas, Chris McCarron, Marylou Whitney, Ogden Phipps, Jerry Bailey, and the author of the Foreword, Carl Nafzger, kept re-appearing in the public record. Coincidence is rife throughout.

There is one other circumstance that you might find revealing. Although this is a book about two of horse racing's genuine treasures, it was a regional publishing company, North Country Books, that decided to risk its money on my idea. Several publishers that specialize in racing and handicapping thought the concept was grand, but the market too small. The decision-makers at these publishers, obviously, don't know the Travers Stakes like we do. That, too, makes me, like Travers and Hunter and Morrissey a century and thirty-nine years ago, regard Saratoga as a place built on dreams.

Above: **The business of horse racing at Saratoga includes auctions where bidders hope their offer is the winner, and so is the horse they take home.** Photograph by Vic Zast

Opposite: **Jockeys must control the pace of eleven-hundred-pound steeds while adjusting their strategy in split-seconds.** Albany (NY) *Times Union* photograph by Skip Dickstein

GREG MONTGOMERY'S TRAVERS POSTER SERIES

GREG MONTGOMERY'S posters, for the most part, are devoid of detail. The artist employs the sparse, timeless style of British Railway Art, linking carefully organized bits and pieces of bright colors that collectively create bold, identifiable images. The effect is a stunning contemporary interpretation of constructivism.

The Silks

Pinnacles

Rain or Shine

Woody's Win

Lady in Red

THE
SARATOGA
RACING SEASON

1991

Jockey's Scales

THE
TRAVERS

123RD RUNNING

AUGUST 22, 1992

Travers Paddock

THE
TRAVERS

125th Running

Saratoga 1993

The Long Wait

THE
TRAVERS

125th Running

Saratoga 1994

Stretch Drive

THE
TRAVERS

126th Running

Saratoga 1995

Out in Front

THE
TRAVERS

127th Running

Saratoga 1996

Wire to Wire

THE
TRAVERS
129th Running

Saratoga 1997

Paddock Parade

THE
TRAVERS
129th Running

Saratoga 1998

Clean Break

THE
TRAVERS
130th Running

Saratoga 1999

By a Nose

THE
TRAVERS
131st Running

Saratoga 2000

First Across

THE
TRAVERS
132nd Running

Saratoga 2001

Driving Home

THE
TRAVERS
133rd Running

Saratoga 2002

Backstretch Move

THE TRAVERS
134th Running

Saratoga 2003

First Race

THE TRAVERS
135th Running

Saratoga 2004

16 Minutes to Post

THE TRAVERS
136th Running

Saratoga 2005

Storm Bird

THE TRAVERS
137th Running

Saratoga 2006

Red Paddock

THE TRAVERS
138th Running

Saratoga 2007

Settling In

THE TRAVERS
139th Running

Saratoga 2008

Street Friends

How the Poster Series Began

By Greg Montgomery

Greg Montgomery spends part of each visit to the track in Saratoga's famous paddock. With a camera or a sketchbook, he collects ideas and images for his posters. Photograph by Paula Rosenberg

I WAS A NEWCOMER to Saratoga in 1985 when I first learned about the Travers Stakes when I saw a small, insignificant poster announcing the race as an upcoming event.

"How could such a monumental event have such a modest poster to promote itself?" I wondered. Shortly thereafter I began work on the 1986 poster depicting the Travers silks.

That first Travers poster was distributed as a party favor at the Travers Celebration sponsored by the Travers Committee. *The Silks* was produced prior to the running of the 1986 Travers. Each poster thereafter was introduced on a similar schedule.

This explains why the subject matter of each poster in the series is not a reflection of that year's race, but often a reflection of the previous year's Travers. It also explains why there are twenty-six Travers posters, not twenty-five. The art for each Travers follows the race, but the posters debut before it is run.

The 1989 poster, the fourth in the series, in fact, was the first to portray the winner of the previous year's race. The yellow silks of Claiborne Farm, worn by jockey Chris McCarron aboard the 1988 Travers winner Forty Niner, comprise the subject matter of that poster.

The most recent poster, dated 2008, portrays Street Sense beating Grasshopper in the 2007 Travers. The special edition release of the *Triple Champs* poster, commemorating my gallery exhibit in August 2008, portrays historic winners in 1930, 1962, and 1978.

The Silks played a significant role in a couple of key areas besides timing. For example, it determined the size used to produce subsequent posters in the series. I initially decided upon the tall, vertical format for economic reasons pertaining to production. But once the design and format came together, I realized that the size enhanced the presentation of my art and provided the posters with a unique look.

Although *The Silks* employs an artistic style that is consistent with the series, the other posters depict scenes instead of inanimate objects, and, as a result, they are more in line with British Railway Art, which describes loosely the technique I have used to enhance the images. The decision to adhere to this technique in the design of the second poster has proved fortuitous. The graphics have remained relevant through the decades. Even the oldest posters look contemporary.

Over the years, my images of the Saratoga horse racing scene have
steadily increased in popularity. Today, my posters and prints hang in
public and private collections throughout the world and in the permanent
collection of the Library of Congress.

The series of Travers and Saratoga posters, which began in 1986, is the
longest continuing series of sporting art produced by one artist for a specific
sporting event. Fifteen of my Travers posters have performed double duty
as covers for Dick Francis's paperback mystery novels. GM

A "map" helped me make the
difficult color choices that brought
fifteen individual elements into
one harmonious whole. Some of
these silks changed position in
the final version.

21

The Silks

THE ORIGINAL STUDIES for the silks and caps on this poster were done as separate little drawings that I would pin to a board in different arrangements. I'd move the silks from row to row, matching rivals, history, and color complexity, then walk across the room to see if any one silk stood out. I must have walked ten miles.

This poster is a study in balance. The silks the jockeys wear are meant to be vivid and eye catching—fifteen unique designs screaming for your attention. The challenge in this poster was to use the distinct, individual geometric shapes to pull these strong designs together into a cohesive whole. Each silk is a work of art. Each placement is deliberate, with color, line, and shape isolated and united on this poster. GM

KEY TO THE SILKS

Payson Stable	Glen Riddle Farm	Bertram R. Firestone
Carr de Naskra	**Man O' War**	**General Assembly**
C.V. Whitney	Loblolly Farms	A.G. Vanderbilt
Chompion	**Temperence Hill**	**Native Dancer**
Harbor View Farm	Pen-Y-Bryn Farm	Goldmills Farms
Affirmed	**Damascus**	**Bold Reason**
Meadow Stable	William Haggin Perry	Calumet Farm
Secretariat	**Loud**	**Alydar**
Ogden Phipps	Marcia W. Schott	Rokeby Stables
Buckpasser	**Willow Hour**	**Key to the Mint**

Opposite: **Originally, only Travers winners were to be on the 1986 Travers Silks poster. But, in the end, I just had to include a little intrigue. Two of the fifteen horses represented by the silks did not win the Travers. Can you find them?**

Opposite: **I wanted a tall, elegant typeface to complement the stately coat-of-arms quality of the silks. A condensed lightweight Garamond was my choice. It has graced fine documents for over five hundred years.**

THE
TRAVERS
CELEBRATION

Saratoga 1986

Beginning of the Bailey Age

Jerry Bailey Steers Wise Times Away from Trouble

1986 Travers Stakes	
117th Running on Saturday, August 16	
Winner	Wise Times
Jockey	Jerry Bailey
Owner	Russell Reineman
Trainer	Philip Gleaves
Time	2:03 2/5

Mud-covered jockey Jerry Bailey guided Wise Times from fifteen lengths behind the leaders to win the first of three Travers career victories. Before retiring, he earned seven Saratoga riding titles.
Skip Dickstein photo for *The Blood-Horse*

The result wasn't made official for eight minutes, while the stewards studied the film and interviewed the jockeys.

Saratoga Springs was experiencing good times when Wise Times won the Travers in the first year that Greg Montgomery began commemorating the race with posters.

A rise in tourism was fueling a rebirth for the city. As gas prices dropped below one dollar a gallon, visitors began to drive up the eastern seaboard in their cars like they once traveled up the Hudson River by steamship.

"The golden era is returning," socialite Marylou Whitney was quoted by *The Saratogian* newspaper as she prepared to host her annual Canfield Casino gala. Each summer, Whitney's elaborate party set things in motion for the August racing season. "You almost feel like Lillian Russell and Diamond Jim Brady are here," Whitney cheered.

When the casinos were closed by Gov. Thomas E. Dewey in 1951, the elegant, old hotels were demolished, and stores began to shut down one by one.

"It seemed for a time that Saratoga would die the normal death," said Joe Dalton, president of the Chamber of Commerce. But in 1962, Gov. Averell Harriman, owner of Log Cabin Stud, passed the Harriman Law, which mandated that Saratoga must have a minimum of twenty-four exclusive racing days, and the phenomenon was on.

Once Saratoga's turnaround began, it seemed that only bad weather could keep tourists away.

But 1986 proved that even rainy days at the racecourse were jammed, as 43,601 turned out for the 117th Travers despite the absence of the 4-5 morning line favorite, Ogygian—winner of six of his last seven starts.

Ogygian's defection was not surprising, as earlier in the week trainer Jan Nerud predicted that the fleet son of Damascus wouldn't run if the going wasn't perfect. A fortnight prior, Nerud proved his mettle as a party pooper by keeping Ogygian, then also the chalk, out of the Jim Dandy because of a sloppy track.

"Hazy, warm, and humid with a thirty percent chance of thundershowers," was the official word from the National Weather Service for Travers Day. But the night before, Mother Nature soaked the racing strip to make it especially hospitable for mudders. Sensing this, with Ogygian walking the shedrow, the public made Danzig Connection its 6-5 choice.

Woody Stephens's Belmont Stakes winner (the trainer's fifth in a row) provided the bettors with a moment of hope, taking the lead from Moment of Hope at the top of the stretch. But then Broad Brush, another proficient off-track performer, swept by him with an eighth of a mile to go.

Sensing Wise Times flying on the outside, Angel Cordero, Jr., decided to move Broad Brush off the rail and toward the middle of the racing surface to force Wise Times even wider. But the tactic had a less-than-desirable outcome. Broad Brush could not keep Wise Times from winning, and his drifting right caused another horse to take up.

Cordero failed to see Personal Flag, being ridden by Jorge Velasquez, moving up between Wise Times and his mount. Velasquez and Personal Flag had to check in deep stretch to avoid clipping heels with the winner and, as a result, finished fourth.

Unaffected by the commotion, Wise Times kept on running and won. The bay colt, owned by Chicagoan Russell Reineman and trained by twenty-nine-year-old British-born Philip Gleaves, recorded a winning time of 2:03 2/5, the slowest Travers since Willow Hour defeated Pleasant Colony on an even sloppier surface in 1981.

The result wasn't made official for eight minutes, while the stewards studied the film and interviewed the jockeys to determine how to handle Broad Brush. When all was said and done, Broad Brush was demoted to fourth, Personal Flag was moved up to third, and Danzig Connection, trying to give Stephens his first Travers victory, was granted second.

It was the first time in Travers history that a horse that didn't win was disqualified. Cordero was given a ten-day suspension for his recklessness, but asked for and received from the stewards a stay in his suspension to ride out the meet. By the way, the popular Puerto Rican rider booted home three winners on the Travers card and ended up as Saratoga's riding king for the eleventh season in a row.

Ironically, the jockey who eventually would surpass Cordero in total Saratoga winning rides, Jerry Bailey, was aboard Wise Times. At one point in the Travers, Bailey had the Mr. Leader colt fifteen lengths behind the pace-setter. But he must have believed that his mount could duplicate his late-charging victorious Haskell Invitational performance on another sloppy track, and Wise Times rewarded his confidence.

In 1986, the Haskell wasn't as much of an influence on the Travers as it grew to be in the 1990s. In fact, Wise Times was only the third horse to win both the Haskell and Travers. Wajima accomplished the double in 1975, a year after Holding Pattern became the first to achieve the feat.

"This ranks up there with one of the biggest wins of my career, especially since there is only one Travers," exclaimed Bailey, obviously not the seer he was made out to be, as a result of his winning ride. Before he was finished as a jockey, Bailey would win seven Saratoga riding titles, three Travers, six Triple Crown races, four Dubai World Cups, fifteen Breeders' Cup races, and five Breeders' Cup Classics.

Pre-race favorite Ogygian was scratched by trainer Jan Nerud when rain soaked the track the night before the Travers. Two weeks earlier, Nerud scratched Ogygian from the Jim Dandy for the same reason. Skip Dickstein photo for *The Blood-Horse*

Left: Jockey Angel Cordero, Jr., aboard Broad Brush, tried to force Wise Times to the center of the track. The tactic not only failed to distract Wise Times, but moved Broad Brush down one place in the final standings when track stewards penalized Cordero for the risky move. New York Racing Association, Inc. photo by Adam Coglianese

Pinnacles

THE SUMMER OF 1986, I took an over-exposed photo of Saratoga's first turn and clubhouse. The faulty exposure helped me to see how the roof, grandstand, track, and infield could be simplified and separated by white space. I began to divide my images into strips of bold color and white. The white of the paper—or negative space—became an important "color" within the artwork. Shape, not graduated tone, created the depth, perspective, and movement that I wanted. Designing areas of "page white" within my illustrations became one of the signature elements of my style.

Original studies for this poster were done by cutting Color-aid® paper and pasting the pieces on a white board. The paper gave me not only sharp edges, but also rich, saturated, solid colors. GM

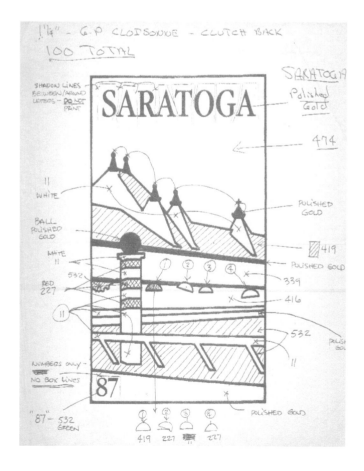

Above left: The powerful graphic style of this poster translates perfectly to the cloisonné lapel pin process. Raised metal outlines are filled with colored sand. When fired, the sand melts into colorful glass swatches.

Left: I created a color guide for the pin manufacturer to follow.

Above: I cut the design for *Pinnacles* out of Amberlith®, a plastic used in screen printing. The orange sections are the areas that will print colors.

THE
TRAVERS
CELEBRATION

Saratoga 1987

Money Can Buy You Love

Java Gold Rewards Rokeby Stables with Fourth Travers Victory

1987 Travers Stakes	
118th Running on Saturday, August 22	
Winner	Java Gold
Jockey	Pat Day
Owner	Rokeby Stables
Trainer	MacKenzie Miller
Time	2:02

Umbrellas added color and kept spectators dry when a drenching rain began to fall as the horses prepared to enter the starting gate. Albany (NY) *Times Union* photograph by James Goolsby

The 1987 Travers was contested for a purse of $1 million, more than any other race in New York Racing Association history.

Right: **Jockey Pat Day swung wide around the turn and brought Java Gold from behind to win on a sloppy track ahead of such stalwarts as Alysheba and Bet Twice.** NYRA photograph by Adam Coglianese

Although Paul Mellon's gray and yellow colors were covered with mud when Pat Day guided Java Gold across the finish line first in the 118th Travers Stakes, that Saturday began a run of nine years in which fans would see the silks of thoroughbred racing's most historic stables on display in the winner's circle of the Midsummer Derby seven times.

Saratoga racing fans have always shown respect for the wealthy and powerful—human and equine alike. The joke in this town is that the mayor-elect is sworn into office with one hand on the Social Register. Although the Spa course is the "Graveyard of Favorites," it is at its most appealing when well-bred horses owned by members of the Jockey Club prosper. Regardless of how fast things change in the resurgent city, a reverence for good standing is one tendency that persists.

For example, even though no three-year-old champion had competed in the Travers since Slew O' Gold in 1983, Saratogians still believed that divisional honors were at issue when the thoroughbreds lined up for the starter. Such was the situation that brought together the winners of all three Triple Crown races, as well as the conquerors of the Jim Dandy, Haskell Invitational, Metropolitan Handicap, Wood Memorial, Florida Derby, Santa Anita Derby, Fountain of Youth, Everglades Stakes, and the Swaps.

Whitney Stakes winner Java Gold, at odds of 3-1, skimmed above the slop like the train of a gown above a littered sidewalk, to defeat a field of eight other horses handily, immediately securing highest standing in his class.

In the colt's wake were such accomplished competitors as Alysheba, Bet Twice, Polish Navy, Cryptoclearance, and Gulch. One sports editor went so far as to compare the rivalry between Alysheba and Bet Twice on a par with Affirmed and Alydar.

Dismissing the ridiculousness, Java Gold produced the fourth triumph in the Travers for Rokeby Stables, placing Mellon only one victory behind all-time leading owners George D. Widener, Jr., and the Dwyer Brothers Stables. Now, that's kingly.

"I think the slop takes a whole lot of validity out of this race as far as the three-year-old title goes," groused Chris McCarron, who finished sixth aboard Alysheba in the $1 million race.

Yes—that's right. The 1987 Travers was contested for a purse of $1 million, more than any other race in New York Racing Association history, except for the races the Breeders' Cup hosted at Aqueduct in 1985. "By increasing it to $1 million, we add to the hype of the Travers," said NYRA President Gerry McKeon. "We make it more of a happening."

Well, not much happened on the racetrack to make the contest extraordinary, except for Java Gold's dominance.

First, ABC-TV slighted the event by providing only thirty minutes of network coverage. The resolution for bragging rights between Alysheba and Bet Twice never materialized. After letting up prior to the first race, the rain resumed when the Travers horses went postward. The winner was separated from the third place horse by nine lengths, and the two-length margin between Java Gold and Cryptoclearance for first money was never in doubt.

Here's what did happen.

Temperate Sil, the Swaps Stakes winner that Charlie Whittingham shipped east from Hollywood Park, tried to overcome his distaste for having mud kicked in his face by avoiding the possibility. But trainer Leroy Jolley entered Gorky as a rabbit for Gulch, so Temperate Sil had company on the lead. The two pacesetters covered six furlongs in 1:10. No Travers winner, other than Man O' War, went that fast before.

Jim Dandy winner Polish Navy took over the lead when they faltered. Bet Twice and Cryptoclearance went after him. On this soggy afternoon, Gulch was never to be heard from. Going widest of all around the turn, Java Gold, a son of Key to the Mint, made his run from last place to third, then put on the afterburners to gun home a final quarter in just over twenty-four seconds. His winning time was 2:02 flat.

"Knowing the kind of horse I was on and the hands he was in, gave me the liberty of riding him with confidence," Day said, one last set of partially-clear goggles atop his head.

Java Gold was trained by MacKenzie Miller, an old-fashioned horseman who began training horses in 1940 and wouldn't hurry a three-year-old for Triple Crown glory. In his tenth year as Rokeby's trainer, the patient Miller was inducted in horse racing's Hall of Fame earlier that summer, so Day's opinion had substance. Moreover, Mellon hand-picked Miller to replace Elliott Burch, who saddled the stable's three previous Travers winners, paying him the ultimate compliment.

Another training traditionalist, Jack Van Berg, was annoyed that Saratoga officials required his horse, Alysheba, to undergo two blood tests before the race. New Jersey state police had information that somebody was trying to drug the favorite—a nasty distraction from a race in which the emphasis should have been on the matchup among graded stakes winners.

When Quadrangle gave Mellon his first Travers victory in 1964, the purse for winning was $52,033. After capturing a race that was longer by a furlong than any he had previously contested, and for carrying 126 pounds for the first time, Java Gold looked deserving of the winner's share of $673,352, despite being a little muddy.

Right: **Pat Day and Java Gold head to the winner's circle. Jockeys wear several pairs of goggles on rainy days. When the race was finished, Day was down to his last pair after spending most of the race in the back of the pack.** NYRA photograph by Adam Coglianese

OWNERS WITH THE MOST TRAVERS STAKES VICTORIES

DWYER BROTHERS STABLES

YEAR	HORSE	SIRE
1881	Hindoo	Virgil
1883	Barnes	Billet
1886	Inspector B	Enquirer
1888	Sir Dixon	Billet
1890	Sir John	Sir Modred

GEORGE D. WIDENER

YEAR	HORSE	SIRE
1939	Eight Thirty	Pilate
1950	Lights Up	Eight Thirty
1951	Battlefield	War Relic
1962	Jaipur	Nasrullah
1963	Crewman	Sailor

ROKEBY STABLES

YEAR	HORSE	SIRE
1964	Quadrangle	Cohoes
1969	Arts and Letters	Ribot
1972	Key to the Mint	Graustark
1987	Java Gold	Key to the Mint
1993	Sea Hero	Polish Navy

Rain or Shine

TO ME, A FIELD OF UMBRELLAS is an irresistible image. Their pop-art color and graphic shapes seem to point everywhere at once. Again, the white of the paper is used to shape the umbrellas and separate the greenery at the top of the image. The umbrellas are so visually arresting they practically vibrate.

I wanted the eye to escape the "noise" of the foreground and quickly move up into the clean open track and be refreshed by the fluid lines and earth colors of the thoroughbreds. The visual weight of the trees and buildings helps to balance the busy foreground and draw your eye up to the race. GM

Above: **This was my initial concept drawing for *Rain or Shine*. I sketched the horses on tracing paper to use as an overlay to help position them.**

Left: **I spent a lot of time choosing my colors. First by selecting just the right hue of Color-aid® paper and creating a cut-paper version of the poster. Then I mixed my silk-screening inks to match those paper colors.**

THE
SARATOGA
RACING SEASON
1988

What's Your Pleasure?

Forty Niner Nips Seeking the Gold in Three Favorites Finish

Above: **Chris McCarron, in Claiborne Farm's yellow silks, moves Forty Niner to the lead down the backstretch, ahead of Seeking the Gold and Brian's Time.** Skip Dickstein photo for *The Blood-Horse*

Forty Niner and Seeking the Gold were sired by the prolific Mr. Prospector and foaled and raised on the same patch of bluegrass.

It's a shame that the Spuyten Duyvil was bought by the Fasig-Tipton Company and closed for good in 1987. For as long as anyone could remember, the little restaurant at the side of the horse auction grounds had been a haven for horse lovers with a thirst and an opinion.

Hanging around the crowd-pleasing watering hole, with its citronella-scented patio and boisterous piano bar, was a Saratoga tradition as developed as drinking the bubbling waters. The venerable establishment—open only during racing season— would have been just the right spot for owners of the first-, second-, and third-place finishers in the 1988 Travers to have gone to continue their argument about which horse was the best three-year-old.

It is a rare Travers Stakes that results in the three favorites finishing one-two-three. But in its 119th running, the Midsummer Derby was decided on a sparkling Saturday, in a close, driving finish featuring Forty Niner, Seeking the Gold, and Brian's Time.

It is certain that the owners of Forty Niner and Seeking the Gold, in particular, would have enjoyed a spirited debate at the restaurant over how a nose caused a difference of several hundred thousand dollars in dividing the $1 million purse.

No doubt Seth Hancock, the thirty-nine-year-old president of Claiborne Farm, the breeder and owner of Forty Niner, was introduced to the Spuyten Duyvil by his father, A.B. "Bull" Hancock, during the fabled breeder's years of selling and buying yearlings at the nearby pavilion.

And it is beyond doubt that Seeking the Gold's owner, Ogden Phipps, was no stranger to a steak and a Scotch in the eatery by virtue of his family's summer residence in Saratoga Springs since the turn of the twentieth century.

The men appeared as opposite as cucumber and watermelon—one boyish, spindly and fair-haired and the other pate-tested and girth-challenged. But they were similar in acumen when it came to owning horses. And in the case of their win and place horses, there was more than a passing kinship.

Forty Niner and Seeking the Gold were sired by the prolific Mr. Prospector and foaled and raised on the same patch of bluegrass. "It means a lot to see the horses off the farm, in addition to our own horses, run well," Hancock was reported to have said by *The Blood-Horse*.

No breeder or owner knows how a horse will perform on the racetrack until the opportunity to compete arrives. When the Travers draw took place the day before the race, one of the few remaining questions surrounding Forty Niner and Seeking the Gold was whether their breeding would carry them one and one-quarter miles.

Forty Niner's strategy for answering the question was to set steady fractions ahead of the pack and try to hang on. Seeking the Gold's plan, not drastically different, was to press the early pace and gather the front runner in.

The Florida Derby winner Brian's Time was made the even-money Travers choice, primarily because his late running style appeared to favor getting the distance. Moreover, two weeks earlier, Brian's Time with Angel Cordero, Jr.—Saratoga's leading rider—had captured the Jim Dandy Stakes by five and a half lengths.

Since returning to the races in July after running out of the money in the Preakness, Forty Niner had raced under three different riders. Although Laffit Pincay, Jr., had partnered the colt to a gritty nose victory over Seeking the Gold in the Haskell, the Panamanian was injured and could not ride in the Travers. Chris McCarron, winless in the Travers throughout his long career, was chosen to ride Forty Niner by trainer Woody Stephens, winless in the Travers throughout his much-lengthier career.

McCarron and Stephens knew their best chance of winning was to make the others try to catch Forty Niner. In the walking ring, Stephens instructed his rider accordingly.

"Speed's holding well, the rail's very fast, so slow him down as much as you can and shut the gate when you turn for home," Stephens told McCarron, a master at getting horses to break quickly from the gate.

Surprisingly, Pat Day aboard Seeking the Gold took the early lead and held it through a first quarter of :24 2/5 before letting his mount slip back to fourth.

Forty Niner inherited the lead and continued at a comfortable pace despite the company of Dynaformer and Kingpost. When Dynaformer ranged up alongside Forty Niner at the half-mile pole, the son of Roberto provided little threat.

"He pinned his ears and spurted for about seventy yards, and I was able to drop over to the rail," McCarron said when his horse easily brushed off Dynaformer. By the top of the homestretch, his colt was ahead of the field by two lengths and running faster than he had on the backstretch.

But the race was far from over. Under steady left-handed encouragement from Day, Seeking the Gold escaped the rail and closed on Forty Niner's starboard with an impressive surge at the eighth pole, and, on the far outside, Brian's Time dismissed Dynaformer to join the hunt.

All three horses ran furiously through the final furlong, and although Forty Niner's margin was fast eroding, he showed no quit or lack of purpose.

"I couldn't say the finish would have been different in a couple more jumps," Day said of Seeking the Gold's second place finish.

"There were two good horses in front of him," said Cordero of Brian's Time. "When I finally got to them, they took off and were two fresh horses."

In defeating Seeking the Gold in the sixth-fastest Travers, Forty Niner joined Battlefield, Native Dancer, Buckpasser, Honest Pleasure, and Chief's Crown as two-year-old champions that won the Travers.

Neither Hancock nor Phipps had the opportunity to reflect further on the race at the Spuyten Duyvil. Although pleased that he won his first Travers, Stephens wasn't much inclined to go out and celebrate anyway.

"I've learned one thing over the years," the seventy-four-year-old Hall of Fame conditioner said, underplaying his acumen by at least one lesson. "To win and go home and to lose and go home" were life's lessons for Stephens.

Favorite melodies from the pianist at the Spuyten Duyvil helped ease the pain of the day's losers and cheer the winners. Photograph property of Leighla Whipper Ford, former co-proprietor of the Spuyten Duyvil, and her daughter Carole Ione Lewis

WOODY STEPHENS' FIVE CONSECUTIVE BELMONT WINS		
YEAR	HORSE	TIME
1982	Conquistador Cielo	2:28.20
1983	Caveat	2:27.80
1984	Swale	2:27.20
1985	Crème Fraiche	2:27.00
1986	Danzig Connection	2:29.80

Woody Stephens' assistant Ken McPeek (far left, wearing white cap) missed having his own Travers winner in a winner's circle photo when Repent fell short of Medaglia d'Oro in 2002. NYRA photograph by Adam Coglianese

Woody's Win

THE KEY TO THIS IMAGE is the balance between its top and bottom. The solid green top is almost a mirror image of the mostly brown bottom. The jockey's crop, torso, and legs form a "Z" shape, which knits the two fields together. To see how delicate the balance is, just cover the jockey's crop. Without it, the eye does not move across the image and the green becomes overpowering. As it is, the green is strong enough to balance the typography below. GM

Above: **I considered several approaches to creating artwork for souvenir tee shirts. I chose the one with a crop similar to the poster, and the shirts were sold at the souvenir tent.**

Right: **This detail of the color comp shows how the shapes were cut out of paper. The white areas are the background showing through.**

THE
SARATOGA
RACING SEASON

1989

Eeeee-zee Does It

No Beating Easy Goer in New York

1989 Travers Stakes	
120th Running on Saturday, August 19	
Winner	Easy Goer
Jockey	Pat Day
Owner	Ogden Phipps
Trainer	Claude R. McGaughey III
Time	2:00 4/5

Easy Goer hinted he was ready to run, giving his handlers a healthy dose of attitude in the paddock area. Skip Dickstein photo for *The Blood-Horse*

A roster of Easy Goer's victims at NYRA tracks reads like a "Who's Few" of racing.

In calling the last of his eighteen Travers Stakes as track announcer, Marshall Cassidy referred to "Eeeee-zee Goer" as "New York's Horse of the Year" when Pat Day eased the gorgeous chestnut under the finish line in the 120th Midsummer Derby.

Easy Goer, Alydar's most accomplished son, was defeated only once in fifteen starts on Empire State soil. That lone loss came as a four-year-old. Easy Goer lost the Metropolitan Handicap at Belmont Park against the national "Horse of the Year," Criminal Type, and the crack sprinter Housebuster.

Nevertheless, Ogden Phipps' homebred raced to nine Grade 1 victories at Aqueduct, Belmont, and Saratoga. He broke his maiden at Saratoga and won the Whitney Handicap and Travers Stakes in back-to-back starts at the Spa as a three-year-old. When away from his friendly surroundings, he lost four of five races, including the Kentucky Derby and Breeders' Cup Juvenile at Churchill Downs, the Preakness at Pimlico, and the Breeders' Cup Classic at Gulfstream Park—the one track outside of New York where he also triumphed.

Lyrics to the anthem "New York, New York" put forth the conceit that if one can make it there, one can make it anywhere. It is an immodest boast, but one with a measure of truth. But that wasn't the case for this great runner who, like Lava Man in California, seemed to have thrived on home cooking but gagged on exotic fare.

Perhaps one of Easy Goer's advantages at home was that he rarely found stiff competition there. A roster of his victims at NYRA tracks reads like a "Who's Few" of racing, with Cryptoclearance the rare "name" horse on his résumé.

For example, the presence of five modestly talented rivals—Clever Trevor, Shy Tom, Doc's Leader, Le Voyageur, and Roi Danzig—made winning the Travers simple for Easy Goer. He raced two wide for a mile, then circled the two horses in front of him, ran alongside Clever Trevor for a furlong, and won.

Except for some gawking at the crowd through the homestretch and a few whacks from Day on his rear end in the final turn, the colt ran to his 1-5 favoritism and completed the mile and a quarter in what is now recorded as 2:00.80. His was the third-fastest Travers Stakes in history. That was the last year in which New York clockers measured the times in fifths of a second, so maybe he went even faster. But although the races in 1990 were clocked in hundredths of a second, they weren't reported this way in the *Daily Racing Form* charts until 1999.

It was not the time that he took to win the race, but the victory itself that

EASY GOER'S NINE GRADE 1 STAKES VICTORIES			
DATE	RACE	DISTANCE	TRACK
October 1, 1988	Cowdin	7 Furlongs	Belmont (Elmont, NY)
October 15, 1988	Champagne	1 Mile	Belmont (Elmont, NY)
April 22, 1989	Wood Memorial	1 1/8 Mile	Aqueduct (Jamaica, NY)
June 10, 1989	Belmont	1 1/2 Mile	Belmont (Elmont, NY)
August 5, 1989	Whitney H	1 1/8 Mile	Saratoga (Saratoga, NY)
August 19, 1989	Travers	1 1/4 Mile	Saratoga (Saratoga, NY)
September 16, 1989	Woodward	1 1/4 Mile	Belmont (Elmont, NY)
October 7, 1989	Jockey Club Gold Cup	1 1/2 Mile	Belmont (Elmont, NY)
July 4, 1990	Suburban H	1 1/4 Mile	Belmont (Elmont, NY)

pleased Phipps. After the race, with the few drops of rain that fell earlier all but gone, Saratoga was lapsing into evening and Phipps began reminiscing. At the age of 81, he had a second Travers victory to show for all his years in racing.

If there was one horse in the past that provided a comparison to Easy Goer, it was his sire, Alydar. Alydar, a Calumet Farm homebred, lost to Affirmed in the Travers but was rewarded with the win on a disqualification. Just as Easy Goer had Sunday Silence to serve as nemesis, Alydar had Affirmed with whom to contend. Both Easy Goer and Alydar were immensely popular with the fans, although neither lived up to their advance.

"I came in a close second twice," Phipps said, recalling Seeking the Gold's loss by a nose to Forty Niner the previous year and Bureaucracy's half-length loss to Gallant Man in 1957. "I've won the race once—with Buckpasser in 1966," he reminded those interested in history. One year later, his son, Ogden Mills "Dinny" Phipps, would stand in the Travers winning circle with Rhythm.

After dismounting, Day said Easy Goer had yet to reach his full potential. "I really don't know how good this colt is going to get," he said. "He has done everything we asked of him. He's maturing and seasoned."

Well, almost everything.

If Easy Goer would have won on the road, against Sunday Silence in the Classics, or in tougher competition throughout his career, he would have been more than "New York's Horse of the Year." He would have been "Horse of the Year," period.

With a little urging from jockey Pat Day, Easy Goer coasted to victory, joining his famed sire, Alydar, as a Travers winner.
NYRA photograph by Adam Coglianese

Lady in Red

THIS IS ONE OF THE BEST examples of how I use white paper to form large and important parts of the final image. The hand, face, neck, and the underside of the lady's hat are all simply unprinted paper. Her racing program is handled the same way. Early drafts of this image had horses shown on the track, but I removed them. I couldn't have the thoroughbreds at the first turn when all the spectators were still looking at the finish line. I greatly simplified the other people and track elements to focus attention on the beautiful young woman. I used shadows to quickly bring you to her eye ... and then to her binoculars. All the lines and shapes in this image are cut with a knife. There are no drawn lines at all. GM

Above: **I experimented by mixing custom colors for *Lady in Red*. I also used the piece to plan the order in which the colors would be printed, and to jot down phone numbers for my helpers.**

Right: **My early sketch was more Victorian, but I chose to create my final *Lady in Red* as modern, simple, and sophisticated.**

Above: **An early study for the poster featured a woman and her red hat.**

THE
SARATOGA
RACING SEASON

1990

The Name Game

Rhythm Gives Phipps Family Back-to-Back Winners

1990 Travers Stakes	
121st Running on Saturday, August 18	
Winner	Rhythm
Jockey	Craig Perret
Owner	Ogden Mills "Dinny" Phipps
Trainer	Claude R. McGaughey III
Time	2:02 3/5

Above: **Trainer "Shug" McGaughey instructed jockey Craig Perret to let Rhythm relax off the pace and run the leaders down once the horse was settled. The strategy had worked in previous victories and earned Rhythm another win in the Travers.** NYRA photograph by Adam Coglianese

It's coincidence—not irony—that those with the largest fortunes were the most fortunate.

Families named Vanderbilt, Whitney, Mellon, and Phipps dominated thorough-bred racing at Saratoga in the second half of the twentieth century. A horse-player could do worse than to bet on an underachiever in their colors going postward in the Whitney, the Adirondack, the Travers, or the Hopeful—the big-money stakes that used to be held on Saturdays when racing was limited to four weeks each August.

Two-year-olds from these stables seemed to blossom in the season like the tomatoes at the Wishing Well or the hand melons served on the Clubhouse Terrace. It's co-incidence—not irony—that those with the largest fortunes were the most fortunate, even when the most optimistic horseplayer least expected them to be.

Rhythm, a Breeders' Cup Juvenile champion but a disappointment for most of his three-year-old season, was bred and owned by Ogden Mills "Dinny" Phipps, the son of Ogden Phipps and grandson of Henry Carnegie Phipps and Gladys Livingston Mills, sister to Ogden L. Mills.

Like the Phipps family members, the oft-criticized son of Mr. Prospector from a mare named Dance Number bore a name that included a reference to his relatives.

Rhythm's nom de course emanated from the Phipps family practice of bestowing its homebreds with something of the sire and the mare that extended beyond the blessings of their bloodlines. The distinctive black silks and cherry red cap of Ogden Phipps could be found in the winner's circle photos of such aptly named horses as Seeking the Gold, Personal Ensign, and Easy Goer.

The name Personal Ensign emerged from the mating of Private Account and a mare by Hoist the Flag. Easy Goer was the progeny of Alydar and Relaxing, whose dam was Marking Time. The name Seeking the Gold, sired by Mr. Prospector, connects cleverly to Con Game on his mother's side.

Considering that the given names of the Phippses are combinations of family names, it's no wonder that the names of their horses are derivatives of their ancestors, too. But although a good name can take a person far in this world when it comes to business, in horse racing it means little. The frustration with Rhythm was that he seldom ran to his illustrious breeding or the reputation of the family that owned him.

Rhythm was winless in the Kentucky Derby prep races, with a displaced palate the given excuse. "He's kind of a moody colt," said jockey Craig Perret, as if the horse's lack of response was the fault of depression.

"I have had some disappointing times with him," added trainer Shug McGaughey, as if talent was the sole requirement for becoming a champion.

After a win in a minor stakes at Belmont in June and a miserable Haskell, Rhythm was made third choice in a field of thirteen horses for the Travers. It was a day in the 90s, unfit for running a colt a mile and a quarter. But without a star in the bunch and with a million dollars on the table, why wouldn't a man with a fast horse saddle up?

The Irish-bred-and-raced Belmont Stakes winner Go and Go was the Travers favorite. Wood Memorial winner Thirty Six Red and Haskell Invitational champion Restless Con were two others to fear. The rest of the field seemed unlikely to win, but each on the right day could confuse the issue.

At the sound of the bell, Thirty Six Red, under Mike Smith, led the baker's dozen out of the gate and into the turn.

Rhythm was next to last, further back than he normally ran. "He couldn't put it all together, and I had to try something different," McGaughey explained later. "We

Left: **The Man O' War Cup is presented to** (from left) **owner Ogden "Dinny" Phipps, trainer "Shug" McGaughey, Ogden Phipps, jockey Craig Perret, Mrs. Walter M. Jeffords, Jr., and Mrs. Ogden Mills Phipps.** Skip Dickstein photograph for *The Blood-Horse*

let him take back of the pace, let him settle, and then just gallop them to the ground."

The strategy worked perfectly, although at one time during the race, McGaughey was worried. "I was starting to think that by the three-eighths pole that we had no chance, but every time he's won this year, it looked like he was hopelessly beaten," the trainer said.

When Thirty Six Red began to feel the effect of making the pace, Shot Gun Scott, racing on the rail throughout, and Sir Richard Lewis, who gained the lead for a moment and then lost it in deep stretch, appeared to be uncatchable.

But Rhythm, flying far to the right of the leaders, made up ground in a hurry throughout the last furlong and eased under the wire ahead by three and a half lengths.

Go and Go, who managed to make it up to third in the middle of the backstretch, was not a factor in the placings, perhaps a victim of change of climate and problems in transit from Europe.

Rhythm completed the Travers on a fast track in a handy 2:02.78.

"Maybe he knows when he's running for a million," Perret quipped afterwards. But McGaughey's strategy of having Rhythm run down a field of slow horses was more likely the reason he won. With his lifetime earnings rising to $1,501,092 after the Travers, Rhythm, as well as the Phipps family, had plenty of dough-re-mi.

The frustration with Rhythm was that he seldom ran to his illustrious breeding or the reputation of the family that owned him.

RHYTHM'S 3-YEAR OLD RACE RECORD				
DATE	RACE	DISTANCE	TRACK	RESULT
February 10	G1 Hutcheson	7 Furlongs	Gulfstream (FL)	7 (8)
March 3	G2 Fountain of Youth	1 1/16 Mile	Gulfstream (FL)	10 (8)
April 7	G3 Gotham	1 Mile	Aqueduct (NY)	5 (7 3/4)
May 21	Allowance 33000	7 Furlongs	Belmont (NY)	1 (1 1/4)
June 9	G3 Colin	1 1/8 Mile	Belmont (NY)	1 (2 1/4)
June 30	G2 Dwyer	1 1/8 Mile	Belmont (NY)	2 (1 1/2)
July 28	G1 Haskell H	1 1/8 Mile	Monmouth (NJ)	3 (2 1/2)
August 18	G1 Travers	1 1/4 Mile	Saratoga (NY)	1 (3 1/2)
September 15	G1 Woodward	1 1/8 Mile	Belmont (NY)	3 (2 3/4)
October 27	G1 Breeders' Cup Classic	1 1/4 Mile	Belmont (NY)	8 (13 1/2)

Jockey's Scales

I WANTED TO SHOW some of what makes the track at Saratoga unique. This wonderful little compound, encircled with a fence of black iron, is the location of the scales. Lush boxes of geraniums and a classic striped awning complete the picture. The black silhouette of a horse in the middle of the scale is not running the wrong way; it is being reflected in a mirror. I used three different reds in the awning to show dimension—bright red in the sun, darker on the side, and darkest in the shade beneath. The geraniums share the sunny red. GM

Left: Artists use sketches and photographs for reference back in the studio. I spend a lot of time at the track with my camera and notebook trying to capture the light and the atmosphere that makes Saratoga so special. This is the image I used to create *Jockey's Scales*. Notice the reflection of the horse in the center of the scale.

Below: *Jockey's Scales* was screen printed, so I had to break the artwork into separate colors. I cut each area of color out of Amberlith® acetate. This is the cutout used to print the dark foliage behind the red flowers at the bottom of the scene.

THE
SARATOGA
RACING SEASON

1991

Playing Catch-up

Slow Learner Corporate Report Brings Victory to Father-Son Team

1991 Travers Stakes	
122nd Running on Saturday, August 17	
Winner	Corporate Report
Jockey	Chris McCarron
Owner	William T. Young
Trainer	D. Wayne Lukas
Time	2:01 1/5

Above: **Jockey Chris McCarron raises his arm in victory as Corporate Report edges Preakness and Belmont Stakes winner Hansel at the wire.** NYRA photo by Adam Coglianese

Gale Brophy, wife of Strike the Gold's part-owner, B. Giles Brophy, knew that it had been forty-nine years since a Kentucky Derby winner had won the Travers. The most recent was Shut Out in 1942, and before Shut Out, it was Whirlaway in 1941. Good things come in threes, but to wait nearly half a century for lightning to strike thrice was too long, she figured.

Clearing the air about recent rumors that trainer Nick Zito was to be fired, Brophy admitted in a press release that her husband was disappointed that the handsome chestnut colt had lost the Preakness, the Belmont, and the Jim Dandy. But she insisted that the team was intact and was looking forward to winning again.

Brophy knew, of course, that reversing a losing trend in the 121st running of the Travers wasn't going to be easy. Preakness and Belmont Stakes winner Hansel, Haskell winner Lost Mountain, and 1990 Juvenile champion Fly So Free, first in the Jim Dandy, were entered in the Midsummer Derby.

The six-horse field also attracted Corporate Report—a D. Wayne Lukas reclamation project who had fractured a coffin bone as a two-year-old and only returned to the races in March. And, completing the competition, there was hopeless Tong Po, whose owners must have needed a box in the clubhouse.

"If we can just get a few more days like this, we'll be in good shape," Zito was reported to have said for Brophy's benefit to the *New York Times* after Strike the Gold galloped ten days before the race. His enthusiasm was genuine, a rare emotion in these ugly times for the racing industry.

Long faces were everywhere in the racing game. Attendance at Belmont had been abysmal before the horses came north to Saratoga. Almost every statistical measure that a business could offer as a barometer of its financial health was dismal.

Earlier that month at the Fasig-Tipton Yearling Sale, a block north of the racetrack, the average price paid for a horse fell by forty percent. At the Keeneland Sales in Kentucky in July, the average price dipped eleven percent. Keeneland's drop occurred even though one buying group—the Maktoum family of Dubai—spent one-third of the seventy-five million dollars taken in.

In keeping with the doom and gloom, Travers Day emerged overcast and humid. Moreover, the race began the way everyone expected and nothing of a surprising nature seemed in store. But what the fans thought might happen never did.

The William T. Young-owned Corporate Report, ridden by Chris McCarron, broke on top. Hansel and Fly So Free pressed the pace, and Lost Mountain took his customary spot near the back of the pack, just behind an overmatched Tong Po in fourth. Far in back, Strike the Gold ran unhurried.

Almost every one of the 48,170 fans expected Corporate Report to be on the lead early, yet only a smattering believed he would be there at the end. He had won only two of his nine races, and those races—the first of his career—were contested at six furlongs. But there he was and there he stayed, cruising the 1/2-mile in :47 2/5 and six furlongs in 1:11 2/5.

By the time the field reached the far turn, favored Strike the Gold was aroused and began a powerful move that swept him past Lost Mountain and Tong Po. In mid-turn, the chestnut son of the stretch-loving Alydar seemed perfectly placed to make his presence felt, four lengths from the lead under jockey Angel Cordero, Jr., and flying.

Jerry Bailey, aboard Hansel, however, expected that no horse would catch his once he passed Corporate Report. And pass him he did, by a head at the quarter pole—a move at the Spa that seldom foretells loss. But Corporate Report would have none of it. He felt the sting from McCarron's right-handed whip on his shoulder and sped along on the rail as if he knew this was his one chance for glory.

Corporate Report had finished ninth in the Kentucky Derby, second in the Preakness, and fourth in the Belmont Stakes—and had seen the heels of Strike the Gold, Hansel, and Lost Mountain before. Running wide out of the turn, Strike the Gold was finished. Lost Mountain never found second gear. All that remained for Corporate Report to get done was to finish off Hansel.

"It's Corporate Report by the length of a white bridle," track announcer Tom Durkin called, as both horses took their final lunges. McCarron raised his riding crop skyward seconds later and shook in the saddle as if dancing. Hansel was vanned off the course. He had suffered a career-ending injury as well as a defeat in the Travers.

D. Wayne Lukas was listed as the trainer of Corporate Report, but winning the race was his son and assistant Jeff's doing. Corporate Report had been under Jeff Lukas's care at Belmont Park leading up to the Travers, and it was Jeff Lukas who gave Bailey the boost in the saddle in the paddock. The elder Lukas was at Del Mar, in residence at Saratoga only to the extent that it was his name in the program.

Sen. Alphonse D'Amato cradled the gold-plated Man O' War Cup in Young's arms and stood alongside for a photo. Thereafter, words were spoken to explain the upset.

"We were playing catch-up throughout the Triple Crown with him, and he was still running well," young Lukas mentioned. "We tried blinkers on him at Monmouth in the Haskell, and they helped. With that, along with the natural improvement of the horse, we went one level beyond what he had been doing, and we were able to win one of these."

"I feel sorry for the people that made him 8-5 and for myself," Zito said, clearly disappointed with Strike the Gold's fourth place finish.

Perhaps the burden of being the Kentucky Derby winner got to him. But whatever the reason the colt took to sulking in the stretch, it wasn't enough to prompt Brophy to remove her man in charge. Zito continued to train the horse.

Above: **Pre-race rumors spread that Nick Zito, trainer of Kentucky Derby winner Strike the Gold, would be fired after losses in the Preakness, Belmont, and Jim Dandy. Zito kept his job, but watched Strike the Gold fade down the stretch in the Travers.** Albany (NY) *Times Union* photograph by Skip Dickstein

Below: **Owner William T. Young** (far left) **and family join Jeff Lukas** (tan coat and dark pants) **and Corporate Report in the winner's circle.** NYRA photograph by Adam Coglianese

Travers Paddock

EUROPE IN THE 1920s saw sensational men's fashion posters. I wanted to create the same continental feeling, and Saratoga's paddock was certainly the place to do it. Like the old advertisements, I used a white outline around much of the image and bright jewel-like colors. This was the only time I modified the "Travers" typography. I thought that a little racing action within the type might be a nice touch. I restricted the racing art to silhouettes and used only black and white so as not to compete with the main art. I love how the tilt of the cane changes the dynamic of the entire piece. GM

Above and below: **I "jazzed up" my type treatment on this poster and included the horses. I cut them out of Amberlith® to burn the screens for printing.**

Right: **I actually created rough concept drawings for two Travers posters and a Saratoga poster in 1992. This sketch, drawn with markers, is one that never made it off the drawing board.**

THE

TRAVERS

123RD RUNNING

AUGUST 22, 1992

Native New Yorker Makes Some Noise

Trip-tested Thunder Rumble Repeats His Surprising Jim Dandy Score

1992 Travers Stakes	
123rd Running on Saturday, August 22	
Winner	Thunder Rumble
Jockey	Herb McCauley
Owner	Konrad Widmer
Trainer	Richie O'Connell
Time	2:00 4/5

The last Travers winner born in the Empire State before Thunder Rumble was Ruthless in 1867.

According to scientific principle, the speed of light is faster than the speed of sound. But lightning struck at the same time thunder rumbled twice during the 1992 Saratoga racing season.

Thunder Rumble was a horse, not a force of nature. A New York-bred colt by the ordinary sire Thunder Puddles, he upset the Jim Dandy Stakes at 25-1 odds, and then repeated his stunning success in the 123rd Travers as fifth betting choice in the field of ten.

At 7-1, Thunder Rumble was a longer price in the Travers than three horses he had beaten in the Jim Dandy, including runner-up Dixie Brass. Although he finished a half-length clear of Dixie Brass in the fastest Jim Dandy time (1:47 2/5) in twenty-nine years, trainer Richie O'Connell was one of the few who believed that Thunder Rumble had the stuff to run as fast a second time.

"I don't tell him he's a New York-bred," O'Connell said, after Thunder Rumble ran the third-fastest Travers ever.

Since Upset's defeat of Man O' War in the 1919 Sanford Stakes, people have called Saratoga the "Graveyard of Favorites," so Thunder Rumble's two triumphs at the Spa course weren't the most stunning developments ever. But considering all the problems that he faced and then overcame, his back-to-back surprises rank right there with the finest.

Those Empire State origins, for example, didn't offer the right kind of birthing address for a Travers Stakes winner. The last Travers winner foaled in New York before Thunder Rumble was the filly Ruthless, the 1867 victress.

In addition, although the colt had won three races earlier that spring, he had not run in any of the Triple Crown races, having contracted a virus before the Wood Memorial. He had finished seventh in a midlevel allowance race in his only competition since March prior to his Jim Dandy start.

What probably persuaded most handicappers that Thunder Rumble had the deck stacked against him, though, was his number ten post position. When the speedy Dixie Brass drew the pole, and Thunder Rumble drew the far outside, it became instantly clear that Thunder Rumble would be running a longer race than his respected adversary.

Thunder Rumble took the long way around the track, running on the outside much of the way. On the first turn, jockey Herb McCauley swung wide around three horses to give Rumble a chance to run down the leaders.
Skip Dickstein photo for *The Blood-Horse*

The rail start for Dixie Brass also suggested to most that he would present a fast-moving target for the other runners. He already had taken top honors that spring in the Withers Stakes and the Metropolitan Handicap, blazing a mile both times in under 1:34.

"The shortest distance between two points is a straight line," Dixie Brass' trainer, Dennis Brida, reminded reporters on the morning of the Travers. "I don't think anyone is foolish enough to go out with us early because of the fractions he can set."

The track was faster than normal on race day, and the weather was clear, with a faint breeze to remind the 46,372 on hand that fall was around the corner. Despite losing his bid to become a Canadian Triple Crown champion at 1-20 odds in the Breeders' Stakes at Woodbine, Alydeed entered the Travers as 8-5 favorite.

As planned, Dixie Brass shot to the front and set fractions of :23, :46 4/5, and 1:10 3/5. In consecutive attempts, long shots Lee n Otto and Tank's Number each bid to wrest the lead from him. Eventually, Alydeed, in third place for most of the race, threatened. Meanwhile, Herb McCauley aboard Thunder Rumble had no choice but to race four wide through the first turn while giving chase.

Approaching the quarter pole, only Devil His Due, Dance Floor, and Thunder Rumble were moving forward, but Thunder Rumble was running four wide again and had more to do than the others. McCauley said, "When I let him out between the three-eighths and the quarter pole, I had a ton of horse." And when let out, Thunder Rumble was truest to his recent form. He gobbled up horses as if they were running in reverse, until reaching the lead with a furlong to go. He eased beneath the wire four and a half lengths the unexpected winner.

As for the three horses that went off at shorter odds than Thunder Rumble, each had an excuse.

"Maybe the mile and a quarter is beyond his scope," Brida offered for Dixie Brass.

"His performance is still a puzzler," Roger Attfield, the trainer of Alydeed, said. "I've said he may be an exceptional miler, but he didn't even run an exceptional mile today."

"I had it clear down the backstretch, but then I look, and here comes that Thunder Rumble," said Mike Smith, the jockey on Furiously.

As often the case when a long shot triumphs, the crowd, unable to comprehend what just happened, fell silent as Thunder Rumble flew past the finishing post. Then a sound like the beginnings of a storm began to swell and, finally, the ovation.

As a fitting conclusion to the amazing day, Gov. Mario M. Cuomo presented the Travers hardware to Konrad Widmer, an economist from Switzerland, who had seen his equine New Yorker in a race but never in a winner's circle.

At the beginning of the race meet, nobody had expected Thunder Rumble to be the meet's star, and yet he ended up that. It was the year of A.P. Indy, so the accolades didn't last past the summer. But for two magic race days in August, like the force of a weather front, they were ear-splitting.

Above: **Once Thunder Rumble got to the front, he cruised to a four-and-a-half-length victory, posting the third fastest time in Travers history.** NYRA photograph by Adam Coglianese

FASTEST TRAVERS TIMES

RANK	HORSE	YEAR	TIME
1	General Assembly	1979	2:00
2	Honest Pleasure	1976	2:00 1/5
3 (T)	Easy Goer	1989	2:00 4/5
3 (T)	Thunder Rumble	1992	2:00 4/5
5 (T)	Loud	1970	2:01
5 (T)	Play Fellow	1983	2:01
7 (T)	Key to the Mint	1972	2:01 1/5
7 (T)	Chief's Crown	1985	2:01 1/5
7 (T)	Corporate Report	1991	2:01 1/5
10	Point Given	2001	2:01 2/5

The Long Wait

I LOVE THIS IMAGE—a young jockey asked to "hold up" by the clerk of the scales. He's tentative, off-balance, and unsure. But the image is perfectly balanced. The dangling stirrups and girth (strap) offset the weight of the numeral and heavy blue shoulder. The large triangular shape above the jockey's shoulder somehow balances the crop and boots below.

It took me weeks to cut the stencils and mix and print the inks of this silkscreen edition. Just printing the yellow girth required putting 125 sheets of paper through the press four separate times. GM

Below left: **From photographs and sketches I created this actual-size working drawing. Based on it, all the screens were cut for the final silk screen printing. As I mixed the inks, I tapped them out side-by-side on this drawing to dry to see how they would look on the finished art. The ink mixing took days.**

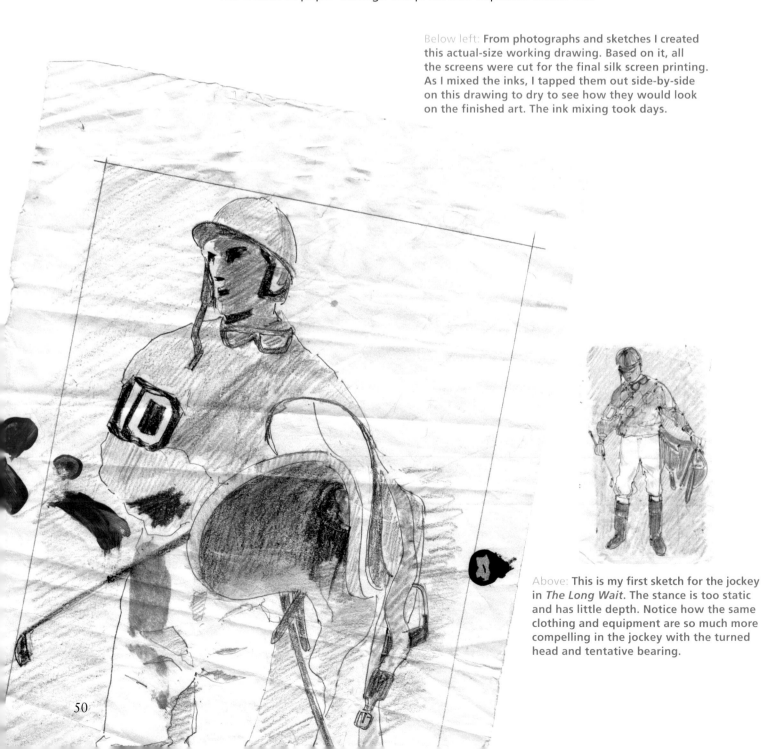

Above: **This is my first sketch for the jockey in *The Long Wait*. The stance is too static and has little depth. Notice how the same clothing and equipment are so much more compelling in the jockey with the turned head and tentative bearing.**

THE
TRAVERS

124th Running

Saratoga 1993

No Explanation for Some Things

Sea Hero Earns a Place in Posterity

1993 Travers Stakes	
124th Running on Saturday, August 21	
Winner	Sea Hero
Jockey	Jerry Bailey
Owner	Rokeby Stables
Trainer	MacKenzie Miller
Time	2:01 4/5

Trainer MacKenzie Miller (left) and owner Paul Mellon watch Sea Hero in the paddock area before the race.
Skip Dickstein photo for *The Blood-Horse*

On Travers Day, both Mellon and Miller posed wearing Panama straw hats in the Saratoga paddock, as if it was the presentation ring at Glorious Goodwood.

Considering that Saratoga Race Course has been operating for many decades, one would expect public reminders of greatness in the forms of paintings, photographs, and statues to be lying all about. Thoroughbred racing revolves around nostalgia. Followers of the sport are enthralled by the memories of close finishes, fast racehorses, daring jockeys, and legendary owners and trainers. Yet, it isn't just the tales being told on porches around town that are keeping legends alive.

Across from the track on Union Avenue, the National Museum of Racing welcomes visitors year-round. The museum inducts new trainers, jockeys, and horses to its Hall of Fame each first Monday of August in the nearby Fasig-Tipton Sales Pavilion. But at the grandstand, no lasting tribute exists, with one exception: a statue of Sea Hero in the paddock.

When an influential member of the racetrack's board asks to have a three-ton bronze of his Travers Stakes winner constructed for public display, there is only one question from his colleagues to surface. Who's going to pay for it?

When that influential board member is Paul Mellon—horseman, industrialist, art collector, and philanthropist extraordinaire—the answer is obvious.

Sea Hero, the Kentucky Derby winner that raced in the gray and yellow silks of Mellon's Rokeby Stables, is one of only three Derby winners in the last sixty-five years to win the Travers. But despite his noteworthy accomplishment, Sea Hero was an unlikely equine subject for a statue.

Fourstardave, for example, was much more the people's horse. The gelded son of Compliance found the winner's circle in eight consecutive Saratoga meets. Perhaps equally deserving is Go for Wand, the only horse buried in the infield. Her grave is marked by a simple headstone, which goes unnoticed. Man O' War, Citation, Secretariat—wouldn't one of these standout performers be more likely than Sea Hero to be honored with a sculpture?

Nevertheless, if Sea Hero ran each of his races the same way that he ran in the Derby and the Travers, the issue about his stature wouldn't surface. But trainer Mack Miller couldn't get the obviously talented but erratic son of Polish Navy to be steady.

In a betting game, the parceling of praise to an animal that frequently loses is like

After bumping Miner's Mark, Jerry Bailey used the whip to urge Kentucky Derby winner Sea Hero across the finish line two lengths ahead of Kissin Kris.
NYRA photograph by Adam Coglianese

SEA HERO'S 3-YEAR-OLD RACE RECORD				
DATE	RACE	DISTANCE	TRACK	RESULT
February 7, 1993	G3 Palm Beach	1 1/6 Mile	Gulfstream (FL)	9 (12 1/2)
February 23, 1993	Allowance 33000	1 1/16 Mile	Gulfstream (FL)	3 (1 1/2)
April 10, 1993	G1 Blue Grass	1 1/18 Mile	Keeneland (KY)	4 (2 3/4)
May 1, 1993	G1 Kentucky Derby	1 1/4 Mile	Churchill (KY)	1 (2 1/2)
May 15, 1993	G1 Preakness	1 3/16 Mile	Pimlico (MD)	5 (8 1/2)
June 5, 1993	G1 Belmont	1 1/2 Mile	Belmont (NY)	7 (15)
August 1, 1993	G2 Jim Dandy	1 1/8 Mile	Saratoga (NY)	4 (7 1/2)
August 21, 1993	G1 Travers	1 1/4 Mile	Saratoga (NY)	1 (2)
September 19, 1993	G2 Molson Million	1 1/8 Mile	Woodbine (ONT)	3 (5 1/4)

Sea Hero's philanthropist owner Paul Mellon suggested that a statue of his horse be created for display to the public. Mellon, a patron of the arts, funded the sculpture created by Tessa Pullan. Photograph by Vic Zast

tipping the roller for snake eyes when your money has been placed on the pass line.

Sea Hero lost his first three races as a three-year-old before capturing the Kentucky Derby. He then promptly dropped his next three decisions as if the Run for the Roses was an accident.

"I wish he could tell me," Miller joked about the horse's in-and-out form. "But darn it, the horse hasn't said a word to me yet," the trainer quipped in explanation.

On Travers Day, both Mellon and Miller posed wearing Panama straw hats in the Saratoga paddock, as if it was the presentation ring at Glorious Goodwood. Sea Hero was the picture of fitness and adorned with a puffy beige shadow roll. The sun bronzed his flanks like a stagelight. The weather gave the effect of a late summer day—not too hot, not too cool, and hardly a trace of humidity. Blue skies made the white, passing clouds look like daisies that Mother Nature tossed on a pond.

When the field broke from the gate, El Bakan shot to the front. Foxtrail sped to his outside, and Cherokee Run ran behind him on the rail. At the half-mile pole, Devoted Brass was fourth with Colonial Affair fifth and Wallenda and Miner's Mark next. Sea Hero had only Kissin Kris, the 5-2 favorite, beat.

Although these horses don't seem like an impressive bunch now, every three-year-old with an important stakes win that spring was represented. Moreover, after six furlongs run in 1:11 3/5 and every betting interest still in contention, the track could have taken wagers all over again and not have been the worse for it.

First, Devoted Brass with Laffit Pincay, Jr., grabbed the lead at the half-mile pole. Then Colonial Affair, the Belmont Stakes winner, made his move under jockey Julie Krone. As Devoted Brass and Colonial Affair exchanged honors in the front of the pack, Chris McCarron, aboard Miner's Mark, got his mount to motoring. In the end, though, it was Sea Hero, Jerry Bailey at the whip, who moved fastest.

Although Sea Hero finished two lengths in front of Kissin Kris at the end, there was a moment of nervousness for everyone. The first place finisher bumped slightly with Miner's Mark at the eighth pole before Bailey straightened him out, giving Nervous Nellies something to worry about. But the bump didn't harm either horse enough to convince the stewards to make anything of it.

The Travers result shed no light on theories about why Sea Hero ran good races on some days and clunkers on others. In his previous three races, the colt finished off the board in uninspiring efforts. But on this, another unpredictable day at the Spa course, Mellon's soon-to-be-bronzed horse shared the stage with no one.

Stretch Drive

THE GAZEBO is another jewel in Saratoga's crown. It is classic Victorian architecture set off by landscaping and the grass of the turf course. It is so elegant and so Saratoga that I had to use it somehow. Initially, I put three horses and jockeys shoulder-to-shoulder beneath the white and gray summer house, but it was too busy. I settled for two riders and used a splash of the white rail to help separate foreground from background. The simple green lawn and uninterrupted treeline help to balance the energy and give the eye a place to rest. GM

I cut the design for *Stretch Drive* out of Amberlith®, one layer for each color. This was the layer for the dark trees and shrubs. My first concept sketch had three jockeys. I deleted the one on the right in my final design.

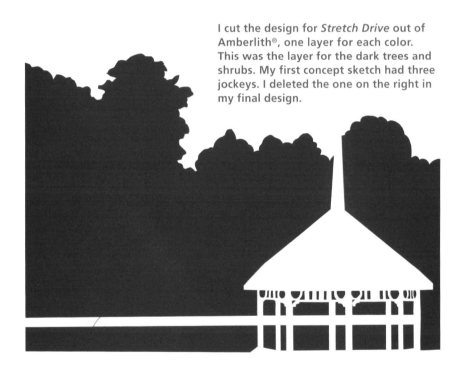

54

THE
TRAVERS
125th Running

Saratoga 1994

The Bull, the Cat, and a Rabbit

Holy Bull Charges to the Front and Stays There

1994 Travers Stakes	
125th Running on Saturday, August 20	
Winner	Holy Bull
Jockey	Mike Smith
Owner	Warren A. "Jimmy" Croll
Trainer	Warren A. "Jimmy" Croll
Time	2:02

In Tabasco Cat, winner of the Preakness and Belmont Stakes, trainer D. Wayne Lukas believed that he had the horse that could beat Holy Bull.

TABASCO CAT ON THE LOOSE

Jeff Lukas was thirty-six years old and the top assistant to his father, D. Wayne Lukas, when he became forever associated with Tabasco Cat. Then two years old, the son of Storm Cat got loose on the morning of December 15, 1993, following a routine bath. The colt charged in the direction of Jeff, who stood his ground and vainly waved his arms to try to stop the charging steed. Tabasco Cat, who would go on to win the 1994 Preakness and Belmont Stakes, slammed into Jeff, who sustained fractures in the base of his skull.

Jeff fell into a coma and contracted pneumonia five days later before he slowly recovered under the treatment of Dr. William Caton. By February, he was allowed to temporarily leave the rehabilitation clinic to visit home, in time for his daughter's first birthday party. Two months later, he returned to the track for the first time since the incident, which left him blind in his right eye and with permanent brain damage. — Jon Forbes

By far, Travers favorite Holy Bull was the most exciting horse of 1994. Those who tried to collar him early came up gasping for air. Those who thought they could catch up with him found themselves with nothing to show for it.

Yet, in Tabasco Cat, winner of the Preakness and Belmont Stakes, trainer D. Wayne Lukas believed he had a horse that could beat him. Unimpressed by Holy Bull's Dwyer and Haskell Invitational victories, Lukas was typically outspoken when comparing the two.

"Look at Holy Bull's record under a microscope. Who was second when he won the Dwyer? Nobody can tell you," Lukas mused, disregarding that the gray son of Great Above had won ten of twelve lifetime starts. To say the least, Lukas could have said that Holy Bull was intimidating.

Furthermore, the trainer's argument might have held merit if Tabasco Cat, a son of Storm Cat, had himself beaten something. But Tabasco Cat's staunchest competition in his Triple Crown triumphs came from Go for Gin, an upset winner of the Derby on a muddy track, and Strodes Creek, the Derby betting favorite for reasons unexplained.

Nevertheless, Lukas must have seen plenty of ability in the colt, and perhaps even something more. In December, the year before, Tabasco Cat changed the life of his son, Jeff, forever. The excitable horse ran over the younger Lukas at Santa Anita, leaving him brain damaged and ending his promising career as a horse trainer.

To his credit, Lukas said after Tabasco Cat won the Belmont Stakes, "I spent thirty-two days of pure hell with Jeff and had some time to think things over. I knew I could never separate Jeff and this horse, but I believed he could be special."

Regardless, Lukas's respect for Tabasco Cat wasn't borne out by the way he approached the Travers. He entered the rabbit Commanche Trail to soften up Holy Bull for his stretch runner's closing kick. Embarrassed by a 1993 which saw him tumble from the top of the nation's trainers' standings, he was going after every big prize as if finishing second was disgraceful. To add the Travers to his total of victories, he would sacrifice a race from another horse to do it.

Commanche Trail, the pacesetter under John Velasquez, did as expected. But Tabasco Cat, the closer, did not. He finished a well-beaten third.

Lukas, a man of many words, chose these to explain why, "I was worried all day about the track," he was reported to have told the *Thoroughbred Times*. "That was a loose, wet couple of inches on the top, and the base was firm. Those are two things he doesn't like: number one, wet; number two, hard."

In any case, Holy Bull ran to Commanche Trail's blistering pace from the opening bell and put him aside after five furlongs. He hit the six-furlong mark in 1:10 2/5 and the mile in 1:35 4/5. Only Man O' War in 1920 and Honest Pleasure in 1976 had won the Travers after setting fractions so suicidal. Then track announcer Tom Durkin alerted the crowd to a threat.

"There is cause for Concern," Durkin boomed into his microphone and startled all in the crowd to take their eyes off the leader and onto the closer. After six furlongs, Concern, a son of Broad Brush, was sixteen lengths back and launching a furious rally under Jerry Bailey. Concern, 10-1 in the wagering, looked even money to catch Holy Bull with an eighth of a mile to go.

As the wire loomed, Holy Bull fought harder. His jockey, Mike Smith, whacked the great champion seventeen times to coax every ounce of effort out of him. Concern kept advancing, with Bailey thinking he had measured the extent of Holy Bull's

THE HISTORY AND ART OF 25 TRAVERS

stamina perfectly. Although Holy Bull had never run this far before, there was no quit in either colt as they raced toward the finish line.

"He had every chance to go by him," Bailey conceded once Holy Bull's head and neck passed under the wire first. "I certainly never got in front of him, and I don't know if I would have if we went around again," he said.

The way Holy Bull's trainer and owner, Jimmy Croll, saw it, "The second he heard that horse coming at him, he dug in again." Regarding Lukas's pre-race comments, he merely added, "Wayne better get a new microscope."

Prior to the race, Lukas had called the 127th Travers field "a Bull, a Cat, a rabbit, and maybe a couple of dogs." As it turned out, the Bull was the rabbit, and the Cat was a dog. Commanche Trail was eased after a mile, and Tabasco Cat finished more than seventeen lengths back. Two months later, Concern won the Breeders' Cup Classic.

Above: **Concern came charging down the homestretch to test the stamina of Holy Bull. Bull rose to the occasion and held on to win by a half length.** NYRA photograph by Adam Coglianese

Left: **Jockey Mike Smith stood high in the saddle, signaling to all that Holy Bull had just won the Travers, shadowed by Jerry Bailey on Concern.** Skip Dickstein photograph for *The Blood-Horse*

TOM DURKIN'S RACE CALL

"It is Holy Bull who runs an eye-opening three-quarters in one-ten and three and he rounds the far turn with a four-length lead. Unaccounted For has now moved into second. Tabasco Cat is still seven lengths from the lead. And Concern begins to hit his best stride; he has ten lengths to make up. And Mike Smith lets The Bull roll! He's in front by five as they come to the quarter pole.

BUT THERE IS CAUSE FOR CONCERN. Concern comes on, second on the outside. Tabasco Cat is well-behind in third. They're coming down to the final furlong. Mike Smith asking Holy Bull for everything he has. Concern is coming hard under Jerry Bailey. It's still Holy Bull, desperately trying to hold.

Concern, a final surge! But it's Holy Bull, AS GAME AS A RACEHORSE CAN BE COMING DOWN TO THE WIRE. HOLY BULL WINS!"

Out in Front

WITH THIS, MY FIRST DIGITAL drawing, I left behind the joys and complexities of silkscreen printing. The beautiful, gray Holy Bull made the transition easy. Graduated colors are difficult in silk screening, but are far more controllable in a drawing program, so I decided to give them a try. I wanted to make the illustration look a bit like an Asian block print. I love the contrasting outline around the horse and the bold shading. Even the background is shaded to create depth. More than most, this image looks three-dimensional to me. GM

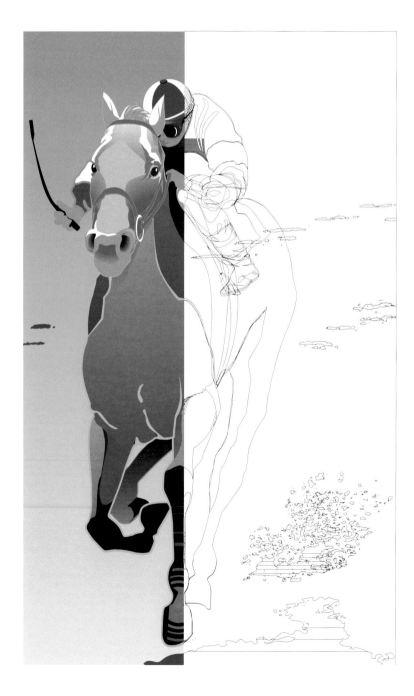

In 1994, technology changed the way I create artwork for the Travers posters. No more cutting colored paper or Amberlith®. Now I use Macro-media FreeHand®, a vector drawing program. Vectors are outlines that I can fill with a solid color or a gradient which transitions from one color to another.

THE
TRAVERS

1 2 6 t h   R u n n i n g

Saratoga 1995

Superstar Turns Second Stringer into Superstar

Victory by Thunder Gulch Convinces Almost Everyone

1995 Travers Stakes	
126th Running on Saturday, August 19	
Winner	Thunder Gulch
Jockey	Gary Stevens
Owner	Michael Tabor
Trainer	D. Wayne Lukas
Time	2:03 3/5

Above: **Thunder Gulch begins to pull away from Pyramid Peak in the stretch.** Albany (NY) *Times Union* photograph by Luanne M. Ferris

"This horse beats horses," Lukas said of his 25-1 Kentucky Derby winner.

Right: **Jockey Gary Stevens said Kentucky Derby winner Thunder Gulch had an easy time running away from the pack to win by four and a half lengths.** NYRA photograph by Adam Coglianese

Of all the great trainers who have saddled Travers Stakes winners, D. Wayne Lukas may be the greatest. A statement like this would outrage some Saratoga racing fans.

Here, on the edge of the rough-hewn Adirondacks, the locals want their trainers bound to their barns and crusty. A man like the eloquent Lukas, an innovator known for jet-setting stakes runners from border to border, is often seen as uncaring.

Give these people H. Allen Jerkens or P.G. Johnson or Woody Stephens—trainers who growl when you ask them a question—and they presume that these fellows must be genuine horsemen. Confront them with the slick-speaking Lukas—big teeth, aviator sunglasses, Stetson, creased chaps, and palomino—and they wonder how anyone so polished could be serious.

Appearances aside, there are other reasons why jealousy abounds. Like all politicians, Lukas knows that job number one is to get elected. Neat as a pin, he works over the swells in the clubhouse as if they were campaign contributors. From one decade to another, he has found that willing investor to buy him the pedigreed athlete that others fail to purchase. And decade after decade, while other trainers have their ups and downs, Lukas has been consistently competitive.

Coincidentally, Lukas and his first Travers winner share a certain characteristic. Thunder Gulch triumphed in the 126th Travers after compiling one of the best records ever. Yet, entering the race, his detractors held a doubt. They were uneasy about the colt's superiority because he, like his trainer, accomplished what he did in a way that they didn't find standard.

"This horse beats horses," Lukas said of his 25-1 Kentucky Derby winner. "You put him on the track and he rises to the occasion. You go back through the record books, and you're gonna have trouble finding credentials like his in the three-year-old division."

Despite his ability to identify a good horse, Lukas didn't realize at first that Thunder Gulch was as talented as he turned out to be. He promoted Timber Country, the Eclipse Award-winning juvenile, as the colt under his shedrow with the best chance of taking home the roses. He ran Thunder Gulch as part of his Derby entry because owner Michael Tabor bred the son of Gulch and because the colt had earned his way to Louisville by winning the Florida Derby.

After winning the Run for the Roses, Thunder Gulch finished third in the Preakness by three-quarters of a length and annexed the Belmont Stakes by two. He then captured the Swaps Stakes at Hollywood Park. But his time in New York was slow and the competition out West was deemed to be marginal, further giving cause for some people to doubt his authenticity.

The competition in the 1995 Travers also was a bit lacking. But with $750,000 at stake, no race is without challenge. Thunder Gulch faced Jim Dandy winner Composer, solid runner Pyramid Peak, Star Standard, Citadeed, Rank and File, and the Panamanian import Malthus. But as expected, Thunder Gulch was best of the seven and came home the victor easily.

The colt's rider, Gary Stevens, placed his mount perfectly in fourth behind Pyramid Peak, Star Standard, and Citadeed in the early running. When he hit the quarter pole, he drew even with Pyramid Peak and then left him wanting.

"The horses I was most worried about were in front of me, and I felt like I had them at any point in the race," he said afterward. "He was pretty much cantering into the stretch. He skipped away from them easily."

Thunder Gulch ended up the winner by four and a half lengths. The ten-time stakes winner's final time was a dawdling 2:03 3/5—just right to keep the controversy about his true quality brewing.

Thunder Gulch paid $3.50, while increasing his own bank account to $2.6 million. Other than Whirlaway in 1941, the only horse to sweep the Triple Crown and win the Travers, only two other horses—Twenty Grand in 1931 and Shut Out in 1942—matched Thunder Gulch by winning the Kentucky Derby, Belmont Stakes, and Travers.

Lukas wanted very much to make Thunder Gulch "Horse of the Year." Following the Travers, he planned to have his colt take on the eventual champion, Cigar, in the Woodward, the Jockey Club Gold Cup, or the Breeders' Cup Classic.

"Yes, Cigar has done everything very impressively," Lukas said, contrasting the champ's stylish romps with Thunder Gulch's workmanlike successes.

After Thunder Gulch won the Kentucky Cup Classic at Turfway Park—his eleventh victory in a stakes race—he lost to Cigar in the Jockey Club Gold Cup. In addition to having to settle for the three-year-old championship, Lukas' colt suffered a condylar fracture of the cannon bone and had to be retired to stud. In his next start, the irrepressible Cigar finished undefeated for the year with a romp in the Breeders' Cup Classic.

Above: **Trainer D. Wayne Lukas was confident in Thunder Gulch, saying the horse always rose to the occasion when he stepped onto the race track.** Albany (NY) *Times Union* photograph by Skip Dickstein

D. WAYNE LUKAS HIGHLIGHTS

Four Kentucky Derby Winners
1988, 1995, 1996, and 1999

Five Preakness Stakes Winners
1980, 1984, 1994, 1995, and 1999

Four Belmont Stakes Winners
1994, 1995, 1996, and 2000

Two Travers Stakes Winners
1991 and 1995

Trained 23 Individual Champions

Led Trainer Standings in Earnings
from 1984–1992 and 1994–1996

Inducted into Racing Hall of Fame in 1999

Wire to Wire

I WANTED TO CREATE the feeling of being surrounded by the action, as though you were riding in the same race. It's a close-up perspective; lots of detail, vivid colors, hard edges and a tight crop, bright, sharp reflections and a straight-at-you, outta-my-way attitude. I used rich earth colors, simple, powerful silks, and a dusty image of the clubhouse to remind you where this action is taking place. GM

I drew this sketch of the magnificent Thunder Gulch to get a better idea of the structure of his handsome face, and to map out all the customary tack surrounding it.

THE TRAVERS

127th Running

Saratoga 1996

Will's Way Walks the Walk

Bond's Streetwalker Takes His Time to Mature and Triumphs

1996 Travers Stakes
127th Running on Saturday, August 24

Winner	Will's Way
Jockey	Jorge Chavez
Owner	William Clifton, Jr.
Trainer	H. James Bond
Time	2:02 2/5

Will's Way had a secret agent, trainer James Bond, spying on the competition in the Travers with video tape. The "007" saddle cloth should have been a clue that Bond would decode the tapes and plan the perfect attack.
Photograph by Vic Zast

In planning for the Travers, Bond plotted Chavez's trip on a chalkboard after studying video tapes of the competition.

Horse trainers come to Saratoga each August, but some dig roots and stay. H. James Bond, the man from Rochester, New York, whose runners in the mornings sport the blue and white saddlecloths with 007 on the side, is a trainer whose roots have sunk more deeply into the local firmament than those of an oak.

For the last dozen years, Bond's barns have been located in town, not inside the main property of the racetrack. Coffee drinkers at the Morning Line food stand can see the trainer's runners coming up Gridley Street, past the Horseshoe Inn Bar and Grill, and through the intersection. The drive-time commuters in their cars on Nelson Avenue show patience, and in fact, one of them, Carol Tarantino, a real estate agent at Roohan's, the city's biggest property agency, rather likes the delay.

"I'm not much of a track person," Tarantino said on the closing day of Saratoga one summer. "But I can't wait for the days when I'm stopped in traffic by horses crossing the street."

Back in 1996, the thirty-eight-year-old Bond stabled his string at the Payson barns between Fifth Avenue and Caroline Street. But even then, he would walk his horses back and forth from the track while traffic waited.

There was no stopping Will's Way from becoming the star of Bond's barn in the spring of that year, except for a few "baby things" which the trainer described as "worn shins."

Bond wasn't able to get Will's Way to the races as a two-year-old. Then the colt missed the Triple Crown stakes even though Bond believed that he was good enough. The colt's best outings in five lifetime starts, aside from a maiden score and subsequent allowance victory at Gulfstream, were a second in the Jim Dandy Stakes and a third in the Flamingo Stakes at Hialeah.

Like Tarantino at the horse crossing, Bond was content to bide his time with Will's Way. Nevertheless, two days before the Travers, the trainer knew that the time had come to abandon patience. "The way he trained this morning, I'm not second-guessing anything," Bond said. "I've never seen him better."

Facing six strong opponents, Will's Way took to the track far from being Bond's secret agent. The chestnut colt had served notice of his form twenty days earlier, when nipped by a nose in the Jim Dandy by Louis Quatorze. Moreover, his breeding suggested that he was the type of horse that could capture a Travers trophy. His sire, Easy Goer, won the 120th Travers in the year that he shadowed Sunday Silence in the Kentucky Derby and the Preakness.

When the gates sprung open, jockey Jorge "Chop-Chop" Chavez eased Will's Way toward the back of the pack and let all but one horse run ahead of him for a mile. With Louis Quatorze, under Pat Day, battling for the front in :23 and :46 1/5, it was

WILL'S WAY'S PRE-TRAVERS PERFORMANCES

DATE	RACE	DISTANCE	TRACK	RESULT
February 10, 1996	Maiden Special Weight	7 Furlongs	Gulfstream (FL)	1 (2 1/4)
March 8, 1996	Allowance	1 1/16 Mile	Gulfstream (FL)	1 (3 1/2)
April 6, 1996	G3 Flamingo	1 1/8 Mile	Hialeah (FL)	3 (6 1/4)
June 22, 1996	Allowance	1 Mile	Belmont (NY)	1 (1)
August 8, 1996	G2 Jim Dandy	1 1/8 Mile	Saratoga (NY)	2 (Neck)

Above: **Jorge Chavez executed trainer James Bond's race strategy perfectly, holding Will's Way near the back while the front runners broke too fast to hang on at the end. Down the stretch Will's Way closed fast and passed Louis Quatorze to win the Travers.** Albany (NY) *Times Union* photo by Luanne M. Ferris

Above left: **Bond stables his runners off racetrack grounds in a residential area of Saratoga. Each morning the horses walk the streets to the track, often stopping traffic on the way.** Photograph by Vic Zast

not very difficult to catch the leader. By the far turn, the two horses were head-to-head until Will's Way began to edge forward.

"It was very tough," said Chavez, relieved that his mount responded to urging when he hit him and opened a three-quarter length lead at the wire.

In planning for the Travers, Bond plotted Chavez's trip on a chalkboard after studying video tapes of the competition. He marked all the key points of the race with Xs and Os to show where he expected the horses to be at different stages. He then instructed Chavez to ride exactly as the chalkboard revealed. As a student, the jockey deserved an "A."

"I knew we were in good shape at the three-eighths pole, but I wanted to save something for the end, because I knew the other horse would fight," Chavez said. And, yes, for a little while, Louis Quatorze did. But the wire came upon Will's Way before it came upon him.

It was a stellar Travers field witnessed by crowd of 45,394 fans. Skip Away, the 7-5 favorite trained by Hubert "Sonny" Hine, was en route to a division title. D. Wayne Lukas saddled Editor's Note, the Belmont Stakes winner. He also had Dr. Caton, an improving sort.

Hine was displeased by the ride his third-place finisher received from Jose Santos. Lukas used the excuse of a "breathing problem" to explain why Dr. Caton missed the board. He said that Editor's Note never fired.

After the Travers, Bond said that he was certain that Will's Way would be a factor in the top races that fall. But it was Skip Away who became a superstar.

Almost all of the horses in Will's Way's class were better than he in the breeding shed. Unbridled's Song, Honour and Glory, and Grindstone, three top three-year-old horses in 1996, became sires of accomplishment in due course.

Regardless, before Will's Way retired from the racetrack, he won the Whitney Handicap at Saratoga as a four-year-old. A year and two weeks after that, Bond walked another promising sophomore across Nelson Avenue for the Travers.

Paddock Parade

THIS IMAGE ALWAYS FEELS so peaceful, cool, and quiet. I wanted to highlight part of the team that makes thoroughbred racing possible: the grooms. Using contrast and detail I first draw your attention to the horse's face, then to the handsome groom, and finally to the regal jockey who sits high above it all. The dark green tree in the background pulls the figures into a group, the architectural element suggests Saratoga, and purple shadows change white paper magically into the surface of the track. GM

Grooms seem to have a special relationship with their charges. They coax and cajole their superstar companions keeping the horses focused and usually out of trouble. Always in the background, they set the stage for the jockey to win and the crowds to delight. What would racing—or weddings—be without them.

THE
TRAVERS

128th Running

Saratoga 1997

Higher Being Hits the Finish Line First

McCarron Triumphs in Stretch with Deputy Commander

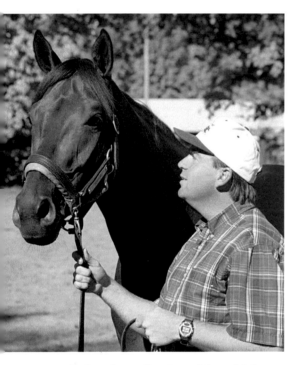

1997 Travers Stakes	
128th Running on Saturday, August 23	
Winner	Deputy Commander
Jockey	Chris McCarron
Owner	Horizon Stable
Trainer	Wally Dollase
Time	2:04

Trainer James Bond conditioned Behrens perfectly for the Travers, but heaven was with Chris McCarron, still grieving his mother's passing, who won on Deputy Commander by nosing out Behrens at the wire. Albany (NY) *Times Union* photograph by Skip Dickstein

Chris McCarron on Deputy Commander (left) battles Twin Spires as Jerry Bailey moves Behrens into contention with Blazing Sword riding the rail. Albany (NY) *Times Union* photograph by Luanne M. Ferris

It's easy to say that thoroughbred racing is all about horses. But it's often that they're the least interesting participants in a memorable race.

Bereaved jockey Chris McCarron was the most lasting story to come out of the 1997 Travers. McCarron rode the winner, Deputy Commander, to a narrow victory on his first mount in four days following the death of his mother, Helen. Her spirit carried him over the finish line, or so it seemed.

The 127th Travers Stakes included no horses that ran in the Triple Crown races. McCarron was to ride Touch Gold, the probable Travers favorite, until the son of Deputy Minister was found to have suffered a cut on his left hind foot. Trainer David Hofmans declared his star out of the race and said that the stable would instead be represented by Jim Dandy winner Awesome Again. Hofmans named Mike Smith to ride the Horizon Stable star, winner earlier that summer of the Queen's Plate in Canada.

Once free to ride another horse, McCarron was chosen by trainer Wally Dollase to partner with Deputy Commander. McCarron learned of the news from his agent while riding in California. He remained riding at Del Mar racetrack until learning of his mother's passing on Tuesday, and then flew to Milton, Massachusetts, for the funeral on Friday, Travers Eve.

Helen McCarron was seventy-four when she passed away, after suffering from brain cancer for years. Yet, death is always unexpected. An inopportune happening, it comes at its own bidding. With the blessing of his family, McCarron arrived in Saratoga less than twenty-four hours later to ride in the Travers.

"I called home, and I put some of the burden on my family," the jockey said after the Travers. "They all gave me their blessing. But that's typical of them. And they said if she can have anything to do with this, she'll give us a little boost, and sure enough, I could feel her presence."

McCarron said, "Typically, after a race I'm not at a loss for words, but I'm having trouble today." Nevertheless, his eloquence was evident on horseback.

The jockey rode the kind of race he rode 7,141 times in his Hall of Fame career. It was perfectly timed, efficient, and ended in the way that all races are supposed to end but only a handful do—with a souvenir photo taken at the finish line and another in the winner's circle.

The winning trainer, Wally Dollase, who had just saddled his first horse at Saratoga, was not the first to give credit where credit was due. That honor went to Hofmans.

Down the stretch Behrens (left), and Deputy Commander traded the lead several times, with the Commander winning in a photo finish so close that spectators didn't know who won until track stewards made the official announcement. Albany (NY) *Times Union* photograph by Luanne M. Ferris

McCarron rode the kind of race he rode 7,141 times in his Hall of Fame career.

"I think Chris was one of the factors why Deputy Commander won," he said. "He's a great rider."

Added Dollase: "We wouldn't even have run if Touch Gold had stayed in the race. I didn't think he could beat Touch Gold right now."

McCarron, heavy-hearted and somber, didn't make his journey without expecting some sort of precious metal, regardless. He rode a stalking pace in third behind the leaders for a mile and then shot to the lead at the top of the stretch. Despite a clear stretch of racetrack in front of him, he knew that his job wasn't over. Behrens, a troubled fourth in the Jim Dandy, collared him.

From the eighth pole to home, the two battled as one—first Deputy Commander, then Behrens, then Deputy Commander, then Behrens, and then at last, Deputy Commander.

"It was a good race," Behrens' jockey, Jerry Bailey, deadpanned. "If I won it, it would have been a great race."

Bailey's opinion aside, enough people in the crowd of 46,532 were pleased by the finish. But few knew who won when the horses passed beneath the wire and even fewer knew what emotional difficulty McCarron was harboring, including Behrens's trainer, James Bond.

Bond was downtrodden by the loss, having believed he would become only the fifth trainer to win the Travers in consecutive years. Before the race, the Saratoga-based trainer promised Behrens' owner, William F. Clifton, Jr., a great race and a victory. In the game of horse racing, you win some and you lose some. To make good on one out of two promises is noteworthy.

"Maybe it was a higher being that decided Chris needed it more than we needed it," Bond was reported to have said to the *Thoroughbred Times*. And then maybe it wasn't. The jockey could ride.

CHRIS McCARRON'S CAREER HIGHLIGHTS
Two Kentucky Derby Winners 1987 and 1994
Two Preakness Stakes Winners 1987 and 1992
Two Belmont Stakes Winners 1986 and 1997
Three Travers Stakes Winners 1988, 1991, and 1997
Five Breeder's Cup Classic Winners 1988, 1989, 1996, 2000, and 2001
Leading Jockey—Races Won 1974 and 1980
Leading Jockey—Earnings 1980, 1981, 1984, and 1991
Inducted into Racing Hall of Fame in 1989

Clean Break

ALL OF THE ENERGY in this poster goes up and out, and your eye follows. The white blinkers on the horse create a focal point that keeps you on the page. These are brilliant, midday, heat-of-August colors, with a hot, hazy sky. And, just to make sure you realize where you are, the ubiquitous gazebo of the famous Saratoga track. GM

I wanted to show the astonishing strength of a race-ready thoroughbred. I did this tonal study to try to understand and simplify the anatomy, and to see how strong sunlight would play on those beautiful muscles.

THE TRAVERS

129th Running

Saratoga 1998

One More Jump

Two Noses Separate Coronado's Quest, Victory Gallop, and Raffie's Majesty

1998 Travers Stakes	
129th Running on Saturday, August 29	
Winner	Coronado's Quest
Jockey	Mike Smith
Owner	Stuart Janney III, Stonerside Farm
Trainer	Claude R. McGaughey III
Time	2:03 2/5

Exercise rider Shannon Ritter guides Victory Gallop through a light workout the morning of the Travers. Her colt ended up behind by a nose in a three-way finsh later in the day. Albany (NY) *Times Union* photo by Skip Dickstein

Cantankerous Coronado's Quest's bad behavior caused trainer Shug McGaughey to hold the ill-mannered colt out of the Triple Crown races. Quest kept his temper under control in Saratoga with just an occasional playful nip at his lead or handler Louie Carrasco's hand. Albany (NY) *Times Union* photograph by Skip Dickstein

Ask collectors of Greg Montgomery's Travers Stakes posters which is their favorite and there's a good chance that the one sold to the public in 1999 will come out on top.

The noses of three horses—the first three across the finish line the prior year—form the left-hand border of the poster. It's a view of the photo finish that only the cameraman sees. Horses race counterclockwise at Saratoga—as they do at all U.S. racetracks—so the noses would be facing the other way if you were a fan watching from the grandstand.

Montgomery's perspective notwithstanding, it's safe to say that the finish of the 129th Travers was thrilling from any vantage point.

Two horses, Victory Gallop, the Belmont Stakes winner and 6-5 favorite, and his Haskell Invitational conqueror, the speed-loving Coronado's Quest, sent off at 8-5, were supposed to be inseparable at the finish line. But Raffie's Majesty, a New York-bred at 11-1 odds, was not. A bob of the head was what separated them, although handicappers with an understanding of pace know differently.

Earlier in the week, Victory Gallop's trainer Elliott Walden, a tall, soft-spoken Kentuckian, entered a rabbit named Sheila's Flag in the Travers. The horse was entered with one purpose—to set fast fractions that would tempt Coronado's Quest, a son of Forty Niner, to chase him. Walden believed that Victory Gallop, who had already shown his liking for the distance, would be better than the speed-favoring Coronado's Quest at 1 1/4 miles and wanted to be certain that the one-and-a-quarter-lengths defeat his horse suffered in the 1 1/8-mile Haskell wouldn't happen again.

It was good thinking while it lasted. Then something happened to change Walden's mind. He saw two horses entered—Dice Dancer and Grand Slam—that figured to do the job of softening up Coronado's Quest for him. At the last minute, he decided to keep Sheila's Flag in the barn and leave the "rabbiting" to others.

Leaving matters in other people's hands or other horses' feet seldom works. The other two pace-setters failed Walden, and the pace was a tepid: 48.93 for the half mile and 1:13.07 for three-quarters. As a result, Victory Gallop had to run much closer to the leaders than expected, and his rider, Alex Solis, had to hope that Coronado's Quest wasn't rested from the crawl.

Mike Smith on Coronado's Quest (right)
holds off Victory Gallop (center)
and late-charging Raffie's Majesty.
Albany (NY) *Times Union* photograph
by Steve Jacobs

"We were closer to the pace than usual," Walden admitted.

Solis said he still thought he had the measure of Coronado's Quest. "We were close to him and I thought I was going to go by him, but he fought back," he said.

That was not the case for trainer Claude "Shug" McGaughey's horse, however, as jockey Mike Smith placed Coronado's Quest in a spot that was perfect for pouncing.

"When I asked him to run he laid it down," Smith told the *New York Times* afterward. "I'm glad the race was written for a mile and quarter and not a mile and a quarter and a jump."

Coronado's Quest won the Travers in 2:03 2/5—not the kind of time to establish an invincible aura. It was his fifth stakes victory in a row, nonetheless, and proved once and for all that the well-bred colt wasn't an underachiever.

In the spring, Coronado's Quest disappointed his trainer and owners Stuart Janney III and Stonerside Farm by exhibiting an unmanageable temper that kept him from participating in the Triple Crown. But before the Travers, he stood like the statue of Sea Hero in Saratoga's paddock.

Lost in the controversy regarding rabbits was the performance of Raffie's Majesty, trained by Saratoga resident James Bond. Although Raffie's Majesty finished third by two noses, his last-second, hold-your-breath dash was most amazing. Given the extra jump that Smith didn't want written, the symmetry of Montgomery's one-two-three finish from the rail out would have been altered. The nose of the horse at the top of the frame would have been first.

> I'm glad the race was written for a mile and a quarter and not a mile and a quarter and a jump.
>
> —Jockey Mike Smith

CORONADO'S QUEST'S FIVE STRAIGHT STAKES WINS				
DATE	RACE	DISTANCE	TRACK	RESULT
April 11, 1998	G2 Wood Memorial	1 1/8 Mile	Aqueduct (NY)	1 (2 1/2)
June 6, 1998	G2 Riva Ridge	7 Furlongs	Belmont (NY)	1 (3 1/2)
July 12, 1998	G2 Dwyer	1 1/16 Mile	Belmont (NY)	1 (5)
August 9, 1998	G1 Buick Haskell	1 1/8 Mile	Monmouth (NJ)	1 (1 1/4)
August 29, 1998	G1 Travers	1 1/4 Mile	Saratoga (NY)	1 (Nose)

By a Nose

I WANTED A DIFFERENT PERSPECTIVE and different background color
for this poster, so I drew these horses as seen from the inside of
the track, right at the finish line. The horses are running right to left,
not the more usual, and comfortable, left to right—like we read.
I used a high, down angle so that the horse closest to the viewer—
the winning horse—would not obscure the other two. The left edge
of the print is the finish line. This was my last silk-screened image.
I pulled many original prints of this image showing a texture to the
track surface (tan background). In the end, I decided that I liked
the simplicity of the untextured track. So, that's the way the poster
appears. Also, it never ceases to amaze me how the application
of a tiny white highlight dot changes a black orb into a flashing,
driven eye. GM

This textured version is not that different
from the cleaner, simpler untextured one
that became my choice for the poster.
It's just busier to my eye and takes away
from the wonderful negative space that
surrounds the charging profiles.

THE
TRAVERS
130th Running

Saratoga 1999

Murphy's Law

Schulhofer Saddles First Travers Winner as Lemon Drop Kid Grows into a Man

1999 Travers Stakes	
130th Running on Saturday, August 28	
Winner	Lemon Drop Kid
Jockey	Jose Santos
Owner	Jeanne Vance
Trainer	Flint "Scotty" Schulhofer
Time	2:02.19

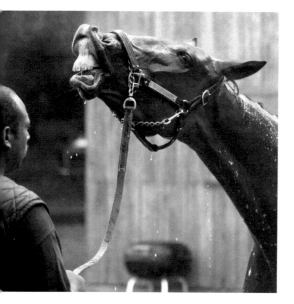

Saratoga is known for its baths, and Lemon Drop Kid shows he enjoys the relaxing waters after his final workout for the Jim Dandy, which he lost by five lengths three weeks before the Travers. Albany (NY) *Times Union* photograph by Skip Dickstein

"Damn, he's got two," *The Blood-Horse* quoted Schulhofer as gleefully telling his co-workers.

Murphy became famous by saying, "If something can go wrong, it will." But there's another of Murphy's laws that proves itself true more often, and that one is, "Things take longer than they do."

Flint "Scotty" Schulhofer, 73, had been training horses for nearly five decades without a Travers Stakes victory before Lemon Drop Kid gave him his first Midsummer Derby score in six tries. Jockey Jose Santos was zero for nine in Travers Stakes rides. But hearing them crow on the day before the race, you wouldn't know it.

Both trainer and jockey believed heartily that Lemon Drop Kid was a mortal lock in the classic. And their reasons for believing in him are why winners aren't always discovered in the *Daily Racing Form*.

One cause for their optimism was that Lemon Drop Kid, who was previously thought to be a ridgling, was discovered not to be. In his three Triple Crown races and the Jim Dandy, Lemon Drop Kid was listed as a horse that had only one testis descended.

"Damn, he's got two," *The Blood-Horse* quoted Schulhofer as gleefully telling his co-workers on the Saratoga backside when he discovered the change in anatomy after a pre-Travers workout. Could the Hall of Fame trainer have thought that the son of Kingmambo might have suffered a bit from the unusual condition?

Whatever the case, there was a sudden gusto to be found in the horse when he worked in the mornings. In fact, Lemon Drop Kid was preparing for the Travers in a style that newspaper reports couldn't account for.

A May foal, Lemon Drop Kid was at an age disadvantage that spring when compared to his rivals in the three-year-old division. But by the time the Travers would be run, he was fully grown and showing the bloom of a competitor at his physical peak. Take, for example, these signs that emerged in the weeks before the race.

In his final Travers prep, Lemon Drop Kid worked three furlongs aggressively in :35 3/5. Unfazed by the exertion, the next day the colt caused a commotion in the barn when he dumped Schulhofer unceremoniously as the Hall of Fame mentor tried to soothe him. Later the same day, the horse heard the bugler's call announcing that runners were coming onto the track, and he rose from his feed on the backstretch as if thinking it was his time to compete.

Creating further optimism in Lemon Drop Kid's camp was the changing weather. Travers Day dawned with an overcast sky, but the track was not sloppy as it was after rain showers doused it on Friday.

A dried-out track was cause for smiles all around at the Schulhofer barn. Believing that a race over the Saratoga surface brought out the best in a horse's second time out, the trainer had used the Jim Dandy three weeks earlier as a prep. But Lemon Drop Kid lost by five and a quarter lengths to Ecton Park. It was a gooey strip he clearly disliked.

Schulhofer noted that Lemon Drop Kid also lost the Peter Pan Stakes at Belmont Park on an off track that he didn't handle well. But the horse came back after that dismal effort to triumph in the Belmont Stakes on a fast track.

Lemon Drop Kid's on-again, off-again tendency to follow each performance with a contrasting one seemed to be the pattern. Schulhofer's horse won the Blue Grass Stakes and then faltered in the Kentucky Derby. He lost the Peter Pan and then triumphed in the Belmont. Would the pattern persist in the Travers?

SCOTTY SCHULHOFER'S TRAVERS RECORD

YEAR	HORSE	FINISH
1987	Cryptoclearance	Second
1991	Fly So Free	Third
1993	Colonial Affair	Fourth
1994	Unaccounted For	Fourth
1998	Deputy Diamond	Sixth
1999	Lemon Drop Kid	First
2000	Postponed	Sixth

Jockey Jose Santos (center) raises his fist in victory after crossing the finish line to win the 130th running of the Travers Stakes. Shane Sellers on Vision and Verse (right) was runner-up with Jerry Bailey, on pre-race favorite Menifee, finishing third. Albany (NY) *Times Union* photograph by James Goolsby

Of course it would. Too much in the way of fate was going on for Lemon Drop Kid—with the inevitability of persistence, the discovery of body parts, the sharpness of form, the drying conditions, and Murphy's little-known law just the least of them. Owner Jeanne Vance's horse was at last ready to show why since day one, Schulhofer told his son, Randy, that Lemon Drop Kid "might be the best horse we've ever had."

At the start of the Travers, Mike Smith aboard Cat Thief engaged Shane Sellers aboard Vision and Verse for the lead. These two were followed by Badger Gold, Ecton Park, and Lemon Drop Kid, heads apart and slightly ahead of Menifee, the 3-2 favorite, who was trapped on the rail. With the pace crawling, a confident Santos kept Lemon Drop Kid within striking distance of the leaders but bade his time until the head of the stretch before taking on Vision and Verse for the lead.

Lemon Drop Kid edged forward to grab a short advantage, but Vision and Verse fought back. With a crowd of 51,371 roaring approval of the duel, the two horses tested each other for a few strides before Lemon Drop Kid gained the advantage once and for all.

"This is the one I've wanted for years," Schulhofer said in the winner's circle. Even Murphy was pleased that he got it.

Jockey Jose Santos and trainer Scotty Schulhofer remove the saddle from Lemon Drop Kid in the winner's circle and celebrate winning the Travers. The victory was a long time coming for both jockey and trainer. Associated Press photograph by Jim McKnight

First Across

THE CONNECTION between the two jockeys is a powerful dynamic. The shadow of the horse's neck pushes you up to the focal point— the red cap of the forward jockey in the plain, blue field. Once you get there, you follow his gaze back to the other horse and rider. This was the first time that I used a low-angle approach, which accentuates the power of the horse, the loft of the jockey, and the grittiness of the track. And that flying dirt was really difficult to do— when you have to draw every grain, lots of dirt is lots of work. GM

Above: **This close-up of the track surface reveals the texture I added to show the explosion that takes place every time a hoof pounds the dirt.**

Left: **My original sketch has the lead horse charging out of the frame, but lacks the wonderful interaction that the jockey's backward glance creates.**

THE
TRAVERS

131st Running

Saratoga 2000

Painting the Canoe

Unshaded is a Shade Better than Albert the Great

2000 Travers Stakes
131st Running on Saturday, August 26

Winner	Unshaded
Jockey	Shane Sellers
Owner	James B. Tafel
Trainer	Carl Nafzger
Time	2:02.59

Elizabeth Contessa, daughter of trainer Gary Contessa, gives a paddock jockey a hug. The metal jockey is painted in Jim Tafel's colors, commemorating Unshaded's Travers victory. Albany (NY) *Times Union* photo by Skip Dickstein

Opposite bottom: **Unshaded's trainer, Carl Nafzger, predicted in the spring that he would be painting the canoe in Saratoga's infield lake with Tafel's yellow and blue colors after winning the Travers.** Albany (NY) *Times Union* photo by Skip Dickstein

It was a crisp, beautiful day that last Saturday in August, dark only in the background that preceded it. One trainer believed in his rider and another didn't. That is an oversimplified summation of the 2000 Travers, a race in which human drama was equal to the competition that took place on the track.

With both Fusaichi Pegasus, the Kentucky Derby winner, and Red Bullet, his Preakness Stakes conqueror, missing from the Midsummer Derby, Unshaded, with Shane Sellers aboard, bested Albert the Great, ridden by Jorge Chavez, by a head. The result was a redemptive experience for almost everyone involved.

Chavez secured the Travers mount on Albert the Great after the accomplished son of Go for Gin ran a dismal seventh out of seven horses in the Jim Dandy, beaten by at least a furlong.

"I can ride one bad and get them beat by three lengths," the jockey Richie Migliore, whom trainer Nick Zito replaced for the Travers, was reported by the *New York Times* to have said, following the embarrassing Jim Dandy defeat. "But I can't ride one bad enough to get him beat by twenty-seven lengths." The actual margin was twenty-eight and a half lengths. It must be difficult to calculate the difference when the rest of the field is so far ahead of you.

Migliore's attempt at humor notwithstanding, Zito decided a change in riders was appropriate. "I say publicly that Richard didn't do anything terribly wrong," Zito told the newspaper. "But those fractions were very fast. I wish he would have given him more of a break."

Zito was referring to the fact that Albert the Great faded badly in the mile and an eighth Travers prep after speeding six furlongs in 1:10.60. To him, Albert the Great's race was a big disappointment, especially since he won four races in a row before it.

Migliore is traditionally one of the leading riders at the Saratoga meet, and Zito's curt dismissal of him seemed unduly harsh. But in typical gentlemanly fashion, the veteran rider acknowledged that the trainer's decision was his professional prerogative and promptly landed another mount on Commendable, the Belmont Stakes winner.

In the Unshaded camp, trainer Carl Nafzger was entrusting his dream to win a Travers to Sellers. The jockey was recently released from treatment for debilitating depression. The affable trainer had failed to win the Travers on three previous occasions. A more unlikely combination was possible, but improbable.

Knowing that Unshaded wouldn't be ready for the Derby, Nafzger had announced as far back as February that he intended "to paint that canoe" in Saratoga's infield lake. Since 1961, it was tradition to decorate the canoe with the Travers winner's colors. He said he was sticking with Sellers, despite the rider's troubles.

"He's had to unload a lot of debris. He's really settled down and become more mature," Nafzger told *The Blood-Horse* about Sellers.

As for his horse, he said that Unshaded also had changed for the better. "He was dumb and immature," Nafzger said.

If ever a match was made in heaven, this was it—unless, of course, you believe that opposites attract.

With these human interests in play, the 131st Travers unfolded like therapy. Migliore aboard Commendable made the fractions, but this time he set a leisurely pace. Behind in second, Chavez rode Albert the Great with uncharacteristic patience.

On the far turn, from as far back as six lengths, Sellers began closing the gap on the leaders, and by the quarter pole, he had Unshaded on even par with Albert the Great, as Commendable receded.

The stretch run was a test of wills, with the horses running nose-to-nose and Chavez and Sellers whipping furiously. It was then that the troubled jockey found the strength to carry on. Despite being leg weary and worn out from his horse's natural obstinacy, Sellers had the son of Unbridled out in front by the eighth pole and kept on riding hard to the wire. Unshaded and Sellers finished a head in front of Albert the Great and Chavez.

"This is a difficult horse to ride," Sellers said afterward. "I dug deep and said 'Shane, give it your all.' And this horse gave it his all."

Sellers, like Nafzger, had never won a Travers before, but unlike Nafzger, who was known to be measured and careful, he was usually a handful.

"I burned a lot of bridges because of my mouth, but I'm a different person now," he gushed. "And to win the Travers is an unbelievable feeling."

Later, Nafzger made it a point to congratulate horse and rider. He was obviously elated that this Travers was history and that he had played an important part in it. "The three-year-old champion has got to win this race," he had said at the post position draw two days before the Travers. Once the race was run and won, he began thinking about the Breeders' Cup.

Based on his February prediction about Unshaded's Travers victory, Nafzger was indeed a canny prognosticator. But he was not a miracle healer.

Unshaded exited the Travers with a tendon injury and didn't race again in 2000.

It turned out that the horse—not the jockey—was damaged.

Shane Sellers celebrated a personal victory over depression and a Travers win aboard Unshaded when he signaled his accomplishments with a raised crop. NYRA photograph by Adam Coglianese

Driving Home

MORE THAN ANYTHING ELSE, with this image I wanted to create the feeling of movement and power. I put a small jockey atop a great horse and reduced the details down to the essentials. The eye follows the jockey's form up to the top of the image, where the cap and crop send you back down again. Finally, the rich brown of the horse sends you left to the girth and jockey, and it all goes around again. I feel like I've just missed seeing the entire jockey—he's just moving too fast.

In my original sketches for the 2001 poster, I actually drew two complete thoroughbreds side-by-side. I had drawn their nostrils flaring, manes flying and all their tack. I showed the two jockeys shoulder-to-shoulder, locked in combat, all eight hooves mid-air—or most of them anyway—and even the track surface and trees beyond. Then I stepped back and looked at it. It was so busy it made me dizzy. So I began to simplify the image, refining it until I could take no more away. I like this simple image so much more. GM

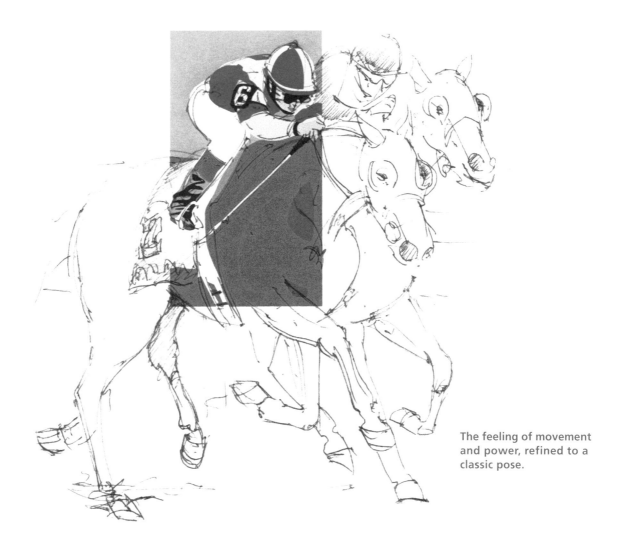

The feeling of movement and power, refined to a classic pose.

THE
TRAVERS

132nd Running

Saratoga 2001

Point of No Return

Point Given is Retired after Delighting a Record Crowd

<table>
<tr><td colspan="2">**2001 Travers Stakes**
132nd Running on Saturday, August 25</td></tr>
<tr><td>Winner</td><td>Point Given</td></tr>
<tr><td>Jockey</td><td>Gary Stevens</td></tr>
<tr><td>Owner</td><td>Thoroughbred Corp.</td></tr>
<tr><td>Trainer</td><td>Bob Baffert</td></tr>
<tr><td>Time</td><td>2:01.40</td></tr>
</table>

The alert ears and focused eyes of Preakness and Belmont Stakes winner Point Given gave his regular exercise rider Pepe Aragon confidence that good things were to come when the bell sounded for the Travers. Albany (NY) *Times Union* photo by Skip Dickstein

Point Given, winner of the Eclipse Award for "Horse of the Year" in 2001, never raced again following his facile three-and-a-half-length victory as the odds-on favorite in the 132nd Travers Stakes.

Perhaps the almost thirteen-hundred-pound chestnut son of Thunder Gulch had hit the ground hard in too many top-level races—he had won four consecutive Grade I races worth at least $1 million each that summer. Or, perhaps the time had come for horses like him to move on to the breeding shed at the slightest hint of injury—the latest trend.

Either way, the 60,486 people at Saratoga Race Course on this sunny, summer Saturday were the last to see him in action. He gave them a show they would not forget.

Prince Ahmed bin Salman of Saudi Arabia, who owned the giant-sized colt and raced him in the name of the Thoroughbred Corp., retired Point Given because of a tendon strain that would have healed in six months and would have allowed him to please fans as a four-year-old. Thus, Point Given was never given the chance to establish a lasting reputation. The talented runner, like Fusaichi Pegasus before him and Smarty Jones afterward, was a brilliant comet that came and went in the blink of an eye.

Ironically, a blink of the eye is not the way you'd describe Point Given's running style. It was more like a locomotive that, once it achieved top speed, was unstoppable. Sports writers took to calling Point Given "The Big Red Train," and his Travers explains why the name was suitable.

"I was on cruise control from the first turn to the stretch," jockey Gary Stevens said, describing the portion of the race in which Point Given stalked Free of Love and E Dubai. Once Free of Love collapsed from the pace on the turn, E Dubai grabbed the lead. Stevens then moved Point Given outside in pursuit of him as he passed the quarter pole.

When Point Given neared E Dubai at the eighth pole, he lugged in so that there was little room between them. "He's a big horse. When he changes leads, he needs a couple of lanes," Stevens explained of the only moment of doubt in Point Given's spectacular performance.

Once the lead switch was accomplished, the big horse gobbled up ground on the leader and finished his chase with a furlong to go. Point Given's move was a churning, grinding sweep that was sustained and resolute. His winning margin was three and a half lengths; the time was 2:01.40.

"He took one deep breath," Stevens said after dismounting. "It was like he hadn't even raced." Navigating a distance of ground was effortless for Point Given, or so it seemed.

But six days later, when Point Given's injury was detected, trainer Bob Baffert

POINT GIVEN'S FOUR CONSECUTIVE GRADE 1 WINNING RACES				
DATE	RACE	DISTANCE	TRACK	RESULT
May 19, 2001	Preakness Stakes	1 3/16 Mile	Pimlico (MD)	1 (3 1/2)
June 9, 2001	Belmont Stakes	1 1/2 Mile	Belmont (NY)	1 (12 1/4)
August 5, 2001	Haskell Invitational	1 1/8 Mile	Monmouth (NJ)	1 (1/2)
August 25, 2001	Travers Stakes	1 1/4 Mile	Saratoga (NY)	1 (3 1/2)

Above: **Owner Prince Ahmed bin Salman holds two fingers aloft in the winner's circle after Point Given crossed the finish line alone to win the Travers. The Saudi prince would be dead before the next year's Travers.** Albany (NY) *Times Union* photograph by Skip Dickstein

Left: **Point Given, also known as The Big Red Train, lived up to his nickname, as his long, powerful strides propelled him down the homestretch. Jockey Gary Stevens said the equine locomotive wasn't even winded when the race was over.** NYRA photo by Adam Coglianese

said he believed the Travers winner might have been hurt in that split second when he loomed alongside E Dubai in the passing lane.

"I really think it probably happened in the race," Baffert said. "But it was so minute that maybe when he was playing around he aggravated it. It's a big blow not only for us, but for the racing community."

No matter when the injury occurred, one thing was perfectly clear in the end: The difference in quality between Point Given and every other three-year-old was wide. The year had produced fine runners such as A P Valentine, Dollar Bill, Congaree, and Monarchos, but none was as impressive and crowd-pleasing as he.

"Never look back," Point Given's trainer, Bob Baffert, said in the Travers winner's circle when some member of the press reminded him that Point Given finished fifth in the Kentucky Derby. "Look forward and enjoy the horse," Baffert said.

He didn't know then that his "Horse of the Year" would be injured and retired a week later and that his client, the forty-three-year-old Saudi prince, would die before the next Travers rolled around.

Backstretch Move

UNLIKE MANY OF THE PREVIOUS POSTERS, this vantage point was imaginary. You would have to be standing on a ladder in the middle of the track to get this view, so I worked from models, hovering over them until I found the right image.

I tried to simplify the grandstand, reducing it to fundamentals—stripes, press box, spires, and ... television monitors, which trail off into the distance. The detail, I put into the horses' muscles. All the action seems to spring from the massive haunches of the closest thorough-bred. The black and white pole locates the race on the track, but, more importantly, stops the eye from following the grandstand up and off the page. It points you quickly back to the action. GM

Since a horse race isn't seen from the vantage point I used in the poster, I needed a reference from this unique viewpoint. An anotomically correct scale model of a thoroughbred worked perfectly.

THE

TRAVERS™

133rd Running

Saratoga 2002

Ordinary Gives Way to Extraordinary

Repent Puts the Heat on Medaglia d'Oro on a Cold, Rainy Day

2002 Travers Stakes	
133rd Running on Saturday, August 24	
Winner	Medaglia d'Oro
Jockey	Jerry Bailey
Owner	Edmund A. Gann
Trainer	Robert Frankel
Time	2:02.53

Fully vested in Medaglia d'Oro at the windows, the dampened crowd came to full throttle as the two horses streaked down the stretch toward a spotlight illuminating the finish line.

Television broadcasters Randy Moss and Kenny Mayne sat wearing ski parkas and gloves on the set that ESPN erected on Saratoga's first turn. From this vantage point, the backdrop of the teeming grandstand, its colorful geraniums, white linen tablecloths, and isosceles-angled roofline produces, on sunny August days, the kind of souvenir image that people not in attendance expect to receive in the mail.

But on this Travers day, slabs of gray sat atop the picture's frame like fissures in anthracite.

Some days at the racetrack can be unbearable. It matters little that you love the sport with all your heart and that you believe a day at the races to be better than a day in heaven. If the weather is dreary when it's supposed to be bright and the temperature is colder than your handicapping, only the truly dedicated are seeking pleasure. The others just want to cash a bet.

Riding the coattails of a 3-5 favorite must have kept the 43,153 faithful in their seats for the 133rd Travers. Medaglia d'Oro, a son of El Prado, was fourth in the Kentucky Derby, eighth in the Preakness, and second in the Belmont. But after he won the Jim Dandy Stakes, no other horse in the Travers seemed his equal. And so he became the chalk.

A good horse race can take place when you least expect it. But not many people anticipated this to be one of them. A sloppy track, the mercury at sixty degrees Fahrenheit, a heavy favorite, and a small field of under-achievers—these were obvious factors that portended mediocrity.

Adding to that doom was the absence of the captivating War Emblem. The Kentucky Derby and Preakness winner had been expected to race, but his principles chose the Pacific Classic at Del Mar on the same date instead. Yet, as veteran turf writer John Pricci said later, "Horse racing isn't like other sports that produce games that are clunkers. In horse racing, there's a close finish or a blow-out that results in a great performance. Either is fun to watch."

Heavily favored Medaglia d'Oro with Jerry Bailey up withstood a late charge by Repent, who handled the sloppy track to make it a two-horse race.
Albany (NY) *Times Union* photograph by Skip Dickstein

It would be inaccurate to conclude that the winner, Medaglia d'Oro, bravely contesting a fast pace on a track that was tiring, and Repent, who came within a half-length of catching him, deserve all the credit for what subsequently transpired. Many of the Travers horses that Saturday played a role in the revival of interest.

Long shot Shah Jehan vied for the early lead. Medaglia d'Oro, with jockey Jerry Bailey aboard, pressed him early. They were joined for a while by Saint Marden, three wide in the early going. But heading for the far turn, it was Medaglia d'Oro all alone as the pace-setter.

Bailey didn't lack for company long, as Quest moved up suddenly on his outside to annoy him. Further back, the duo of Repent, an accomplished closer, and Puzzlement, a Jim Dandy also-ran, advanced. The activity caused a stir in the crowd, although it was nothing compared to what happened next.

Puzzlement couldn't sustain his challenge when the homestretch arrived. But with two furlongs to go, it was clear that the race for third place wouldn't include either Repent or Medaglia d'Oro. One of these two would make certain it was his name that would go on the Man O' War Cup.

Repent, a son of Louis Quatorze, was a Kentucky Derby hopeful before injuring himself in April. Following surgery to remove a chip in his ankle, trainer Ken McPeek gave the colt four works to make him ready for this effort. Most horse conditioners contend that four works aren't enough to make a horse fit after such a long layoff, especially for a mile and a quarter. Yet Repent seemed to relish the off going and glided over the slop easily.

McPeek explained Repent's strong performance simply. "I thought we owned him at the eighth pole," he said. As a matter of fact, McPeek believed jockey Edgar Prado had timed Repent's move against Medaglia d'Oro perfectly.

In contrast, the view from the winner's saddle was worrisome. "I knew he was there at the eighth pole," said Bailey. "I knew he was still there at the sixteenth pole." During the course of the stretch, Bailey never fully believed he could withstand Repent's charge.

Ironically, Medaglia d'Oro's fast early fractions might have helped him more than hurt him. Shah Jehan, Saint Marden, and the winner sped :23.14 for the first quarter and :46.82 for the half. It was what Medaglia d'Oro's trainer Bobby Frankel wanted. Experienced race watchers know that a horse on the lead is dangerous at Saratoga, and few on top at the quarter pole are caught at the end. Bailey might have been worried, but there was no need for it.

Fully vested in Medaglia d'Oro at the windows, the dampened crowd came to full throttle as the two horses streaked down the stretch toward a spotlight illuminating the finish line.

To their ultimate satisfaction, owner Edmund A. Gann and Frankel, disdaining umbrellas, descended to the winner's circle. There, a blanket of red and white flowers was spread over Bailey's lap. Unfazed by the weather, the Hall of Fame rider sat aboard their triumphant bay, awaiting the flash of the cameras.

Top: **Upstate New York is famous for its occasional cool and damp summer days. Jackets and umbrellas were the order of the day for Travers 2002.** Albany (NY) *Times Union* photograph by Steve Jacobs

Bottom: **It wasn't a good day to run in second place as Edgar Prado did aboard Repent.** AP Photo/Jim McKnight

First Race

THIS POSTER WAS ORIGINALLY DESIGNED with only three people in it—the three at the first table. I carefully placed them, turning their heads and chairs and hats. I used subtle colors that were stylish but wouldn't distract from where I really wanted you to look— toward the lead thoroughbred, racing down the stretch. It worked beautifully. I looked where they were looking. Everything was clean and simple.

So I showed the piece to friends and colleagues. Their response was pretty unanimous and troubling. Everyone thought it was "great, but why is the place so empty?" Hmmm. What looked to me as "uncluttered" looked to almost everyone else as "unattended."

So I brought some more people into the picture. Even the *Lady in Red* made an appearance. But I still wanted to keep the true focus on the racing horses—the stars of the show.

It is of note that the shadows on the columns, the back of the empty chair, and the wrinkles on the tablecloth all bracket or point to the lead horse. GM

One of the reasons I named this poster *The First Race* is to partially explain why no one is eating, the napkins are still folded, and the glasses are filled only with water. One assumes that before the second race, a server will come and solve those problems deliciously.

THE
TRAVERS
134th Running

Saratoga 2003

Ten Most Wanted, Not the One Most Wanted

Hometown Hero Funny Cide and His Rival Empire Maker Stay Away

2003 Travers Stakes
134th Running on Saturday, August 23

Winner	Ten Most Wanted
Jockey	Pat Day
Owner	Reddam, Jarvis, Chisholm, et al
Trainer	Wally Dollase
Time	2:02.14

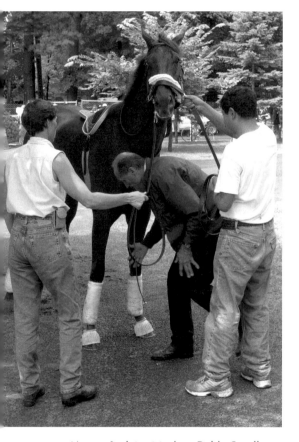

Above: **Assistant trainer Robin Smullen (from left), trainer Barclay Tagg, and groom Santos Cardoza examine fan favorite Funny Cide.** AP Photo/Tim Roske

Right: **Tagg answers questions as to why he scratched Funny Cide from the Travers. Smullen detected a rattle in the horse's chest and Tagg scratched his charge rather than risk injury.** Albany (NY) *Times Union* photograph by Skip Dickstein

In the summer of Seabiscuit, stores up and down Broadway were jam-packed with T-shirts and mouse pads and coffee mugs that paid homage to a different horse. Funny Cide, the New York-bred gelding with the catchy name and a busload of rag-tag owners, was coming home after a failed attempt at winning the Triple Crown, and he was being given a hero's reception.

The Stadium Café, the sports bar in town, began serving Funny Cide beer. The Price Chopper supermarket, which sells the *Daily Racing Form* and *Pink Sheet*, began selling Funny Cide cider.

Saratoga Springs resident Jack Knowlton, the managing partner of Sackatoga Stables, announced shortly after the Belmont Stakes that the Travers was the target for Funny Cide, their Kentucky Derby winner born on a farm a stone's throw from Saratoga Race Course. Even in this sometimes sleepy hamlet on the edge of the Adirondacks, preparations to mark its occasion were proceeding at a feverish pace.

Caught up in the hoopla, Knowlton himself opened a Funny Cide souvenir shop down the street from Sperry's Restaurant—a horse industry haunt with its own share of Derby memorabilia. Knowlton's wife, Dorothy, the proprietor of a shoe boutique, decorated the storefront with racing plates.

To Funny Cide's many admirers, the Travers became more than a horse race—it became a marketing phenomenon. But to those connected to Funny Cide, it became a quest. "I'm not letting anything get in the way of the Travers," Knowlton's trainer, Barclay Tagg, proclaimed. "We'll prep in the Haskell and then run in the Travers. That's the race I want to win most," he declared, adding to the feverish anticipation.

Meanwhile, Brooklynite Bobby Frankel had similar thoughts, if not the same appreciation of birthright. The Hall of Fame trainer had saddled Juddmonte Farms' Empire Maker to beat Funny Cide in the Wood Memorial and the Belmont. Following the Triple Crown, he announced that the Travers would determine once and for all which of the two horses was better. A rivalry was scripted.

Although Empire Maker failed in his Travers prep—finishing second in the Jim Dandy to Strong Hope—and Funny Cide ran third in the Haskell, the trainer, the

fans, and the press were itching for the rematch. And from the way all the parties were acting, there was more at stake than a $1 million bounty.

When all this was taking place, Frankel and Empire Maker's jockey, Jerry Bailey, were out of favor with the locals because of their lack of remorse over ending Funny Cide's Triple Crown bid. This was soft ground to be standing on for Bailey, who owns a home on Saratoga Lake. But Frankel seemed to relish his role as villain, saying prior to the Belmont, "If everyone hates me after the Belmont, then I've done my job." Ever politic, Bailey took a more neutral line. "We beat him," he said. "That's horse racing."

It was a good thing for Frankel that he trained another accomplished three-year-old because the anticipated face-off between Funny Cide and Empire Maker unraveled on the Thursday before the Travers. Just before entries were drawn for the race, Frankel revealed that Peace Rules, the Haskell Invitational winner, would substitute for Empire Maker because Funny Cide's two-time conqueror was ill. "He's a hell of a substitute," Bailey declared, eschewing diplomacy.

To heap disappointment upon misfortune, trainer Barclay Tagg followed suit on Friday and proclaimed Funny Cide out. He reported that Funny Cide had a mysterious rattle in his chest. Exercise rider Robin Smullen detected the condition in a workout. "I'm not taking any chances with him," Tagg reported, a lame way of saying he was unable to follow through on his promise to run the horse before the home crowd.

The defections didn't prevent a record Travers crowd of 66,122 from gathering, although a sliver of resignation persisted in the picnic grounds. Even though it had been speculated for weeks that the two horses might not make it to the Travers, hope drives the sport, and that summer there was an abundance of the virtue in Saratoga.

In the absence of the marquee players, Illinois Derby winner Ten Most Wanted, owned by eleven men from California, including the trainer Wally Dollase, won the Travers. It was only the third win in nine career starts for the enigmatic son of 1997 Travers winner Deputy Commander. Dollase became just the second trainer to win the Midsummer Derby with a sire and his son.

Ten Most Wanted's rider, Pat Day, won his fourth Travers, tying three other jockeys for most winning rides in the race. Day tracked the leaders Peace Rules and Strong Hope for most of the race before sweeping wide to capture the lead in the homestretch. Dollase added blinkers to keep Ten Most Wanted focused, a move opposite the one he made to assist Deputy Commander to victory. Obviously benefiting from the change, his horse strode beneath the finishing post four and three-quarter lengths ahead of the rest.

"I thought they'd run along pretty quick, so I was just going to let my horse coast along there," Day explained.

"With these two horses you don't have an option," Bailey said of the speed duel between his mount, Peace Rules, and Strong Hope.

Despite no Funny Cide and Empire Maker, on a sunny, humidity-free afternoon, Saratoga records were set for on-track handle ($9,390,940) and overall handle ($40,907,482). "It's been a spectacular day," said NYRA Chairman and CEO Barry Schwartz, hiding any disappointment he, too, might have felt about losing Funny Cide and Empire Maker.

All this, supposedly, represented an historic afternoon. But it wasn't the unforgettable afternoon of unparalleled rivals that everyone expected.

Above: **Jockey Pat Day on Ten Most Wanted swung wide entering the home stretch to beat Jerry Bailey aboard Peace Rules.** Albany (NY) *Times Union* photo by James Goolsby

Travers Winningest Jockeys

FOUR-TIME TRAVERS WINNERS	
Jim McLaughlin	1881, 1883, 1886, 1888
Eddie Arcaro	1938, 1942, 1944, 1951
Braulio Baeza	1966, 1969, 1972, 1975
Pat Day	1983, 1987, 1989, 2003

THREE-TIME TRAVERS WINNERS	
Eric Guerin	1952, 1953, 1963
William Shoemaker	1957, 1962, 1967
Jerry Bailey	1986, 1993, 2002
Chris McCarron	1988, 1991, 1997

16 Minutes to Post

16 MINUTES TO POST depicts a quiet scene in the paddock just before a race at Saratoga Race Course. Saratoga's famous paddock gives trainers and grooms a choice of where they saddle and prepare their mounts. Some prefer the open, manicured areas beneath the great trees. Others opt for the relative quiet and seclusion of the tented or covered areas.

I tried to present horses in both of these venues and to show some unique color there as well. I couldn't resist the rack full of colorful jockeys silks and the wonderful old "digital" clock with its light bulbs ticking down the minutes to post time.

The mood is warm and bright and peaceful. GM

Originally the poster was going to be *17 Minutes to Post*, but the numeral "17"—seen in this sketch—created a back-lit pointer sending the viewer's eys up and off the page. "16" does the opposite. On the poster, the opening in the "6" points in and down and creates kind of a bull's eye to help keep you there. The rear horse, facing right, balances the scene's overall leftward movement.

THE
TRAVERS

135th Running

Saratoga 2004

Worth Ruining a Nice Pair of Shoes

Birdstone Beats the Rain, but Marylou Does Not

2004 Travers Stakes	
135th Running on Saturday, August 28	
Winner	Birdstone
Jockey	Edgar Prado
Owner	Marylou Whitney
Trainer	Nick Zito
Time	2:02.45

Belmont Stakes and Travers winner, Birdstone, was alert and playful after his morning workout at the Oklahoma training track. He stayed in Saratoga until he was shipped to Lone Star Park in Grand Prarie, Texas for the 2004 Breeder's Cup. Albany (NY) *Times Union* photograph by Skip Dickstein

The 2004 Saratoga racing season was only one week old when an announcement about the star of the upcoming Travers Stakes blew up the coast from Philadelphia with the wallop of a Rocky Balboa knockout punch.

Smarty Jones, the rags to riches three-year-old that thrilled the nation by winning the Kentucky Derby and the Preakness Stakes, was retired to stud unexpectedly. The bruising of four fetlocks—the equivalent of sprained ankles—was given as the reason.

"He doesn't owe us anything and we owe him a lot," said owner Pat Chapman matter-of-factly to the colt's legions of followers. She, along with her husband Roy, believed that repair to the horse's limbs was impossible and went along with the decision of the experts at Three Chimneys Farm, where the horse would stand at stud.

It was a quote she would soon regret, after learning that her decision might have been hasty.

Chapman's pronouncement, however, didn't provide the most aggravating news for the New York Racing Association, proprietors of Saratoga Race Course. That came when the District Attorney's office in Albany, then occupied by future Gov. Eliot Spitzer, installed Getnick & Getnick, a state-appointed oversight agency, to monitor its activities.

First the marquee contestant for the Travers was lost to injury, and then the insult of intervention arrived in its wake.

Nevertheless, time marches on, and an unlikely replacement for Smarty Jones emerged at the top of the three-year-old division. Purge, who finished well behind Smarty Jones in two races at Oaklawn Park in the spring, won the Jim Dandy Stakes for trainer Todd Pletcher and was promptly installed as the 2-1 Travers Stakes favorite by oddsmaker Don LaPlace.

Purge was a nice horse, but a Travers favorite—not. "How can the Belmont winner and Haskell winner not be favored?" asked Lion Heart's trainer, Patrick Biancone, referring to his horse as well as the Nick Zito-trained Birdstone.

In spoiling Smarty Jones's bid for a Triple Crown, Birdstone had rallied from behind at 36-1 in the Belmont. Moreover, the miraculous finish of his upset in early June was not a feat that handicappers might expect to be duplicated in August. It was a lot to ask of a horse that had been on the sidelines for three months.

With this as the murky backdrop, the outcome of the 135th Travers was made clear with a lightning bolt. As thunder rattled the lodgepoles and strikes of white appeared at the edges of the weather front, Birdstone, in near darkness, collared his stablemate, The Cliff's Edge, to reward the New York-born Zito with his first Travers winner.

Birdstone gave Marylou Whitney her first Travers victory, too, although the Whitney family—Saratoga's most beloved collectors of horse racing silver—had several of the race's Tiffany-designed Man O' War Cups in the trophy room.

But it was the weather, not the record-making achievements of this Travers, which people will remember. As so often occurs in the shadow of the Adirondacks at the end of a summer afternoon, a torrent of rain—the likes of which makes the track at Saratoga more suitable for arks than for animals—fell immediately after the contestants raced past the finish line. This time around, the threat of getting wet froze all but the owner in the grandstand.

Whitney engaged her triumphant horse as he pranced back to the winner's circle in the downpour. Putting aside all concern for her stylishly expensive shoes, she dashed down from her clubhouse box and onto the track. Ankle deep in mud, with water

Above: **Marylou Whitney storms the track, wading through ankle-deep mud to celebrate Birdstone's victory with jockey Edgar Prado and her winning team.** AP Photo/Jim McKnight

pelting down on her fancy haberdashery, the Saratoga socialite sealed her horse's place in Travers lore with an act of unmitigated abandonment. "Did we just swim the English Channel?" the grande dame of Saratoga joked.

Yet, Birdstone's dash through the stretch ahead of the storm and the field was no laughing matter. The diminutive son of Kentucky Derby winner Grindstone had just won his second of the two most prestigious New York races for three-year-olds. His Travers win went along with his victory as a two-year-old in the most prestigious New York race for juveniles—the Hopeful.

"This is a dream come true," Whitney said, as thunder drowned out the cheers of the fans left stranded in the grandstand. "I think the gods came out and did this to sort of congratulate him."

Zito, too, believed that miracles occurred. "There's a reason the rain held off. If it had come earlier and they would have sealed the track, we would have scratched," he confessed.

And a decision like that, with Smarty Jones on the sidelines, would have left the 2004 Travers truly dry.

As thunder rattled the lodgepoles and strikes of white appeared at the edges of the weather front, Birdstone, in near darkness, collared his stablemate, The Cliff's Edge, to reward the New York-born Zito with his first Travers winner.

WHITNEY FAMILY VICTORIES IN THE TRAVERS STAKES			
YEAR	HORSE	TRAINER	OWNER
1929	Beacon Hill	J.G. Rowe, Jr.	Harry Payne Whitney
1931	Twenty Grand	J.G. Rowe, Jr.	Greentree Stable
1942	Shut Out	J.M. Gaver, Sr.	Greentree Stable
1954	Fisherman	S.E. Veitch	C.V. Whitney
1960	Tompion	J.J. Greely, Jr.	C.V. Whitney
1968	Chompion	Ivor G. Balding	C.V. Whitney
2004	Birdstone	Nicholas Zito	Marylou Whitney

Storm Bird

ONE OF THE GREATEST thoroughbred races of 2004 was almost run underwater. During the 2004 Travers, an enormous summer thunderstorm struck. Growing darker and more massive by the minute, the storm clouds turned day into night. Only the low-angle yellow lamps at the finish line illuminated the eerily darkened track. It had begun to rain earlier, but as jockey Edgar Prado rode the Belmont Stakes winner, Birdstone, across the finish line, the skies opened up. To say that it poured rain does not begin to describe the deluge and winds that followed. You couldn't see ten feet. It was not a race that anyone who darted through or danced in the rain will soon forget. And so, my twentieth anniversary poster, *Storm Bird*.

The white of the paper became the massive thunder cloud. You can follow the path of white around and down to the lead horse, Birdstone. Striated clouds near the jockey's back are intended to look like wings. The similar wing-shaped mauve cloud in front of Birdstone was reversed in direction to keep your eye on the page and on the lead horse.

I experimented with different cloud patterns and blends for weeks before finally arriving at this final configuration. GM

The ominous clouds that provided the canopy for Birdstone's run to victory in the Travers created both the atmosphere for that day and for the poster. My original study of the gathering thunderstorm served as the reference for the dramatic cloud formation in *Storm Bird*.

THE
TRAVERS
136th Running

Saratoga 2005

Social Graces Give Way to Street Smarts

Flower Alley Beats Bellamy Road

2005 Travers Stakes	
136th Running on Saturday, August 27	
Winner	Flower Alley
Jockey	J.R. Velasquez
Owner	Melnyk Racing Stable
Trainer	Todd Pletcher
Time	2:02.76

The citizens of Saratoga Springs pride themselves on their social graces. After all, this is a city where a gentleman named George Washington once basked in the relaxation of the spa and where the Philadelphia Orchestra and New York City Ballet are in residence each summer for the indulgence of lovers of music and movement.

Visitors flock to this Victorian retreat for all sorts of reasons, but you'd have to look far and wide to find someone on the backside of Saratoga Race Course who has come here without a horse, or an interest in horses. If you like racing better than baths, sidle up to a stranger and start a conversation, and you'll make a connection *sans doubte*.

But beware—hypocrisy knows no limits when a man with a horse meets a man with another horse.

Even so, owner Bill Bianco appeared to be telling the truth when he tipped a tout in the opposite direction of his 2005 Travers Stakes contender, Roman Ruler.

"Which was the best horse you ever owned?" the tout asked Bianco, expecting the owner to answer Roman Ruler, a dark brown son of Fusaichi Pegasus who was 2-1 in the Travers on the strength of his recent win in the Haskell Invitational Handicap.

"Buzzards Bay," Bianco answered unflinchingly. His surprising remark took place moments after he watched Roman Ruler work out on the track from the gap where the horses cross over Union Avenue from the barns at Oklahoma.

Bianco owned Buzzards Bay in partnership with David Shimmon and raced the once prominent Kentucky Derby hopeful under the Fog City Stable name before

Above: **Dana Barnes exercises Roman Ruler fresh off a win in the Haskell Invitational. This son of Fusaichi Pegasus was one of the pre-race favorites for the Travers.** Albany (NY) *Times Union* photograph by Skip Dickstein

Right: **Jockey John Velasquez held Flower Alley off the pace until the head of the stretch. Bellamy Road, coming off a twenty-week layoff, faded as Flower Alley got the win.** Albany (NY) *Times Union* photograph by Skip Dickstein

Shimmon and he sold the horse to Gary Broad. But Buzzards Bay never achieved his potential to the extent that Roman Ruler did, and the tout was taken back by the comparison.

Bianco's non-endorsement of Roman Ruler led the tout to focus on the two other logical contenders in the Travers—the heralded Bellamy Road and Flower Alley, the Jim Dandy Stakes winner. The way he figured it, even though morning line favorite Bellamy Road would lead from the bell, he would fade from the debilitating effects of a twenty-week layoff. Flower Alley, third choice at 3-1, would break from the outside and run back of the pace setter until fatigue did the leader in.

He wasn't the only one with that vision.

"It unfolded the way we thought it would and the way we hoped it would," Flower Alley's trainer, Todd Pletcher, said afterward.

For Bianco, Roman Ruler, his rider Jerry Bailey and his trainer Bob Baffert, it didn't.

Kinsman Stables farm manager Ed Sexton and trainer Nick Zito were surprised by the outcome, but not disappointed. "I thought Bellamy Road was really something," Zito said in defeat.

Jockey Javier Castellano gave Bellamy Road a proper send-off, and the big bay colt by Concerto ran off to an effortless lead. There were more than a few fans in the crowd who thought then that the race was over. But John Velasquez, aboard Flower Alley, had a better plan, if not sounder orders.

In the saddling enclosure, both Pletcher and Eugene Melnyk, the horse's owner, reiterated to Velasquez that Flower Alley would have to play the role of the stalker. Velasquez kept Flower Alley in check, then summoned a response from his mount by loosening the reins at the top of the stretch. Together, horse and rider spent less than the next furlong in overdrive.

"The real key was around the three-quarters, when Johnny turned up the pressure," Pletcher said on the public record about Velasquez's timing. "If it was going to be a fight with Roman Ruler, he was going to have to come get us," the trainer said, remembering that Roman Ruler beat Flower Alley in the Dwyer Stakes by getting the jump on him.

As for Bellamy Road, he faded like a colored bed sheet that was left out in the sun too long. It was a shame that this happened, too.

Lots of casual racing fans bet on Bellamy Road because he was owned by George Steinbrenner. Back in May, when Steinbrenner's seventeen-and-a-half-length winner of the Wood Memorial was installed as the Kentucky Derby chalk, the press room at Churchill was inundated with calls from newspapers' editors instructing writers to prepare two stories instead of one. If Bellamy Road had won the Run for the Roses for the Yankees owner, the Derby would have been front page news like in the old days.

Eugene Melnyk, the owner of Flower Alley, didn't get this kind of coverage after the Travers. Neither did Bill Bianco, but then why would he?

Melnyk, a generous contributor to Anna House—the backstretch facility run by the Belmont Child Care Association that was built with his money—won his first Travers Stakes after two previous tries. Some Saratogians, especially those with a proper sense of manners, would say that a man like he was deserving of more attention.

But Melnyk, who twenty years ago used to sit in the picnic grounds after driving nine hours from Toronto to view the races with his buddies, put the day in perspective. "There can't be a bigger thrill in racing," he decided, heedless of the slight in his ink.

EUGENE MELNYK'S TRAVERS STAKES TRIES		
YEAR	HORSE	RESULT
1998	Archers Bay	Fourth
2003	Strong Hope	Third
2005	Flower Alley	First

Above: **Eugene Melnyk, owner of Flower Alley, hugs Hall of Fame jockey Angel Cordero, Jr., who helped condition the Travers champion.** Albany (NY) *Times Union* photograph by Skip Dickstein

As for Bellamy Road, he faded like a colored bed sheet that was left out in the sun too long.

Red Paddock

I DO LOVE SARATOGA'S PADDOCK. This beautiful green oval with the dazzling red-flower edging is the staging area for the day's dramas. It goes from bustling action and crowds to peaceful, shady repose about ten times a day.

Shadow plays a powerful role in this design. The fence line shadow leads you in, pointing you directly at the horse and groom, where the mass of dark treetops stops you. I used a dappled light on the trees to soften the dense shape and point you down, once again, to the horse and groom. The compound shadows on the fence are compelling, yet simple. GM

This is such a wonderful place. Just find a spot along this fence and enjoy the flowers, trees, and the peace. Before long, some of the world's fastest horses and most fascinating people will literally walk a path to your door.

on the rail - paddock
GM

THE
TRAVERS
137th Running

Saratoga 2006

More Show-off than Showdown

Sheikh Mohammed's Bernardini Lives Up to Expectations

2006 Travers Stakes	
137th Running on Saturday, August 26	
Winner	Bernardini
Jockey	Javier Castellano
Owner	Darley Stable
Trainer	Tom Albertrani
Time	2:01.60

Trainer Todd Pletcher (right) **said privately that favorite Bernardini would have to fall down for Bluegrass Cat to win.** Albany (NY) *Times Union* photo by Skip Dickstein

Nothing stirs the imagination more than an electrifying performance, and in his Travers, Bernardini made the lights of Broadway seem dim.

A anticipation surrounding the Travers Stakes showdown between Bernardini, winner of the Preakness and Jim Dandy Stakes, and Bluegrass Cat, who twenty days earlier had won the Haskell Invitational Handicap, was more of a contrivance than a reality.

"He'd have to fall down, and then maybe we'd have a shot," Bluegrass Cat's trainer, Todd Pletcher, discreetly revealed to a stranger he met at a party the evening before the draw, referring to the sensational Bernardini.

But at Thursday morning's selection of post positions, Pletcher provided a different opinion to the public at large. "My horse ran well in the Haskell, and I'm hoping that he's kept his form, even though the race is a little closer to his last race than we'd like," he said, standing in the grassy paddock where the draw was held. It was a public remark that provided his owner the requisite hope.

Bernardini's trainer, Tom Albertrani, was more optimistic in his post-draw remarks. Albertrani had been touting Bernardini since racing returned to Saratoga in late July. He predicted victory for the handsome A.P. Indy colt in the Jim Dandy, the major tune-up for the Travers, after the big bay worked five furlongs in less than a minute.

"He reminds me a lot of Cigar, in how easy he does things," Albertrani remarked with some prompting at a National Museum of Racing and Hall of Fame panel session on the Monday before the meet began. Yet few people gave the relatively obscure Brooklyn-born trainer much notice. On the racetrack, it is customary for trainers to talk positively about their runners and glowingly of the competition, and this was just more of that. Or was it?

Albertrani was speaking from experience. During the 1990s, he had served as an assistant to Bill Mott when Cigar won sixteen straight races, including the Breeders' Cup Classic. But now, in the service of Sheikh Mohammed bin Rashid Al Maktoum of the United Arab Emirates, in whose maroon and white Darley Stable silks Bernardini competed, he knew that a low profile was required. "There's more to this horse than we've seen," was all Albertrani said.

Travers Day came up cloudy. Nevertheless, 40,785 fans descended upon the grounds, and a field of six three-year-olds faced the starter. As Bernardini paraded past the packed grandstand, he tossed jockey Javier Castellano to the track and the crowd gasped. The outrider let the horse buck a couple times more and then settle, and Castellano promptly mounted him again.

The misstep caused fans to remember the pre-race irregularities of the Preakness, in which Barbaro burst through the gate prematurely and then broke down a few strides after the start. But there was no trauma this time around.

Although Bernardini had defeated all challengers in the weeks following that ill-fated Preakness, he was still chasing Barbaro for the hearts of the public. He had come to prominence in the very race that brought about Barbaro's downfall, and the fans could find little love for him while the Derby winner was fighting for his life. The fact that he was owned by a Middle Eastern sheikh did not boost his Q Scores.

On the other hand, nothing stirs the imagination more than an electrifying performance, and in his Travers, Bernardini made the lights of Broadway seem dim.

The sheikh's Jim Dandy winner took the early lead. He set slow fractions of :48 flat for the 1/2-mile and 1:12.30 for six furlongs with Bluegrass Cat a length or so off his tail. Many of the fans were surprised by the early move, because High

Cotton was anticipated to be the pacesetter. Could having Bernardini and Bluegrass Cat at the front mean a match race?

When the pair reached the apex of the last turn, jockey John Velasquez urged Bluegrass Cat to collar the front-runner, and Castellano, biding his time until then, signaled his mount to respond. "I wanted him to do what he wanted and let him be comfortable," Castellano said afterward. But when the time to start running approached, his mount knew it was time.

With a tap of the whip and a loosening of the reins for encouragement, Castellano roused Bernardini to a four-and-a-half-length lead at the top of the stretch. The horse increased his advantage another three lengths en route to the wire. Nevertheless, it was not simply the margin that made the winner appear invincible.

Although the winner's time of 2:01.60 was an ordinary mark, the victory was so conclusive that the jockey patted Bernardini's neck twice with a sixteenth of a mile to go and raised a finger to the skies just before the finish line.

Castellano continued his showboating in the winner's circle. He plucked flowers from the garland of carnations that was draped over Bernardini's withers and tossed them in all directions as if they were souvenirs for someone to press into a scrapbook.

"I wanted all the people to recognize he's a special horse," the jockey said later, as if calling undue attention to himself would reflect positively on the Travers winner.

Meanwhile, Prince Rashid, the sheikh's twenty-five-year-old son, took out his cell phone to call Dubai. "My father couldn't be here, but he was so happy," the young prince said after the call.

Whether the clubhouse faithful considered Bernardini's Travers an encroachment upon their dinner hour, or simply saw his triumph as too blasé, the boxes emptied long before the trophy presentation ended.

Top left: **Bernardini led most of the way and ran away from Bluegrass Cat for an easy win.** Albany (NY) *Times Union* photograph by Skip Dickstein

Top right: **Exuberant jockey Javier Castellano gestures heavenward after tossing carnations to Bernardini admirers.** Albany (NY) *Times Union* photograph by Skip Dickstein

Above: **Castellano, to the left of trainer Tom Albertrani, pumps his first in the air, as New York Governor George Pataki applauds Bernardini, and the Shiekh's son, Prince Rashid, hoists a trophy.** Albany (NY) *Times Union* photograph by Skip Dickstein

DUAL PREAKNESS AND TRAVERS STAKES WINNERS			
YEAR	HORSE	TRAINER	OWNER
1878	Duke of Magenta	R.W. Walden	G.L. Lorillard
1880	Grenada	R.W. Walden	G.L. Lorillard
1920	Man O' War	L. Feustel	Glen Riddle Farm
1941	Whirlaway	Ben Jones	Calumet Farm
1953	Native Dancer	W.C. Winfrey	A.G. Vanderbilt
1967	Damascus	Frank Y. Whiteley Jr.	Mrs. Edith W. Bancroft
2001	Point Given	Bob Baffert	Thoroughbred Corporation
2006	Bernardini	Tom Albertrani	Darley Stable

Settling In

NO ONE NEEDS TO TEACH thoroughbreds how to run, but they do need to learn how to start. *Settling In* highlights the most important six feet (two meters) on the racetrack: the starting gate. Every race-horse must learn how to enter and leave the tight green box before he can race. Young and veteran horses alike are repeatedly brought to the gate and trained not to fear its confinement or sounds. With such powerful animals in such small spaces many things can and do happen. It can be a dangerous place where a wise jockey waits for his mount to ... settle in.

This poster has a very limited pallet—mostly green. It's the contrast and design that make it work. The white ironwork, like a halo, points to the jockey's head, as do the powerful chevrons on his back. His arm and his gaze direct you to the thoroughbred, and the dark green shape on the right keeps you on the page.

The assistant starter's arm, the downward loop of the reins, and the horse's dark tail all point you back up at the jockey again. GM

When this young man reached up over his head to hold on, it simply made the image for me. It was the perfect pose. I loved what the movement did to the chevrons on his back and how it forced a slight forward lean. Perfect. He held it long enough for me to get the image. For me, that's being lucky at the racetrack.

THE TRAVERS

138th Running

Saratoga 2007

Derby Winner Returns Luster to the Travers

Street Sense Catches Grasshopper

2007 Travers Stakes	
138th Running on Saturday, August 25	
Winner	Street Sense
Jockey	Calvin H. Borel
Owner	James B. Tafel
Trainer	Carl Nafzger
Time	2:02.69

Jockey Calvin Borel pilots Kentucky Derby winner Street Sense through a speed workout in preparation for the Travers. Albany (NY) *Times Union* photograph by Skip Dickstein

Asmussen had the nerve to insult Saratoga racing fans by referring to their Midsummer Derby as just another horse race.

By the summer of 2007, the Travers Stakes was one of twenty-eight races in North America that offered a purse of $1 million or more.

In a world where the accumulation of money supersedes the accomplishment of history in the hierarchy of values, the legendary stakes race had become an arbitrary stop on the way to the $5 million Breeders' Cup Classic for many trainers.

One such trainer was Steve Asmussen—the trainer of Curlin, the eventual "Horse of the Year."

"What's the difference between the Breeders' Cup Classic and the Travers? Five million to one," Asmussen said, crassly ignoring the prestige which comes from winning the Midsummer Derby.

Although stabled in the shade of Saratoga's comforting pine trees, Curlin was not going to race there, and Asmussen cared little about what racing fans thought. "I think Graveyard of Champions and the best horse I've ever had shouldn't go in the same sentence," the *Thoroughbred Times* reported the trainer to have said as he spelled out an agenda that omitted the Travers from Curlin's dance card.

Asmussen's rebuke of the Travers was distressing, but it was also telling in terms of how far tradition had fallen as an influence in the modern day. Horses were rarely raced on three weeks' rest anymore, so the $1 million Haskell Invitational at Monmouth—a previously popular prep for the Travers—and the $1 million Jockey Club Gold Cup, a test against older horses, became Asmussen's chosen path for Curlin.

The unfortunate decision left Street Sense, the Kentucky Derby winner, to carry the day as the Travers' sole attraction. But when temperatures skyrocketed to the mid-90s and the prospect of less than even-money became the hard, cold fact of the matter, he alone wasn't enough. A disappointing crowd of 38,909 people—nearly two thousand fewer than the year before—coughed up the $10 admission ticket and $25 seat price. Thank goodness, the true blue got their money's worth.

For example, the prelude featured wise-guy speculation that the Phipps Stable's Sightseeing might provide Street Sense at least a mild challenge. Entered by Shug McGaughey, a two-time Travers winning trainer, Sightseeing was bred for the mile and a quarter and had run third against Street Sense when the son of Street Cry won the Jim Dandy.

C.P. West, trained by Nick Zito, who won the Travers with Birdstone in 2004, was another contestant given a semblance of chance. The bay son of the young sire Came Home drilled four furlongs in an eye-opening :46.3 seconds a week prior to the Travers, providing a sign that he might steal the race. After all, C.P. West made the pace in the Jim Dandy and relinquished it as deep into the nine furlongs as the eighth pole, losing to Street Sense by less than two lengths.

A third challenger, Grasshopper, a lightly-raced son of Dixie Union, had demonstrated his talent against older horses in an allowance race the day after Street Sense won the Jim Dandy. Although the Travers was Grasshopper's first stakes, he looked to be formidable in any company. Obviously, by entering him, owner Will Farish, the former Ambassador to Britain, and his trainer, Neil Howard, showed that they believed in him.

So it came to pass that C.P. West sprung to the lead. But by the time the field hit the backstretch, it was the 9-1 Grasshopper with Robby Albarado in front. Meanwhile, Calvin Borel aboard Street Sense had the Derby winner in third, much closer to the pace than usual, and unexpectedly wide.

Borel, given the nickname "Bo-rail" for his propensity for riding near the fence, probably figured that his mount could win from anywhere. Or, perhaps he had learned the previous Saturday in winning the Alabama Stakes with Lady Joanne that the crown of the track was accommodating.

Whatever the reason, only four trainers had won the Alabama and Travers in the same year since 1901 and, with the 1-4 Street Sense beneath him, Borel wanted very badly to raise Nafzger to that echelon. In addition, no Kentucky Derby winner since Thunder Gulch had triumphed in the Travers, so history was in sight several ways.

On the other hand, Albarado, aboard Grasshopper, was of a different frame of mind. Unwilling to fade as the Kentucky Derby winner came alongside him at the top of the homestretch, Grasshopper dug in and battled Street Sense head-to-head all the way to the sixteenth pole. There, Street Sense inched his way forward, abetted by Borel's left-handed call to action.

It was not certain if Albarado meant Street Sense or Borel, when he said afterward, "At every point, I thought I could beat him." Although of the same Cajun ancestry, Albarado and Borel had little in common. Nevertheless, they had ridden against each other often. No doubt, this time around, the elder of the two Bayou natives scheduled his mount's closing move more precisely. Bo-rail, racing off the rail, caused Street Sense's winning margin to be a half length.

"This horse is something we're very proud of," remarked Street Sense's eighty-one-year-old owner, Jim Tafel.

"The second time around is just as sweet to me," said Nafzger. His statement was a reference to 2000, when he won the Travers for Tafel with Unshaded.

Yes, the Travers was an inconvenience for some trainers, but not him. He was rewarded for having come to Saratoga en route to the Breeders' Cup and proud of it.

Two horses battled stride for stride down the homestretch. Calvin Borel on Street Sense took a peek at Robby Albarado on Grasshopper as they came to the wire. Albany (NY) *Times Union* photograph by Skip Dickstein

Below: **Nafzger looks over Street Sense during preparation for the 132nd running of the Preakness, where Curlin edged Street Sense at the wire in a photo finish. The trainer skipped the Belmont, shipped his horse to Saratoga, and won both the Jim Dandy and the Travers Stakes.** Albany (NY) *Times Union* photograph by Skip Dickstein

DUAL KENTUCKY DERBY AND TRAVERS STAKES WINNERS

YEAR TRAINER	HORSE OWNER
1877 W. Astor	Baden-Baden J. Williams
1881 J. Rowe Sr.	Hindoo Dwyer Brothers
1917 R.F. Carmen	Omar Khayyam Wilfried Viau
1931 James G. Rowe, Jr.	Twenty Grand Greentree Stable
1941 Ben Jones	Whirlaway Calumet Farm
1942 J.M. Gaver, Sr.	Shut Out Greentree Stable
1993 MacKenzie Miller	Sea Hero Rokeby Stables
1995 D. Wayne Lukas	Thunder Gulch Michael Tabor
2007 Carl Nafzger	Street Sense James B. Tafel

Street Friends

BREEDERS' CUP and Kentucky Derby winner Street Sense came to Saratoga with quite a résumé—and didn't disappoint. It was the way that jockey Calvin Borel treated his horse that caught my eye.

After the race, even before dismounting, Borel cooled his ride with great splashes of water and ebullient affection. It was heartwarming to watch. Borel is clearly a world-class rider, but just as clearly a genuine character. So, when, in the last few strides of one of the most important races of his career, he turned in the saddle to take a long look under his arm at Robby Albarado on the charging Grasshopper, I knew that had to be the image for this poster. Friends in fast company, what could be better?

The format of my posters, however, presents a real challenge when I try to show two full race horses and their riders. The intensity of this race with the horses practically on top of each other allowed me to crop a strong vertical image. There is so much going on here that the challenge was to simplify and use planes of color and shadow, so necessary to create the depth and capture the moment. GM

As you can see, I had originally planned to show the head-to-head duel between Calvin Borel and Robby Albarado. It was so thrilling to watch. Borel's determination was so evident on his face with Albarado squeezing by on the rail. But, an instant later, Borel looked back under his arm at his competitor and tied the two together forever. I had to use the second shot as the reference for the poster.

THE
TRAVERS™

139th Running

Saratoga 2008

Travers History Is a Rich Tapestry

There Have Been Good Travers and Great Travers—Each Worth Watching

Greg Montgomery's tribute to previous Travers Stakes is a triptych of two of the most memorable races of all time and a showdown between Hall of Fame horses that became a controversial end to a noteworthy rivalry.

The artist's vintage race masterpiece, produced in limited edition to commemorate the first exhibit of the complete collection of his Travers and Saratoga posters at the Arts Center Gallery in Saratoga Springs, captures three unique occasions when the Travers transcended the boundaries of sport.

At the left of the poster's horizontal plane, the viewer sees Jim Dandy sprinting clear of Gallant Fox in the 1930 Travers. In the center, the image has Jaipur and Ridan nose-to-nose in 1962. On the right, Alydar catches up with Affirmed after the finish line of the 1978 Travers, the final time the two captivating adversaries met.

"The level of excitement created by each race can't be separated, and so I didn't want to separate the images," Montgomery said, in explaining the triptych. "For all those people who have been coming to Saratoga year after year, the thrills are indivisible. The three races should be drawn as one."

Perhaps the three Travers that Montgomery illustrated are indeed part of a collective experience. But any series, especially one of nearly one hundred fifty horse races, is, at a minimum, brimming with peculiarities. Likewise, the history of the earliest Travers, written so many years ago, has conveniently been edited many times to suit various purposes. The result is a rich tapestry.

For example, one would not have to be a skeptic to conclude that the 1864 Travers Stakes was created solely to put money into the pockets of the owners of Saratoga Race Course. After all, chicanery in the nomination process was claimed by the owners of Norfolk, and it may have prohibited the undefeated son of Lexington—one of only two horses to ever defeat the winner—from participating.

On the other hand, it was common practice then for men who developed the racetracks to own the best horses. The best horse that August 2 was Kentucky, co-owned by Saratoga Racing Association president William R. Travers and John Hunter, the first chairman of the Jockey Club.

The three-year-old bay son of Lexington, the sire of nine of the first fourteen Travers winners, led the favorite Tipperary by four lengths to the finish line for the lion's share of the $2,940 purse.

"Propriety reigned supreme, and the whole affair was so thoroughly respectful that we may justly quote the now progressing Saratoga meeting as a model institution," it was written in the *New York Times*, two days after Kentucky's conquest of four other runners was finished, portending a condition that continues in existence today.

As the first race on the new racetrack's opening day card, the Travers inaugurated a tradition of Saratoga racing in August and, of course, a standard for how racing was to be conducted. "Neither pains nor expenses have been spared to render it perfect in all its departments," the *Times* reported.

This we know for sure, Kentucky negotiated the race's 1 3/4 mile distance in 3:18.75 before a boisterous, well-heeled, and thoroughly pleased mass. Gilbert W. Patrick, also known as Gilpatrick—the leading jockey of several generations—was aboard for the winning ride. Then to prove his mount's outcome no fluke, Gilpatrick rode the gallant steed to consecutive Saratoga Cup triumphs.

Although Kentucky won twenty-one of twenty-three starts in four years on the racetrack, the career-perfect Norfolk, his Jersey Derby conqueror, and eventually Lodi, who faced Norfolk twice in ballyhooed West Coast races, were considered, at the time, his superiors. Regardless, Kentucky, for winning the first Travers, became the most famous of the three.

As a matter of fact, the mantle of fame became a byproduct for many horses that won or lost Saratoga's showcase. Twenty Travers winners, for example, have been elected to Racing's Hall of Fame, and other runners that were upset in their Travers, like Gallant Fox and Affirmed, have joined them. In addition, there are Travers victors such as Street Sense (2007), Point Given (2000), and Thunder Gulch (1995) that may someday be elected.

It is noteworthy that females, at least in the form of equines, dominated the earliest Travers. Talented fillies Maiden (1865), Ruthless (1867), The Banshee (1868), and Sultana (1876) captured four of the first dozen runnings. Not unexpectedly, females ever since have left their mark on Travers history.

Female owners, in fact, have graced the winner's circle so many times that their gender is not even noticed. Unfortunately, no woman has ever been the jockey of a Travers winner and only one woman has trained one. Mary Hirsch gave Eddie Arcaro the leg up for Anne Corning on Thanksgiving in 1938. And, with typical chauvinism, the press by and large failed to report her accomplishment with fanfare.

In any regard, the decades in which fillies won established Saratoga as a place where co-habitation was invited. By the turn of the twentieth century, the Travers was the highlight of summer, resulting in lavish parties, attracting a summer colony of the upper crust and thirty thousand fashionable spectators. When New York, at the urging of Tammany boss Richard Croker, banned the pari-mutuel system of betting in 1888, "turf exchanges" began to flourish faster than hot tips from a cold-hearted tout, and the bookies' biggest clients were the ultra-wealthy who lodged at the grand hotels. When Man O' War tied the track record in 1920, a bevy of socialites unparalleled in the land came to roost in the clubhouse.

Nevertheless, money is often a license for misbehavior, and the Travers has seen its share of petty miscreants. Only the filly Prudery, owned by Harry Payne Whitney, was expected for the 1921 race. Then the gambler Arnold Rothstein entered Sporting Blood, presumably to prevent a walkover and earn second place money. At the last minute, however, trainer/owner Sam Hildreth entered Ronconcas Stable's Grey Lag, causing Prudery's odds to drop like a pigeon's dinner, as Sporting Blood's odds rose accordingly. Before anyone had a clue to what was happening, Grey Lag scratched, Sporting Blood won, and Rothstein, with his wagers and purse money, exited the track with a half-million dollars.

By the way, it was Rothstein who most people believe fixed the 1919 World Series in which the Chicago White Sox became the "Black Sox." Although Rothstein proclaimed innocence to his dying day, he nonetheless met his death by being shot for cheating at poker, and this begs a question about his argument.

Twenty years after Sporting Blood, Calumet Farm's Whirlaway became the only Triple Crown champion to win the Travers. With jockey Alfred Robertson substituting for the suspended Eddie Arcaro, the chestnut colt trailed the two other horses in the Travers for all but the stretch before making a fast track of the heavy going. One can presume that while all this was happening, the fans recalled 1930, when another Triple Crown champ could not cope with the elements. But when Whirlaway's patented stretch kick hit full throttle, they soon realized the day would be special. Whirlaway was sent off at odds of 3-20, and his Travers was the eleventh of his thirteen victories that year.

Top: **Man O' War with jockey Clarence Kummer paints a picture of perfection in the Dwyer Stakes post parade. Man O' War lost only once in his career, and that was at Saratoga as a two-year-old. But he made amends in the 1920 Travers.** Photograph from the NEA Service, Inc. Collection, Browne Popular Culture Library, Bowling Green State University

Center: **Eddie Arcaro, the greatest jockey of his time, often paired up with the greatest horses of his time, including two Triple Crown winners—Whirlaway (1941) and Citation (1948). Each year, the New York Turf Writers Association honors his memory by presenting the Eddie Arcaro Award to an "Outstanding Jockey."** Photograph courtesy of the Albany (NY) *Times Union* newspaper

Top: **Whirlaway, pictured here in the Churchill Downs winner's circle, is the only horse to capture the Triple Crown and the Travers. Affirmed would have been the second until Saratoga's stewards reversed the results of his tenth confrontation with Alydar.** Albany (NY) *Times Union* archive, from postcard at National Racing Museum

Bottom: **Street Sense was only the third Kentucky Derby winner to win the Travers since 1942. Jockey Calvin Borel rode the Carl Nafzger-trained bay to both victories.** Photo by Eric Patterson Photography

A year after Whirlaway, Arcaro got the Travers victory that his suspension denied him—his second of four, in fact, one that augmented his aforementioned ride on Thanksgiving. In 1942, the man called "Banana Nose" rode Shut Out, another Kentucky Derby winner, in the Travers and triumphed. His timing was perfect, because racing at Saratoga was cancelled the following summer and would not be renewed until 1946. He could have triumphed in one of the three Travers Stakes held at Belmont Park in the next years, but then his achievement would have been part of a different Saratoga lore.

Unbelievably, Shut Out fell to second in the balloting for top three-year-old to Alsab, who, in turn, finished second to Whirlaway—a rival he beat in a match race—in the Horse of the Year voting. But, after Shut Out, only three Derby winners have captured the Travers—Sea Hero (1993), Thunder Gulch (1995), and Street Sense (2007).

When the odds-on Buckpasser, owned by Ogden Phipps, captured the 1966 Travers, he accomplished something no horse his age had before. The victory lifted his career earnings to $1,038,369, making Buckpasser, a bay son of Tom Fool, the first three-year-old to win $1 million.

The next year, Edith W. Bancroft's Damascus, without rival Dr. Fager to worry about, beat three overmatched competitors by twenty-two widening lengths on a sloppy track, with Bill Shoemaker taking him from last to first after trailing by nearly sixteen lengths. It was the third and last Travers winner that Shoemaker would pilot, despite a career in the saddle that lasted twenty-three more years.

Horse of the Year Arts and Letters brought the race's most glowing decade to a close in 1969. After winning the Jim Dandy by ten lengths, the Belmont Stakes-winning Rokeby Stables star took the 100th Travers by six and a half, equaling the track record of 2:01 3/5. Observers say the well-bred colt by Ribot could have gone even faster, but jockey Braulio Baeza decided enough was enough and hand-rode him home.

Saratoga's track record for a mile and a quarter belongs to Bertram Firestone's General Assembly, a son of Secretariat, who raced to victory in 1979. General Assembly romped by fifteen lengths in two minutes flat in the slop, leaving in his wake the fast filly Davona Dale, the favorite. In winning, the handsome chestnut colt knocked a fifth of a second off the record held by Firestone's 1976 Travers winner, Honest Pleasure.

In 1982, Runaway Groom paid $27.80 for a $2 win ticket in becoming the only Travers winner to beat all the winners of the Triple Crown races. The Kentucky Derby winner Gato del Sol, Preakness Stakes winner Aloma's Ruler, and Belmont Stakes champion Conquistador Cielo trailed Runaway Groom home in the Travers, but the Canadian three-year-old champion could not beat even one horse in his next start—the Lawrence Realization Stakes at Belmont.

These noteworthy races notwithstanding, Montgomery selected the correct trio of Travers to honor the race's past. Undoubtedly, someone who attended the 1930, 1962, and 1978 Travers will be paging through this book and might argue otherwise. Horse racing, after all, despite the indisputable clarity of its results, is about disagreement. But, by all accounts, it will be difficult, if not impossible, to prove.

TRAVERS STAKES WINNERS

FROM 1864 TO PRESENT—SARATOGA RACE COURSE—SARATOGA SPRINGS, NEW YORK

YEAR	WINNER	YEAR	WINNER	YEAR	WINNER	YEAR	WINNER
1864	Kentucky	1900	not run	1936	Granville	1972	Key to the Mint
1865	Maiden	1901	Blues	1937	Burning Star	1973	Annihilate 'em
1866	Merrill	1902	Hermist	1938	Thanksgiving	1974	Holding Pattern
1867	Ruthless	1903	Ada Nay	1939	Eight Thirty	1975	Wajima
1868	The Banshee	1904	Broomstick	1940	Fenelon	1976	Honest Pleasure
1869	Glenelg	1905	Dandelion	1941	Whirlaway	1977	Jatski
1870	Kingfisher	1906	Gallavant	1942	Shut Out	1978	Alydar
1871	Harry Bassett	1907	Frank Gill	1943*	Eurasian	1979	General Assembly
1872	Joe Daniels	1908	Dorante	1944*	By Jimminy	1980	Temperence Hill
1873	Tom Bowling	1909	Hilarious	1945*	Adonis	1981	Willow Hour
1874	Attila	1910	Dalmatian	1946	Natchez	1982	Runaway Groom
1875	D'Artagnan	1911	not run	1947	Young Peter	1983	Play Fellow
1876	Sultana	1912	not run	1948	Ace Admiral	1984	Carr de Naskra
1877	Baden-Baden	1913	Rock View	1949	Arise	1985	Chief's Crown
1878	Duke of Magenta	1914	Roamer	1950	Lights Up	1986	Wise Times
1879	Falsetto	1915	Lady Rotha	1951	Battlefield	1987	Java Gold
1880	Grenada	1916	Spur	1952	One Count	1988	Forty Niner
1881	Hindoo	1917	Omar Khayyam	1953	Native Dancer	1989	Easy Goer
1882	Carley B.	1918	Sun Briar	1954	Fisherman	1990	Rhythm
1883	Barnes	1919	Hannibal	1955	Thinking Cap	1991	Corporate Report
1884	Rataplan	1920	Man O' War	1956	Oh Johnny	1992	Thunder Rumble
1885	Bersan	1921	Sporting Blood	1957	Gallant Man	1993	Sea Hero
1886	Inspector B.	1922	Little Chief	1958	Piano Jim	1994	Holy Bull
1887	Carey	1923	Wilderness	1959	Sword Dancer	1995	Thunder Gulch
1888	Sir Dixon	1924	Sun Flag	1960	Tompion	1996	Will's Way
1889	Long Dance	1925	Dangerous	1961	Beau Prince	1997	Deputy Commander
1890	Sir John	1926	Mars	1962	Jaipur	1998	Coronado's Quest
1891	Vallera	1927	Brown Bud	1963	Crewman	1999	Lemon Drop Kid
1892	Azra	1928	Petee-Wrack	1964	Quadrangle	2000	Unshaded
1893	Stowaway	1929	Beacon Hill	1965	Hail To All	2001	Point Given
1894	Henry of Navarre	1930	Jim Dandy	1966	Buckpasser	2002	Medaglia d'Oro
1895	Liza	1931	Twenty Grand	1967	Damascus	2003	Ten Most Wanted
1896	not run	1932	War Hero	1968	Chompion	2004	Birdstone
1897	Rensselaer	1933	Inlander	1969	Arts and Letters	2005	Flower Alley
1898	not run	1934	Observant	1970	Loud	2006	Bernardini
1899	not run	1935	Gold Foam	1971	Bold Reason	2007	Street Sense

* The 1943, 1944, and 1945 Travers were run at Belmont Park in Elmont, New York.

Triple Champs

IN DESIGNING every other poster in this series, I began by capturing and simplifying some racing scene or image. Whether the image was of a horse winning a race or a trainer saddling his runner in the paddock, it was an image which I captured and developed, not built out of whole cloth.

This triple was different. It would be three posters in one, a seamless portrayal of the passage of time from Jim Dandy on a muddy track in 1930 to Alydar and Affirmed on a sparkling day in 1978—events in time that I never experienced. To accomplish this challenge, I decided to create a set emulating the famous "East Coast Joys" series of 1931 by the noted British poster artist, Tom Purvis for London and North Eastern Railway (LNER).

Each individual poster was meant to work alone and as a continuous scene. Each scene had to be accurate in its details—weather, architecture, clothing, and colors. Each panel's action had to be commensurate with history. None of the images could dominate the others. And, since the triple was a piece of commemorative art that was to embody my entire series, I wanted to sprinkle in elements from as many of the previous posters as feasible.

More than a thousand hours later, here is the set. I wish Tom were around to see it. GM

TWENTY-FIVE

THE ARTS CENTER GALLERY

1930 TRAVERS · JIM DANDY

GREG

YEARS OF THE TRAVERS

SARATOGA SPRINGS, NEW YORK · AUGUST 2-31, 2008

1962 TRAVERS · JAIPUR AND RIDAN

1978 TRAVERS · ALYDAR AND AFFIRMED

MONTGOMERY

Jim Dandy Scores Historical Upset

Mud Lover Beats a Pair of Celebrated Rivals

1930 Travers Stakes
61st Running on Saturday, August 16

Winner	Jim Dandy
Jockey	Frank Baker
Owner	Chaffee Earl
Trainer	J.B. McKee
Time	2:08

Arriving at Saratoga, President Franklin D. Roosevelt, then governor of New York State, his wife Eleanor, and their sons, John and Franklin, were joined for lunch in the clubhouse by two Groton School schoolmates—William W. Woodward, owner of Gallant Fox, and Harry Payne Whitney, owner of Whichone. *Albany (NY) Times Union photograph from George S. Bolster Collection, Saratoga Springs History Museum.*

The track was heavy, owing to steady rain Friday night, more rain in the morning and another shower around one o'clock on race day.

Retired heavyweight boxing champion Gene Tunney and Saratoga "Cottage Colony" stalwarts John Hay "Jock" Whitney and his fiancée, Elizabeth Altemus, typified the breadth of clubhouse society at the 61st running of the Travers Stakes that pitted Triple Crown winner Gallant Fox against Whichone.

But their kind was small in number compared to the masses that filled the historic wooden grandstand and blanketed the broad lawn that extended from the building to the racing strip. During the nationwide broadcast of the race by Clem McCarthy, fellow radio announcer George Hicks said the crowd was the biggest the popular track on the edge of the Adirondacks ever hosted.

On the eve of the Travers, two extra Specials from New York arrived at the railway station on Broadway. Higher-ups from Tammany Hall engulfed the United States and Grand Union hotels. The porches of these elegant "Victorian Ladies" embraced talk of the times that touched upon everything from government to gossip.

Temptation raged at the Canfield Casino and in the night clubs at Brown's Beach and on Saratoga Lake. Only a swell willing to peel off a double sawbuck for the maitre d' could access the Arrowhead Inn, where the notable Paul Whiteman Orchestra was performing. Another tough date to engage was the Piping Rock Club, where Vincent Lopez and the Hotel St. Regis Orchestra provided an incomparable selection for dancing.

Earlier in the week, Gov. Franklin D. Roosevelt received a citizen's complaint that eighteen gambling houses and fourteen brothels were operating in Saratoga. He ordered an investigation, which, of course, turned up nothing.

Satisfied with the due diligence—such as it was—and safe in the knowledge that his reputation wasn't threatened, Roosevelt came to Saratoga for Travers Day and lunched with his wife, Eleanor, at the track restaurant before moving on to his box for the races.

Estimates of the crowd at the racecourse that Saturday ran as high as forty thousand people. After the Beverwyck Steeplechase, the infield was opened to the public—the first time this rare accommodation had been offered in years. In addition, it was reported that twenty-five thousand programs were sold. To satisfy the demand, the Turf Printing Corporation whipped up three additional print runs totaling three thousand to serve fans who didn't get a copy from the first batch.

On the opposite side of the grandstand, ushers with ropes cordoned off the path to the elms where the horses were saddled. The Travers was carded as the fifth of six races, with a post time of 5:20 P.M. There were five horses entered, but only four looked the starter in the eye.

The track was heavy, owing to steady rain Friday night, more rain in the morning and another shower around one o'clock on race day. "It sucked the boots off your feet if you tried to walk through it," recalled witness Richard Cherry, in a 2001 article by Bill Mooney in the *New York Times*.

In those days, Saratoga Race Course did not have pari-mutuel betting, but the bookmakers had Gallant Fox at 3-5 and Whichone at 7-5. Sun Falcon was chalkboarded at 40-1 and Jim Dandy at 100-1. Obviously, the ten-furlong Travers was seen by the bettors to be a match race, including many Gallant Fox doubters who considered the odds mighty tasty on Whichone.

The Travers was to be the third meeting of the two horses, each of whom had beaten the other once before. As a two-year-old, Whichone defeated Gallant Fox in the Belmont Futurity, thus capturing the Juvenile Championship. Because he nursed a quarter crack for most of the spring as a three-year-old, Whichone was still considered by many to be superior to his rival, despite finishing behind Gallant Fox in the Belmont.

That summer, Harry Payne Whitney's sturdy brown colt had won three times at Saratoga in the two weeks leading up to the Travers. On August 6, Whichone won the Saranac Handicap. On August 9, he won the Whitney Stakes. Three days later, he captured the Miller Stakes, and on August 16, he was ready to run again. Obviously, four races in ten days seemed a mere stroll in the park for the great-grandson of Hanover, who himself had won thirteen times in ten weeks during one stretch of his fifty-race career.

Gallant Fox, a son of Sir Gallahad III, was owned by William Woodward's Belair Stud. The bay colt had captured in succession the Wood Memorial, Preakness, Kentucky Derby, Belmont, Dwyer Stakes, and Arlington Classic. His jockey for those triumphs, Earl Sande, was called upon to ride in the Travers, while Raymond "Sonny" Workman, Whitney's contract rider, had the leg up on Whichone. Trainers "Sunny Jim" Fitzsimmons for Gallant Fox and Tom Healy for Whichone were fast friends. Every element required for an epic confrontation was present.

When the flag fell, the four starters broke perfectly. Sande sent Gallant Fox, who had drawn outside, straight to the front. Workman followed on Whichone. The two brilliantly fast colts raced ahead of the slower two on the crown of the track, where the footing seemed safest.

Above: **Seldom a winner, Jim Dandy nonetheless stood in Saratoga's chalked winner's circle twice during his long, often disappointing, career. But horses that have accomplished ten times more than he are not as famous for their exploits.** Photo provided by the *Thoroughbred Times*, Keeneland Cook collection

Left: **Many years later, trainer "Sunny Jim" Fitzsimmons** (left) **and jockey Earl Sande reminisced of Gallant Fox in the Aqueduct paddock. The Hall of Fame duo took Belair Stud's pride to the track for the Travers as a Triple Crown winner and exited the race as one of two champions to lose to the 100-1 long shot, Jim Dandy.** NYRA photo by Mike Sirico provided by the *Thoroughbred Times*

DUAL JIM DANDY AND TRAVERS STAKES WINNERS	
YEAR	**HORSE**
TRAINER	**OWNER**
1969	Arts and Letters
Elliot Burch	Rokeby Stables
1981	Willow Hour
James E. Picou	Marcia W. Schott
1984	Carr de Naskra
Richard Lundy	Virginia Kraft Payson
1992	Thunder Rumble
Richard O'Connell	Braeburn Farm
2002	Medaglia d'Oro
Robert Frankel	Edmund A. Gann
2005	Flower Alley
Todd Pletcher	Melnyk Racing Stable
2006	Bernardini
Tom Albertrani	Darley Stable
2007	Street Sense
Carl Nafzger	James B. Tafel

Harry Payne Whitney was a thorough-bred owner who was unafraid of racing his horses. He started nineteen horses in the Kentucky Derby and won with two of them. His Whichone raced three times in two weeks at Saratoga before facing nemesis Gallant Fox in the Travers won by Jim Dandy. Bert and Richard Morgan photo provided by the *Thoroughbred Times*

Below: Jim Dandy's "eggshell hooves" made him an ordinary horse on hard tracks. But for the Travers, Chaffee Earl's underachiever found a track that was soft and gooey, and he showed his heels to two champions. Photograph courtesy of AP Images

Just before the mile marker, Gallant Fox pushed ahead. But it was obvious that he was laboring. Whichone ran at him, then, and gained a slight advantage. Neither rider nor anyone in the crowd noticed the two trailers—until suddenly, the mud-splattered blue silks with white sleeves worn by Frank J. Baker aboard Jim Dandy appeared on the rail.

Obviously relishing the off going, Jim Dandy steadily made up ground on the leaders and stormed to the front while approaching the three-eighths pole. Gallant Fox offered a final response, but Sande knew that his attempt to catch Jim Dandy, well ahead of the field in deep stretch, would end in vain. At the eighth pole, the rider began easing the Triple Crown hero home.

For Whichone, the end was merciful, although equally unrewarding. Whitney's horse pulled up lame, and Workman walked him back to the unsaddling area instead of jogging him there.

In the aftermath of Jim Dandy's enormous upset, it was written that his victory by six lengths shouldn't have been a stunner. According to the *New York Times*, the horse's trainer, James B. McKee, appeared confident from the day he left San Francisco, where owner Chaffee Earl kept Jim Dandy stabled. As Earl's horse boarded a train at the Tanforan Race Track for Saratoga, Earl told the assembled, "Now you see the winner of the Travers. He will beat them all whether the track is fast or muddy."

Others, however, noted that Jim Dandy was always a decent racehorse but had "eggshell hooves"—thinly walled so they bothered him on fast tracks and caused him to rarely hit the board when racing on such surfaces. A year before, as a two-year-old, Jim Dandy had won Saratoga's Grand Union Hotel Stakes at odds of 50-1 in the mud, thus proving that a cushion of slop made a world of difference to him.

With the Travers as his goal, Jim Dandy ran at Saratoga on August 8 and finished eighth in a field of nine. His earnings for the year before loading into the Travers starting gate were only $125. He also was entered in the fourth race on the same card, suggesting that Earl and McKee might have been less confident than they claimed.

It took Saratoga Race Course officials thirty-four years to immortalize Jim Dandy's Travers victory. In 1964, favored Malicious out-gamed Quadrangle in the first ever Jim Dandy Stakes, coming out on top in a four-horse field that matched the number in Jim Dandy's Travers. Seven Jim Dandy Stakes winners, including the most recent three, have gone on to be Travers winners.

The initial Jim Dandy trophy was presented to Greentree Stable's Mrs. Charles Shipman Payson and her brother, John Hay "Jock" Whitney. Upon receiving his accolades, Whitney likely reflected on the day that Gallant Fox and Whichone were beaten.

1930 TRAVERS • JIM DANDY

Too Close to Call

Jaipur and Ridan Race Head to Head

1962 Travers Stakes	
93rd Running on Saturday, August 18	
Winner	Jaipur
Jockey	William Shoemaker
Owner	George D. Widener
Trainer	W.F. Mulholland
Time	2:01 3/5

Jaipur developed his credentials as the odds-on Travers favorite by winning the Belmont. Owner George D. Widener led Jaipur to the winner's circle with Willie Shoemaker in the saddle. Photograph by Mike Sirico provided by NYRA

It was one of those years between eras. The 1950s left a world longing for change. And the 1960s—a time in which life was turned upside down—had just begun.

But in 1962, the citizens of Saratoga Springs, for the first time in many Augusts, were beginning to believe that constancy could be a condition.

During the previous decade, Sen. Estes Kefauver had punctured their emotions and their economy. The Tennessee senator's zealous effort to wipe out organized crime had contributed to the end of the city's casinos. Not unexpectedly, as the casinos shut down, the city's hotels and restaurants began to close, throwing uncertainty over the future of horse racing on Union Avenue.

Sensing discontent in the electorate, Gov. Nelson A. Rockefeller, who provided in the state's budget for concurrent racing at Aqueduct and Saratoga a few years before, finally came to understand that the tiny city in the Adirondack foothills was cut from the cloth of gamblers.

Encouraged by John Hay "Jock" Whitney, publisher of the *New York Herald Tribune* and co-owner of Greentree Stable, Rockefeller visited Saratoga Race Course for the first time and enjoyed what he discovered. Rockefeller toured the backstretch and ate breakfast on the Clubhouse Terrace in the morning, stopped by the Museum of Racing afterward and concluded his day by watching the Whitney Stakes from a finish line box.

To most Saratogians, the visit by the governor provided ample assurance that their track would retain its exclusive racing dates. At the same time, state and local agencies and private entities began pouring $50 million into the city's renaissance. Money would go toward a school for the mentally retarded, a new wing at Saratoga Hospital, and $3.5 million in improvements at the Spa, including renovation of the palatial Victoria Pool. But the funding caused other changes to occur, and even those that seemed silly proved substantial.

In 1962, nine holes (with $2.50 greens fees) were opened at the new Saratoga Spa Golf Course. Skidmore College was planning to move its campus. A $2.5 million Saratoga Performing Arts Center and a convention hotel, ultimately the Holiday Inn, were placed on the drawing boards. Most notably, the Northway (I-87) was opened from Albany to Malta. By 1963, it would allow people to drive from the capital to South Glens Falls.

Each day brought change and each change made Saratoga a better place, with one exception. A federal government grant of $1.8 million led to the razing of the culturally-rich West Side and creation of an unsightly parking lot where once stood a vibrant neighborhood. By the end of the '60s, such pleasure dens as The Palace, Jack's Harlem Club, and Miss Hattie's on Congress Street would disappear. But in 1962, there was as much "good life" to be found as in any other period of the city's history. The enthusiasm for racing reflected it.

A diverse crowd of 26,183 fans descended upon the racecourse on a pleasant, warm day for the 93rd Travers. Alas, Bermuda shorts made a fashion statement in the clubhouse. Yet, for the most part, the dress was expensive, suffocating, and conservative.

Almost all of the ladies wore black, white, or navy—hems slightly below the knee. "First Call" was played by a real bugler named Pat Renzi, sporting red coat and fur derby, instead of the phonograph machine used after Karl Rissland retired. The voice of Fred "Cappy" Caposella was back to call the races. A new fan-like water fountain in the infield lake gave reason to turn gazes away from the canoe.

The blue canoe, for the first time, was painted in Calumet Farm's "devil's red"—the colors of the previous Travers Stakes winner.

Although Jaipur's victory over Ridan stood as the official result, to this day, people who watched Jaipur win aren't certain that what they saw really happened. But considering the turmoil of the times, it was only fitting that the finish of the race was surrounded by a strong sense of disbelief.

"I had the sense that Jaipur won. But, honestly, I couldn't tell. Nobody expected Ridan to get the distance," said Mike Fitzgerald, who watched from the roof.

Fitzgerald, then a twenty-year-old college student, worked summers at the track as a handyman and spent most of his time on call. "I took that small elevator up to the steward's stand and found a spot near the camera eye. There was no better place to nail the finish. But, boy, it was close."

"There was refined jeering when Ridan came East for the Travers," Red Smith wrote in the *Herald Tribune*, when trainer Leroy Jolley, the twenty-four-year-old son of the owner, brought Ridan to Saratoga from Chicago. But despite losing the 1 1/4 mile American Derby at Arlington to Black Sheep in his previous start, Ridan was indeed an accomplished runner.

Mrs. Moody Jolley's colt, a son of Nantullah, was seven for seven as a two-year-old. He finished second in the Kentucky Derby and Preakness and won the mile Arlington Classic, the 1 1/8 mile Blue Grass Stakes, the 1 1/8 mile Florida Derby and the seven-furlong Hibiscus as a three-year-old. In his sophomore season, Ridan had four victories, four places, and one show in ten starts. And prior to the Travers, he had beaten Jaipur the one time they had faced each other.

In comparison, George D. Widener's Jaipur was raced exclusively in the East, winning the Jersey Derby at Garden State, the Belmont in New York, and the Choice Stakes at Monmouth in succession as a three-year-old. He also captured the Gotham and the Withers at Aqueduct in the spring before loping home tenth in the Preakness.

When, at last, the break came, there were six to seven people deep standing behind the clubhouse reserved section seats. A mighty roar went up as the gates sprung and Ridan, under Manny Ycaza, went to the lead, while Jaipur, ridden by Willie Shoemaker, clung to him. There were five other horses in the race, including Cicada—a filly that had never missed the board in twenty-eight starts. Cyane and his stablemate, Smart, attracted support at the windows, and Military Plume, victorious at a mile in his last start, was a tempting long shot.

Regardless, all eyes were glued to Ridan and Jaipur as they sizzled through the turn. The duo made its way up the backstretch pressed close on each other. It was a match race, all right, and a reasonably fast one at that, with a mile in 1:35 2/5 and no sign of either horse backing off.

Then Ridan, on the inside, drifted slightly on the turn, and showed the first sign of wear. Shoemaker let Jaipur go after him, but Ridan was resolute. Amazingly, the pace quickened and Jaipur kept up with it. Jaipur stuck his nose in front after the two horses passed the quarter pole, and he kept it there, barely, for stride after unrelenting, heart-thumping stride to the wire.

"I ran down from the roof after the winner's circle presentation," Fitzgerald remembers. "On the path under the stands where the riders walk to return to the jockey quarters, I saw Burt Mulholland, all gnarled and grumpy, madder than hell at Shoemaker."

Ridan, under Bill Hartack, displayed his blazing speed to the field in the Blue Grass Stakes at Keeneland in Lexington, KY. But horseplayers were unsure if the quick colt could sustain it for the ten-furlong Travers. Keeneland Library/Skeets Meadors photograph

WILLIE SHOEMAKER'S TRAVERS STAKES

YEAR	HORSE	RESULT
1957	Gallant Man	First
1962	Jaipur	First
1963	Candy Spots	Fourth
1967	Damascus	First
1987	Temperate Sil	Eighth

A mighty roar went up as the gates sprung and Ridan, under Manny Ycaza, went to the lead as Jaipur, ridden by Willie Shoemaker, clung to him.

123

Right: **When two horses run a mile and a quarter neck to neck on the lead, both are rarely in a photo finish for the win. But Jaipur, on the outside, nipped Ridan in what many people believe to be the greatest Travers ever.** Photo courtesy of AP Images

The official photo finish that the stewards studied before proclaiming Jaipur the winner provided the only means to determine with certitude which horse finished first. Jones Precision Photo Finish provided by NYRA

"'I told you not to go out like that,'" Fitzgerald heard Jaipur's seventy-eight-year-old trainer say. "And Shoemaker just listened."

Mulholland was the only one who thought that the ride "the Shoe" gave his horse wasn't brilliant.

To this day, Fitzgerald believes that another horse might have won if he hadn't been knocked sideways at the break by Cicada and by Smart at the eighth pole. "Fifty yards past the line, Military Plume flew by them."

The charts lend support to Fitzgerald's account.

In finishing a length behind Jaipur and Ridan, Military Plume ran faster than any of the four previous Travers winners sent out by the family of his owner, Mrs. Walter M. (Kay) Jeffords.

The grey son of Princequillo fell far back in the running when he was impeded early on. Then Cyane spooked when he saw something in the infield and veered into his stablemate Smart, who, in turn, caused Military Plume, running fastest of all, to slow noticeably.

Nobody, except perhaps Fitzgerald, paid much attention to the commotion. In the greatest race ever run, either Jaipur or Ridan broke Man O' War's Travers record. That's all that anybody knew, at the finish.

TRAVERS STAKES WINNERS OF KAY AND WALTER M. JEFFORDS

YEAR	HORSE	JOCKEY	TRAINER	OWNER	TIME
1926	Mars	Frank Cotiletti	S.D. Harlan	Walter M. Jeffords	2:04 3/5
1946	Natchez	Ted Atkinson	Oscar White	Walter M. Jeffords	2:08
1952	One Count	Eric Guerin	Oscar White	Mrs. Walter M. Jeffords	2:07 2/5
1958	Piano Jim	Bobby Ussery	Oscar White	Walter M. Jeffords	2:05 4/5

1962 TRAVERS • JAIPUR AND RIDAN

Unresolved Ending

Affirmed Beats Alydar but Loses

1978 Travers Stakes
109th Running on Saturday, August 19

Winner	Alydar
Jockey	Jorge Velasquez
Owner	Calumet Farm
Trainer	John M. Veitch
Time	2:02

Exercise rider Charlie Rose knew from the horse's behavior and from his Whitney Stakes victory that Alydar would beat Affirmed. But he had no idea the outcome would result from a disqualification.
Photograph from the NEA Service, Inc. Collection, Browne Popular Culture Library, Bowling Green State University

The Chinese were celebrating the Year of the Horse. But for every American racing fan, 1978 was clearly the Year of Two Horses. Affirmed, a tenacious copper colt owned by Louis Wolfson's Harbor View Farm, was the Triple Crown champion. Alydar, a golden giant that raced in Calumet Farm's "devil's red" silks, was his rival.

In the spring and summer, these two legendary combatants stood head and shoulders over all other three-year-olds. They had faced each other nine times, and in most of their races, the margin of victory was, well, marginal.

Saratoga Race Course and the 109th Travers was the setting for their tenth and final meeting. Of course, before the race was run, nobody realized that the two captivating colts would never face each other again. Expectations were sky-high, a record crowd was anticipated, and there was plenty of bluster in the air as the day approached.

Laz Barrera was telling people that Affirmed, a son of Exclusive Native, would defeat his handsome rival, a son of Raise a Native, as he had in seven of their previous meetings.

"If those two were fighters, Alydar would never receive another chance because he has already lost so many times," the Cuban-born trainer, a boxing fan, said as he watched his champion gallop on the track two days before the showdown. "He's perfect. He looks a little bigger each day. He's just right," Barrera said.

John Veitch thumped his chest a little less aggressively as he looked ahead to Alydar's final workout.

"We'll just blow him out three-eighths Friday and that'll be that," Veitch told Kay Coyte of *The Saratogian* newspaper. Charlie Rose, Alydar's exercise rider, was bolder. "I know I've said that before, but this time I think we'll get him," Rose predicted.

August life in Saratoga Springs had changed in the sixteen years since the last awe-inspiring rivalry, between Jaipur and Ridan. For example, the newspaper's social page reporter Jeannette Jordan could only cajole forty-four families to reveal their seasonal whereabouts in her customary "Cottage List."

Every burglar worth a rap sheet knew that Col. and Mrs. Cloyce Tippett (the former Elizabeth Altemus Whitney) lived at 181 Phila St. But how handy it must have been to read that Dell Hancock and Helen Alexander were at 294 Lake St., that Mr. and Mrs. John R. Gaines were in residence at 695 North Broadway, and that Mr. and Mrs. Nicholas Brady were up the street from the Gaineses at number 748.

That summer, Mrs. Tippett—the "Queen of Llangollen Farm"—had restored "The Outlaw," a black and yellow road coach from the late 1920s. Covered in her purple and fuschia stable colors, she would drive her gleaming team and wagon on selected days to the Reading Room, the "members only" house that sat on the northwest corner of the racecourse's property. Once there, friends such as Lillian and Ogden Phipps, Señor and Mrs. Horatio Luro, and Libby Schaffer would meet her for lunch on the porch.

As a sign of respect, officials of the New York Racing Association saved a grassy spot for Tippett's bays and grays to graze. Of course, the makeshift range wasn't opened until after the stout-hearted, well-muscled animals led a homestretch parade that gave folks in the grandstand a charge. With one hand on a gold cup of Moët et Chandon, Tippett would wave from "The Outlaw" to cheers and applause.

Such whimsical portrayals of pomposity, if not dead, were at least dying in the late '70s. In coming decades, the public was more likely to catch a glimpse of high society in seersucker suits and sun dresses under the shady paddock elms or, if lucky, to make the invitation list at lavish soirees such as the New York Turf Writers' dinner.

But there was one place where anyone could go to have a look or be seen. Set in the pines at the peak of a knoll, Villa Balsamo was John Guerriero and Joe Balsamo's August-only restaurant. The restaurateurs owned and operated Don Peppe's opposite Aqueduct Racetrack in Ozone Park, Long Island. But ornate Villa Balsamo, occupying the abandoned Shutts Mansion on the road to Ballston Spa, was their summer place to rid cash-laden horseplayers of their stinginess. In its third year of operation, the Italian eatery was packing them in.

What was being said when horse people got together for eggplant parmagiana? Not unexpectedly, many diners praised the improvements at Saratoga Race Course. A candy-striped, canvas-covered saddling marquee was erected to replace the old wooden paddock, which in turn was outfitted with betting machines. Televisions were hung in the trees and a small play area with a sand box and slides went in. Seventy-five picnic tables were set up on the apron at the head of the stretch.

But not all the small talk was positive. On the Tuesday before the Travers, track superintendent Joe King visited the press box to defend the condition of the racing strip. The deaths of three horses had prompted an outcry from trainers, including Barrera.

"It won't get as fluffy as we'd like it until dry weather and sunny days come," general manager John Mangona told *The Saratogian*, and as soon as he did, the clouds disappeared.

The Travers was run on a fast track, on a fine summer day. The crowd began to form at 5:30 A.M., and by early afternoon, more than fifty thousand fans jammed the stands and filled the infield, breaking the attendance record by five thousand people.

It was obvious that these equine idolaters wanted a replay of the Belmont Stakes. All who saw that amazing race considered it one of the greatest ever. Affirmed ambled along on the lead for a half-mile before Alydar moved up to challenge him. Both horses were still at each other's throats with an eighth of a mile to go. At the wire, Affirmed had a head in front.

After the Belmont, Affirmed rested before winning the Jim Dandy, catching front runner Sensitive Prince in what horsemen call a "tightener." Alydar took a different road. He won the Arlington Classic and the Whitney Stakes, winning in a rush by ten lengths.

The public favored Affirmed at 7-10. Alydar was second choice at even money. There were two other horses in the field. Nasty and Bold earned his way in by winning the American Derby. Shake Shake Shake was a stakes winner in Puerto Rico.

It took the length of the clubhouse turn for Affirmed to snare the lead from Shake Shake Shake. Angel Cordero, Jr., aboard Shake Shake Shake, pushed the Triple Crown champion and jockey Laffit Pincay, Jr., substituting for Steve Cauthen, out to the middle of the track, before fading into second.

Along the backside, Alydar remained at the back, until Jorge Velasquez raced him rapidly through the gap on Shake Shake Shake's inside. Affirmed, three wide, kept a half-length advantage on Alydar.

When Shake Shake Shake faltered completely, Alydar was alone on the rail, Affirmed slightly ahead of him on his right. The two rivals raced that way for several hundred yards—Alydar following his nemesis and hoping to catch him.

Pincay decided then to move his mount closer to the rail, but in doing that

Top: **Steve Cauthen, aboard Affirmed, nearest the rail, keeps an eye of Alydar, as the two horses battle for the lead in the stretch of the Belmont Stakes. The race gave Affirmed the Triple Crown and left Alydar as the first horse to finish second in all Triple Crown races.** Photo courtesy of AP Images

Bottom: **Trainer Laz Barrera had to find a new rider for Affirmed when the wonderboy Steve Cauthen was injured. Cauthen's replacement caused the foul that denied Affirmed victory in the Travers.** NYRA photo by Bob Coglianese provided by the *Thoroughbred Times*

RIVALRY RESULTS BETWEEN AFFIRMED AND ALYDAR IN TEN STAKES

Affirmed 7, Alydar 3

DATE RACETRACK	STAKES RACE WINNER
June 15, 1977 Belmont Park (NY)	Youthful Affirmed
July 6, 1977 Belmont Park (NY)	Great American Alydar
August 27, 1977 Saratoga Race Course (NY)	G1 Hopeful Affirmed
September 10, 1977 Belmont Park (NY)	G1 Futurity Affirmed
October 15, 1977 Belmont Park (NY)	G1 Champagne Alydar
October 29, 1977 Laurel Park (MD)	G1 Laurel Futurity Affirmed
May 6, 1978 Churchill Downs (KY)	G1 Kentucky Derby Affirmed
May 20, 1978 Pimlico (MD)	G1 Preakness Affirmed
June 10, 1978 Belmont Park (NY)	G1 Belmont Affirmed
August 19, 1978 Saratoga Race Course (NY)	G1 Travers Alydar

Velasquez stepped high in his irons and Alydar lost six to seven lengths.

forced Velasquez to check Alydar. The Hall of Fame rider must not have seen Alydar, because the last time he looked to his left there was Shake Shake Shake, and now Shake Shake Shake wasn't there anymore.

Velasquez stepped high in his irons and Alydar lost six to seven lengths. Although the horses didn't touch, Pincay's move was enough of a foul to take Affirmed's number down.

"The other horse (Shake Shake Shake) dropped back and I think Pincay didn't know where he was," Veitch said after the race. "Jorge said he thought he was going down."

By the top of the stretch, Affirmed had an unchallenged lead, plenty in reserve from a moderate pace, and a quarter mile of track ahead.

To his credit, Alydar kept running. Velasquez had him rolling down the homestretch, but the favorite cruised under the finish line a length and three-quarters ahead.

The official result played out like "The Sopranos" finale. After seasons of intriguing characters, storylines, plot twists, and denouements, Pincay's indiscretion burdened the sport's ultimate show—the Travers face-off between Affirmed and Alydar—with an ending that had no resolution or clarity.

"It was a discouraging day," said Veitch, even though he accepted the Man O' War Cup. "Pincay robbed my horse out of justifying my belief that he was as good as Affirmed."

"I don't like to win that way, but you take it any way it comes," Velasquez added.

"It never should have happened, what happened," Barrera insisted, although he didn't shift all the guilt to Pincay. He blamed Cordero for pushing Affirmed wide in the first place. Cordero didn't explain why he did it, but there's no denying the fact that the popular "King of Saratoga" knew many ways to win races.

A year later, Barrera was still sticking to his guns. "If I could run that race again today, I would do nothing different. No horse could beat Affirmed," he insisted.

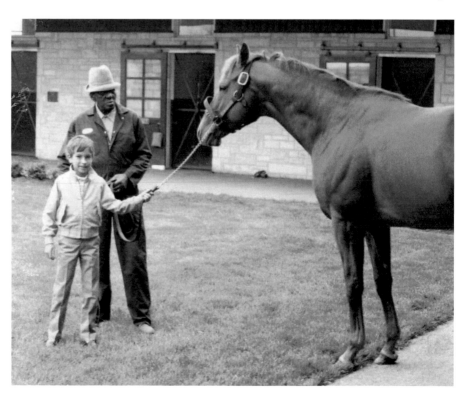

The Triple Crown champion Affirmed in retirement at Spendthrift Farm, Kentucky, in 1980. Jon Zast, the author's son, holds the halter strap on the handsome chestnut. Photo by Vic Zast

1978 TRAVERS • ALYDAR AND AFFIRMED

51835 FIFTH RACE—1 1-4 Miles. (Man o' War, Aug. 21, 1920—2:01⅘—3—129.) Sixty-first Running TRAVERS STAKES. $5,000 Added. 3-year-olds. Allowances. Net value to winner $27,050; second, $4,000; third, $2,000; fourth, $500.

Aug.-16-30-Sar

Index	Horses	A	Wt	PP	St	½	¾	1	Str	Fin	Jockeys	Owners	O	H	C	P	S
51509	JIM DANDY	w	120	2	1	$3^{1\frac{1}{2}}$	3^{3}	$1^{1\frac{1}{2}}$	1^{3}	1^{8}	F Baker	C Earl	50	100	100	10	out
(50339)	GALLANT FOX	wB	126	4	4	2^{3}	2^{3}	2^{h}	2^{nk}	2^{6}	E Sande	Belair St'd Sta	3-5	13-10	1-2	out—	
(51656)	WHICHONE	wB	126	3	2	1½	1^{h}	3^{8}	3^{8}	3^{3}	R W'kman	H P Whitney	7-5	8-5	8-5	1-6	out
51407^{3}	SUN FALCON	wB	117	1	3	4	4	4	4	4	F Co'letti	W S Kilmer	30	40	30	3	out

Time, :25, :59⅗, 1:13⅗, 1:42, 2:08. Track heavy.

Winner—Ch. c, by Jim Gaffney—Thunderbird, by Star Shoot (trained by J. B. McKee; bred by Mr. W. S. Dudley).

WENT TO POST—5:20. OFF AT ONCE.

Start good and fast. Won easily; second and third the same.

JIM DANDY was restrained back of the early pace, moved up fast on the inside rounding the stretch turn, shook off the leaders and drew away at the end. GALLANT FOX forced the pace from the start, moved away when settled on the back stretch on the outside, was carried wide turning for home, but could not overtake the winner. WHICHONE was hustled into command at the start, displayed good speed in the going, but tired badly in the stretch and pulled up very lame. SUN FALCON was outrun from the start and had no mishaps.

Scratched—51407 Caruso, 120.

SIXTH RACE
Sar 14041
August 18, 1962

1 1-4 MILES. (Lucky Draw, Aug. 24, 1946, 2:01⅗, 5, 121.) Ninety-third running TRAVERS. $75,000 added. 3-year-olds. Allowances. By subscription of $100 each, which shall accompany the nomination; $750 additional to start with $75,000 added. The added money and all fees to be divided 65 per cent to the winner, 20 per cent to second, 10 per cent to third and 5 per cent to fourth. Weight, 120 lbs. Winners of two races of $35,000 in 1962, 3 lbs.; extra; three such races or one of $60,000 in 1962, 6 lbs. extra. Non-winners of a race of $25,000 at a mile or over or two of $10,000 at such a distance allowed 3 lbs.; of a race of $20,000 or two of $10,000 at any distance, 6 lbs. The winner shall have his name inscribed on the Man o' War Cup, and a gold plated replica will be presented to the owner. Trophies will be presented to the winning trainer and jockey. Closed Wednesday, Aug. 1, with 24 nominations.

Value of race $82,650. Value to winner $53,722.50; second, $16,530; third, $8,265; fourth,, $4,132.50. Mutuel Pool, $269,335.

Index	Horses	Eq't	A Wt	PP	¼	½	¾	1	Str	Fin	Jockeys	Owners	Odds to $1
13908Mth^{1}	—Jaipur	b	126	2	2^{5}	2^{5}	2^{2}	1^{h}	1^{h}	1no	W Sho'aker	G D Widener	.65
13935AP^{2}	—Ridan		126	1	1½	1^{h}	1^{h}	$2^{1\frac{1}{2}}$	2^{2}	2^{1}	M Ycaza	Mrs M Jolley	2.65
13989Sar^{1}	—Military Plume	b	114	4	7	7	7	7	4^{h}	3¾	J Sellers	Mrs W M Jeffords	23.30
13970Sar^{1}	—Smart		114	7	4^{1}	5^{1}	5^{h}	4^{h}	5^{2}	4^{2}	P J Bailey	Christiana Stable	a-6.30
13908Mth^{2}	—Cyane		120	3	3½	3^{h}	3½	3^{2}	3^{h}	5^{2}	E Nelson	Christiana Stable	a-6.30
13949Atl	—Flying Johnnie	b	114	6	6^{4}	6^{6}	6^{6}	6^{1}	7	6^{1}	C Burr	Jopa Stable	27.15
13987Sar^{3}	—Cicada		118	5	5^{1}	4^{4}	4^{1}	5^{2}	6½	7	R Ussery	Meadow Stable	10.05

a-Coupled, Smart and Cyane.

Time, :23⅘, :47⅖, 1:11, 1:35⅖, 2:01⅗ (equals track record). Track fast.

$2 Mutuel Prices:			
3-JAIPUR	3.30	2.30	2.20
2-RIDAN		2.70	2.60
4-MILITARY PLUME			3.00

Dk. b. c, by Nasrullah—Rare Perfume, by Eight Thirty. Trainer, W. F. Mulholland. Bred by Erdenheim Farms Co.

IN GATE—4:48. OFF AT 4:48 EASTERN DAYLIGHT TIME. Start good. Won driving.

JAIPUR raced on even terms with RIDAN from the break and they continued as a team in a torrid duel. JAIPUR, on the outside of RIDAN, had a slight lead at the quarter pole and won narrowly in a race in which neither horse gave way. RIDAN, showing brilliant speed, was unable to shake off JAIPUR while saving ground throughout. He raced courageously to the end and was beaten narrowly in a thrilling duel. MILITARY PLUME was sharply impeded at the break when CICADA rammed into him. He dropped far out of it in the early stages, but came on strongly from the five-sixteenths pole to the wire, while racing in the middle of the track. SMART, unhurried early, was going well at the end, while racing between horses. CYANE, also impeded at the start, moved up early to follow the pacemakers, while racing on the rail. He changed course in the final eighth when RIDAN came in slightly, but was tiring at the time. FLYING JOHNNIE was outrun throughout. CICADA bore in sharply immediately following the break, impeding MILITARY PLUME and CYANE. She then failed to display any speed in the running. Scratched—13989Sar^{2} Zab.

EIGHTH RACE
Saratoga
AUGUST 19, 1978

1 ¼ MILES. (2.00⅕) 109th running THE TRAVERS. Purse $100,000 Added. 3-year-olds, weights, 126 lbs. By subscription of $200 each, which shall accompany the nominations; $500 to start, with $100,000 added. The added money and all fees to be divided 60% to the winner, 22% to second, 12% to third and 6% to fourth. Starters to be named at the closing time of entries. The winner shall have his name inscribed on the Man o' War Cup and a gold plated replica will be presented to the owner of the winner. Trophies will also be presented to the winning trainer and jockey. Closed with 14 nominations.

Value of race $104,800, value to winner $62,880, second $23,056, third $12,576, fourth $6,288. Mutuel pool $505,467, Minus place pool $6,151.61, OTB pool $342,816. OTB Minus Place Pool $9,082.68

Last Raced	Horse	Eqt.	A.	Wt	PP	¼	½	¾	1	Str	Fin	Jockey	Odds $1
8Aug78 ^{8}Sar^{1}	[D]Affirmed		3	126	3	$2^{1\frac{1}{2}}$	2^{2}	$1^{\frac{1}{2}}$	$1^{1\frac{1}{2}}$	1^{2}	$1^{1\frac{3}{4}}$	Pincay L Jr	.70
5Aug78 ^{8}Sar^{1}	Alydar		3	126	4	4	3^{1}	2^{2}	2^{hd}	2^{1}	$2^{3\frac{3}{4}}$	Velasquez J	1.00
22Jly78 ^{8}Bel^{1}	Nasty And Bold	b	3	126	1	3^{hd}	4	4	3^{4}	3^{10}	3^{15}	Samyn J L	15.90
5Aug78 ^{8}Mth^{5}	Shake Shake Shake		3	126	2	1^{hd}	1^{hd}	$3^{\frac{1}{2}}$	4	4	4	Cordero A Jr	20.40

[D]-Affirmed Disqualified and placed second.

OFF AT 5:46, EDT. Start good, Won ridden out. Time, :24, :48, 1:11⅗, 1:36⅘, 2:02 Track fast.

$2 Mutuel Prices:			
4-(D)-ALYDAR	4.00	2.10	—
3-(C)-AFFIRMED		2.10	—
1-(A)-NASTY AND BOLD		—	—
(No Show Wagering)			

Alydar—Ch. c, by Raise A Native—Sweet Tooth, by On-And-On. Trainer Veitch John M. Bred by Calumet Farm (Ky).

AFFIRMED away in good order, prompted the pace while racing outside SHAKE SHAKE SHAKE into the backstretch, took over just after going a half, came over racing into the far turn interfering with ALYDAR, settled into the stretch with a clear advantage and held sway under good handling. AFFIRMED was disqualified and placed second following a stewards inquiry and a foul claim by the rider of ALYDAR. ALYDAR, never far back while being reserved early, moved through along the inside to go to the leaders midway along the backstretch, was taken up sharply when AFFIRMED came over at the far turn, dropped back several lengths after coming out, came again to make a bid leaving the turn but wasn't able to gain on the winner during the drive. NASTY AND BOLD, unhurried for six furlongs made a run along the inside approaching the stretch but weakened under pressure. SHAKE SHAKE SHAKE showed early foot while saving ground, drifted out slifhtly after entering the backstretch and was finished soon after going six furlongs.

Owners— 1, Harbor View Farm; 2, Calumet Farm; 3, Meadowhill; 4, Acevedo F.

Trainers— 1, Barrera Lazaro S; 2, Veitch John M; 3, Johnson Philip G; 4, Martin Jose.

EIGHTH RACE
Saratoga
AUGUST 16, 1986

1 ¼ MILES. (2.00) 117th Running THE TRAVERS (Grade I). $250,000 Added. (Plus $50,000 Breeders' Cup Premium Awards.) 3-year-olds. By subscription of $500 each which should accompany the nominations $4,000 to pass the entry box with $250,000 added. The added money and all fees to be divided 60% to the winner, 22% to second, 12% to third and 6% to fourth. Weight, 126 lbs. Starters to be named at the closing time of entries. The winner shall have its name inscribed on the Man o'War Cup and a gold-plated replica will be presented to the owner. Trophies will be presented to the winning trainer and jockey. Closed Wednesday, July 30, 1986 with 25 nominations. Breeders' Cup Fund Awards to: Wise Times, Danziq Connection, Personal Flag.

Total purse $344,500. Value of race $339,500; value to winner $203,700; second $78,290; third $39,840; fourth $17,670. Nominator Award $5,000. Mutuel pool $499,366, OTB pool $191,478. Exacta Pool $239,104. OTB Exacta Pool $185,808.

Last Raced	Horse	Eqt.	A.	Wt	PP	¼	½	¾	1	Str	Fin	Jockey	Odds $1
26Jly86 ^{9}Mth^{1}	Wise Times		3	126	3	$6^{\frac{1}{2}}$	$6^{\frac{1}{2}}$	5^{hd}	$5^{2\frac{1}{2}}$	5^{3}	1^{hd}	Bailey J D	5.80
26Jly86 ^{9}Mth^{5}	[D]Broad Brush	b	3	126	5	3^{2}	3^{5}	$3^{2\frac{1}{2}}$	3^{2}	1^{hd}	$2^{1\frac{1}{4}}$	Cordero A Jr	2.50
26Jly86 ^{9}Mth^{3}	Danzig Connection		3	126	4	$2^{1\frac{1}{2}}$	$2^{\frac{1}{2}}$	2^{5}	1^{hd}	$2^{\frac{1}{2}}$	3^{hd}	Maple E	1.20
26Jly86 ^{9}Mth^{2}	Personal Flag		3	126	2	5^{4}	$5^{2\frac{1}{2}}$	6^{3}	$4^{2\frac{1}{2}}$	4^{hd}	$4^{1\frac{3}{4}}$	Velasquez J	3.60
30Jly86 ^{3}Sar^{3}	Scrimshaw	b	3	126	7	7	7	7	$6^{1\frac{1}{2}}$	6^{14}	$5^{4\frac{1}{2}}$	Guerra W A	36.50
3Aug86 ^{8}Sar^{2}	Moment Of Hope		3	126	6	$1^{1\frac{1}{2}}$	$1^{\frac{1}{2}}$	$1^{\frac{1}{2}}$	2^{3}	3^{2}	6^{22}	Venezia M	19.40
30Jly86 ^{3}Sar^{1}	Waikiki Star	b	3	126	1	4^{1}	$4^{2\frac{1}{2}}$	4^{2}	7	7	7	Cruguet J	21.60

[D]-Broad Brush Disqualified and placed fourth.

OFF AT 5:43. Start good, Won driving. Time, :23⅘, :48⅖, 1:12, 1:37, 2:03⅖ Track sloppy.

$2 Mutuel Prices:			
4-(D)-WISE TIMES	13.60	5.00	4.00
5-(E)-DANZIG CONNECTION		3.20	2.60
3-(C)-PERSONAL FLAG			3.20

$2 EXACTA 4-5 PAID $35.20.

B. c, by Mr Leader—Trying Times, by He's a Pistol. Trainer Gleaves Philip. Bred by Nuckols Bros (Ky).

WISE TIMES, unhurried while outrun for a mile, settled suddenly while racing wide after entering the stretch and continued on with good courage to wear down BROAD BRUSH in the final yards. The latter, allowed to follow the early leaders while racing well out in the track, dropped back approaching the end of the backstretch, continued wide into the stretch, caught the leaders a furlong out and failed to last after coming out and impeding PERSONAL FLAG about 70 yards from the finish. BROAD BRUSH was disqualified and placed fourth following a stewards inquiry. DANZIG CONNECTION prompted the pace, moved up outside MOMENT OF HOPE soon after entering the stretch, dueled for the lead to the final sixteenth and weakened. PERSONAL FLAG, reserved to the far turn, moved up along the inside nearing the stretch, came out between horses for the drive and was moving with WISE TIMES when forced to check by BROAD BRUSH about 70 yards from the finish. SCRIMSHAW, badly outrun for a mile, raced very wide into the stretch and failed to seriously menace while making up ground late. MOMENT OF HOPE raced well out from the rail while making the pace, held on well to the final furlong and gave way. WAIKIKI STAR stopped badly. WISE TIMES, DANZIG CONNECTION and MOMENT OF HOPE raced with mud caulks.

Owners— 1, Reineman R L; 2, Meyerhoff R E; 3, De Kwiatkowski H; 4, Phipps O; 5, Peters Betty M; 6, Four Fifth S Stable; 7, Firestone B R.

Trainers— 1, Gleaves Philip; 2, Small Richard W; 3, Stephens Woodford C; 4, McGaughey Claude III; 5, Kelly Larry; 6, Dunham Bob G; 7, Penna Angel.

Scratched—Ogygian (5Jly86 ^{8}Bel^{1}).

EIGHTH RACE
Saratoga
AUGUST 22, 1987

1 ¼ MILES. (2.00) 118th Running THE TRAVERS (Grade I). Purse $1,000,000 added. 3-year-olds. By subscription of $1,500 each which should accompany the nomination; $3,000 to pass the entry box, $7,500 to start, with $1,000,000 added. The added money and all fees to be divided 60% to the winner, 22% to second, 12% to third and 6% to fourth. Weight, 126 lbs. Starters to be named at the closing time of entries. The winner shall have his name inscribed on the Man o' War Cup and a gold plated replica will be presented to the winning owner. Trophies will be presented to the winning owner, trainer and jockey. Closed with 19 nominations Wednesday, August 5, 1987. Value of race $1,123,000; value to winner $673,800; second $247,060; third $134,760; fourth $67,380. Mutuel pool $805,751, OTB pool $803,715. ExPl$321,117.OTB ExPl$646,094TriPl$220,041.OTB TriPl$352,927

Last Raced	Horse	Eqt.	A.	Wt	PP	¼	½	¾	1	Str	Fin	Jockey	Odds $1
8Aug87 ^{8}Sar^{1}	Java Gold		3	126	3	8^{6}	8^{2}	9	6^{3}	3^{2}	1^{2}	Day P	3.20
9Aug87 ^{8}Sar^{3}	Cryptoclearance		3	126	2	9	9	8^{2}	3^{2}	$1^{1\frac{1}{2}}$	$2^{6\frac{3}{4}}$	Cordero A Jr	7.90
9Aug87 ^{8}Sar^{1}	Polish Navy		3	126	1	3^{1}	3^{2}	$3^{\frac{1}{2}}$	1^{hd}	$2^{\frac{1}{2}}$	$3^{1\frac{1}{2}}$	Romero R P	9.70
8Aug87 ^{8}Sar^{2}	Gulch		3	126	4	$6^{1\frac{1}{2}}$	$6^{\frac{1}{2}}$	6^{hd}	4^{1}	5^{4}	4^{2}	Santos J A	a-9.90
1Aug87 ^{9}Mth^{1}	Bet Twice		3	126	8	$4^{\frac{1}{2}}$	$4^{1\frac{1}{2}}$	4^{2}	2^{2}	4^{1}	5^{8}	Perret C	4.20
1Aug87 ^{9}Mth^{2}	Alysheba	b	3	126	6	$7^{1\frac{1}{2}}$	7^{5}	7^{3}	$7^{\frac{1}{2}}$	6^{6}	$6^{9\frac{1}{2}}$	McCarron C J	2.50
1Aug87 ^{9}AP^{1}	Fortunate Moment		3	126	5	5^{hd}	$5^{\frac{1}{2}}$	$5^{1\frac{1}{2}}$	8^{6}	8^{8}	7^{hd}	Fires E	23.90
26Jly87 ^{9}Hol^{1}	Temperate Sil		3	126	7	$1^{1\frac{1}{2}}$	$1^{\frac{1}{2}}$	1^{hd}	$5^{\frac{1}{2}}$	7^{3}	8^{13}	Shoemaker W	5.30
8Aug87 ^{8}Sar^{7}	Gorky		3	126	9	2^{3}	2^{7}	2^{6}	9	9	9	Graell A	a-9.90

a-Coupled: Gulch and Gorky.

OFF AT 5:46. Start good. Won driving. Time, :23⅖, :46⅕, 1:10, 1:36⅖, 2:02 Track sloppy.

$2 Mutuel Prices:			
4-(C)-JAVA GOLD	8.40	5.40	3.80
3-(B)-CRYPTOCLEARANCE		6.40	3.80
2-(A)-POLISH NAVY			5.00

$2 EXACTA 4-3 PAID $90.60. TRIPLE 4-3-2 PAID $526.00

B. c, by Key to the Mint—Javamine, by Nijinsky II. Trainer Miller Mack. Bred by Mellon Paul (Va).

JAVA GOLD, away in good order, was unhurried while dropping back around the first turn and into the backstretch and was trailing at the far turn. He settled suddenly after starting the turn, angled out to continue a rally approaching the stretch, caught CRYPTOCLEARANCE with a sixteenth remaining and drew off under brisk urging. CRYPTOCLEARANCE, badly outrun to the end of the backstretch, swung out while beginning to [illegible] but wasn't able to withstand the winner while drifting out under pressure. POLISH NAVY, reserved early, commenced to rally nearing the end of the backstretch, reached the front from between horses approaching the stretch but tired during the drive. GULCH, outrun early while saving ground, moved between horses while advancing nearing the stretch but lacked a late response. BET TWICE, reserved for six furlongs, moved fast to loom a threat from the outside approaching the stretch, held on well until inside the final three-sixteenths and gave way. ALYSHEBA failed to be a serious factor. FORTUNATE MOMENT tired badly. TEMPERATE SIL saved ground while making the pace, held on well for seven furlongs but had nothing left. GORKY, hustled along after breaking slowly, prompted the pace while racing outside TEMPERATE SIL to the far turn and stopped suddenly. JAVA GOLD, CRYPTOCLEARANCE and TEMPERATE SIL raced with mud caulks.

Owners— 1, Rokeby Stable; 2, Teinowitz P; 3, Phipps O; 4, Brant P M; 5, Cisley Stable & Levy Blanche P; 6, Scharbauer Dorothy & Pamela; 7, Pinkley Jerry R; 8, Whittingham C; 9, Brant P M.

Trainers— 1, Miller Mack; 2, Schulhofer Flint S; 3, McGaughey Claude III; 4, Jolley Leroy; 5, Croll Warren A Jr; 6, Van Berg Jack C; 7, Vanier Harvey L; 8, Whittingham Charles; 9, Jolley Leroy.

EIGHTH RACE
Saratoga
AUGUST 20, 1988

1 ¼ MILES. (2.00) 119th Running THE TRAVERS (Grade I). Purse $1,000,000 added. 3–year–olds. By subscription of $1,500 each, which should accompany the nomination; $3,000 to pass the entry box, $7,500 to start, with $1,000,000 added. The added money and all fees to be divided 60% to the winner, 22% to second, 12% to third and 6% to fourth. 126 lbs. Starters to be named at the closing time of entries. The winner shall have its ame inscribed on the Man o'War Cup and a gold plated replica will be presented to the winning owner. Trophies will lso be presented to the winning trainer and jockey. Closed Wednesday, August 3 with 17 nominations.
Value of race $1,088,500; value to winner $653,100; second $239,470; third $130,620; fourth $65,310. Mutuel pool $1,235,337. Exacta Pool $720,577. Triple Pool $375,099.

Last Raced	Horse	Eqt.A.Wt	PP	¼	½	¾	1	Str	Fin	Jockey	Odds $1
30Jly88 ^{9}Mth^{1}	Forty Niner	3 126	5	2^{3}	$1^{1/2}$	$1^{1/2}$	$1^{1/2}$	1^{2}	1no	McCarron C J	2.20
30Jly88 ^{9}Mth^{2}	Seeking the Gold	3 126	1	1^{1}	3^{1}	$4^{2 1/2}$	3^{hd}	$2^{1/2}$	$2^{3/4}$	Day P	2.50
7Aug88 ^{8}Sar^{1}	Brian's Time	b 3 126	4	6	6	6	$4^{1/2}$	3^{1}	$3^{5 1/2}$	Cordero A Jr	1.00
7Aug88 ^{8}Sar^{2}	Evening Kris	3 126	6	5^{1}	$5^{1 1/2}$	$5^{1/2}$	5^{12}	4^{1}	4^{3}	Bailey J D	14.80
7Aug88 ^{8}Sar^{8}	Dynaformer	b 3 126	3	4^{4}	2^{hd}	$2^{1 1/2}$	$2^{1 1/2}$	5^{22}	5^{38}	Davis R G	34.10
7Aug88 ^{8}Sar^{7}	Kingpost	3 126	2	$3^{1/2}$	4^{5}	$3^{1/2}$	6	6	6	Vasquez J	22.50

OFF AT 5:46 Start good, Won driving. Time, :24⅕, :48⅗, 1:13⅕, 1:37⅘, 2:01⅖ Track fast.

$2 Mutuel Prices:

5–(E)–FORTY NINER	6.40	3.40	2.60
1–(A)–SEEKING THE GOLD		3.60	2.60
4–(D)–BRIAN'S TIME			2.20

$2 EXACTA 5–1 Paid $16.40. $2 TRIPLE 5–1–4 Paid $27.00.

Ch. c, by Mr Prospector—File, by Tom Rolfe. Trainer Stephens Woodford C. Bred by Claiborne Farm (Ky).

FORTY NINER away in good order, moved to the fore entering the backstretch, raced slightly out from the ail while going easily, moved to the inside while drawing clear after entering the stretch and lasted over SEEKING THE GOLD in a furious drive. The latter gained a clear lead along the inside on the first turn, was nhurried when replaced entering the backstretch, rallied while continuing to save ground leaving the far turn, ased out from behind FORTY NINER to continue his bid inside the final furlong and finished strongly, just nissing. BRIAN'S TIME outrun early moved between horses to reach contention nearing the stretch and ontinued on with good energy. EVENING KRIS unhurried early, made a run from the outside leaving the far urn but tired during the drive. DYNAFORMER moved to the leaders from the outside entering the backstretch, rompted the pace while racing outside FORTY NINER to the stretch, then was steadied slightly while tiring etween horses a furlong out. KINGPOST away in close quarters restrained behind the leaders approaching the ackstretch, raced within easy striking distance to the far turn and stopped badly.

Owners— 1, Claiborne Farm; 2, Phipps O; 3, Phillips J W; 4, Brennan R; 5, Allen Joseph; 6, Warner M.

Trainers— 1, Stephens Woodford C; 2, McGaughey Claude III; 3, Veitch John M; 4, Gleaves Philip; 5, .ukas D Wayne; 6, Carpenter Dianne.

EIGHTH RACE
Saratoga
AUGUST 19, 1989

1 ¼ MILES. (2.00) 120th Running THE TRAVERS (Grade I). Purse $1,000,000 Added. 3–year–olds. By subscription of $1,500 each, which should accompany the nomination; $3,000 to pass the entry box; $7,500 to start, with $1,000,000 added. The added money and all fees to be divided 60% to the winner, 22% to second, 12% to third and 6% to fourth. Weight, 126 lbs. Starters to be named at the closing time of entries. The winner shall have its name inscribed on the Man o' War Cup and a gold plated replica will be presented to the winning owner. Trophies will also be presented to the winning trainer and jockey. Closed Wednesday, August 2 with 17 nominations.
Value of race $1,088,500; value to winner $653,100; second $239,470; third $130,620; fourth $65,310. Mutuel pool $1,210,623. Exacta Pool $626,049. Triple Pool $567,402.

Last Raced	Horse	Eqt.A.Wt	PP	¼	½	¾	1	Str	Fin	Jockey	Odds $1
5Aug89 ^{8}Sar^{1}	Easy Goer	3 126	5	4^{2}	3^{hd}	3^{2}	2^{5}	$1^{1 1/2}$	1^{3}	Day P	.20
15Jly89 ^{9}AP^{1}	Clever Trevor	3 126	2	$1^{1 1/2}$	$1^{1/2}$	1^{2}	1^{1}	2^{6}	2^{9}	Pettinger D R	5.60
29Jly89 ^{9}Mth^{3}	Shy Tom	3 126	1	$5^{1/2}$	5^{2}	5^{3}	3^{4}	3^{3}	$3^{5 3/4}$	Santos J A	15.30
6Aug89 ^{10}Mtn^{1}	Doc's Leader	b 3 126	3	6	6	6	4^{2}	4^{6}	4^{8}	Fox W I Jr	49.30
29Jly89 ^{9}Mth^{5}	Le Voyageur	3 126	4	3^{hd}	4^{3}	$4^{1 1/2}$	5^{1}	5^{4}	5^{11}	Romero R P	8.80
6Aug89 ^{8}Sar^{3}	Roi Danzig	b 3 126	6	2^{3}	2^{4}	2^{2}	6	6	6	Maple E	13.60

OFF AT 5:43; Start good. Won ridden out. Time, :23⅕, :46⅘, 1:10⅗, 1:35⅗, 2:00⅘ Track fast.

$2 Mutuel Prices:

5–(E)–EASY GOER	2.40	2.20	2.10
2–(B)–CLEVER TREVOR		3.00	2.10
1–(A)–SHY TOM			2.10

$2 EXACTA 5–2 PAID $5.60. $2 TRIPLE 5–2–1 PAID $20.00.

Ch. c, (Mar), by Alydar—Relaxing, by Buckpasser. Trainer McGaughey Claude III. Bred by Phipps O (Ky).

EASY GOER, four wide into the first turn while well in hand, commenced to rally approaching the end of the backstretch, moved up alongside CLEVER TREVOR midway of the far turn, continued outside that rival while prompting the pace to the upper stretch, ducked in slightly after taking over nearing the final furlong and drew away under a hand ride. CLEVER TREVOR quickly sprinted to the front, raced well out from the rail while making the pace under good handling, shook off ROI DANZIG soon after going a half, responded readily when first challenged by EASY GOER midway of the far turn, then wasn't able to handle that one while besting the others. SHY TOM, unhurried while outrun early, made up some ground along the inside approaching the stretch but tired during the drive. DOC'S LEADER failed to reach serious contention. LE VOYAGEUR was finished approaching the end of the backstretch. ROI DANZIG quickly reached contention from the outside, went up after CLEVER TREVOR entering the backstretch but gave way soon after going six furlongs.

Owners— 1, Phipps O; 2, McNeill D C & Cheri; 3, Young W T; 4, Loccisano Mary Ann; 5, Calumet Farm & Marcus Betty; 6, De Kwiatkowski H.

Trainers— 1, McGaughey Claude III; 2, VonHemel Donnie K; 3, Lukas D Wayne; 4, Meyer Jerome C; 5, Biancone Patrick L; 6, Stephens Woodford C.

SEVENTH RACE
Saratoga
AUGUST 18, 1990

1 ¼ MILES. (2.00) 121st Running THE TRAVERS (Grade I). Purse $1,000,000 added. 3–year–olds. By subscription of $1,500 each, which should accompany the nomination; $3,000 to pass the entry box; $7,500 to start, with $1,000,000 added. The added money and all fees to be divided 60% to the winner, 22% to second, 12% to third and 6% to fourth. Weight: 126 lbs. Starters to be named at the closing time of entries. The winner shall have its name inscribed on the Man o'War Cup and a gold–plated replica will be presented to the winning owner. Trophies will also be presented to the winning trainer and jockey. Closed Wednesday, August 1 with 26 nominations.
Value of race $1,178,500; value to winner $707,100; second $259,270; third $141,420; fourth $70,710. Mutuel pool $1,201,880. Exacta Pool $1,001,254 Triple Pool $743,798

Last Raced	Horse	M/Eqt.A.Wt	PP	¼	½	¾	1	Str	Fin	Jockey	Odds $1
28Jly90 ^{10}Mth^{3}	Rhythm	b 3 126	3	$11^{1/2}$	13	12^{5}	7^{1}	$3^{1 1/2}$	$1^{3 1/2}$	Perret C	6.50
14Jly90 ^{8}AP^{7}	Shot Gun Scott	3 126	1	2^{1}	$2^{1 1/2}$	1^{hd}	$2^{1/2}$	2^{1}	2^{nk}	Clark K D	f-55.50
5Aug90 ^{8}Sar^{4}	Sir Richard Lewis	b 3 126	2	4^{hd}	$5^{1/2}$	2^{hd}	1^{hd}	$1^{1 1/2}$	$3^{3 1/2}$	Stevens G L	a-7.30
28Jly90 ^{10}Mth^{2}	Baron de Vaux	b 3 126	7	5^{1}	$4^{1/2}$	$5^{1 1/2}$	$5^{1 1/2}$	5^{1}	$4^{1 1/4}$	Cruguet J	18.70
28Jly90 ^{10}Mth^{6}	Profit Key	3 126	6	6^{1}	6^{1}	6^{5}	6^{3}	7^{hd}	$5^{1/2}$	Santos J A	a-7.30
28Jly90 ^{10}Mth^{7}	Secret Hello	3 126	9	$9^{1/2}$	8^{hd}	9^{hd}	8^{3}	8^{8}	6^{nk}	Day P	15.80
9Jun90 ^{8}Bel^{1}	Go And Go	b 3 126	12	$7^{2 1/2}$	3^{hd}	$4^{1/2}$	$4^{1/2}$	$6^{1 1/2}$	7no	Kinane M J	1.70
1Aug90 ^{1}Sar^{4}	Thirty Six Red	3 126	5	$1^{1/2}$	1^{hd}	3^{2}	3^{4}	$4^{1/2}$	8^{16}	Smith M E	5.40
5Aug90 ^{9}Crc^{2}	Rowdy Regal	b 3 126	8	13	10^{hd}	$11^{1/2}$	$11^{1 1/2}$	11^{6}	$9^{3/4}$	Chavez J F	f-55.50
28Jly90 ^{10}Mth^{4}	Yonder	3 126	11	12^{hd}	$11^{1/2}$	7^{hd}	9^{hd}	$9^{1/2}$	10^{4}	Bailey J D	9.90
28Jly90 ^{10}Mth^{5}	Tee's Prospect	3 126	13	8^{1}	$9^{1 1/2}$	8^{hd}	10^{3}	$10^{1 1/2}$	$11^{7 1/4}$	Cordero A Jr	25.30
28Jly90 ^{10}Mth^{1}	Restless Con	3 126	4	$3^{1/2}$	7^{5}	$10^{1/2}$	12^{6}	12^{7}	$12^{6 1/2}$	Doocy T T	9.20
29Jly90 ^{8}Bel^{1}	Solar Splendor	3 126	10	$10^{1 1/2}$	12^{hd}	13	13	13	13	Maple E	10.80

a–Coupled: Sir Richard Lewis and Profit Key.
f—Mutuel field.

OFF AT 4:51 Start good, Won driving. Time, :23⅕, :47⅖, 1:11⅖, 1:36⅖, 2:02⅗ Track fast.

$2 Mutuel Prices:

2–(B)–RHYTHM	15.00	7.80	5.60
12–(L)–SHOT GUN SCOTT (f–field)		37.00	12.00
1–(A)–SIR RICHARD LEWIS (a–entry)			7.40

$2 EXACTA 2–12 PAID $1,203.40 $2 TRIFECTA 2–12–1 PAID $7,151.00

B. c, (Mar), by Mr Prospector—Dance Number, by Northern Dancer. Trainer McGaughey Claude III. Bred by Phipps O M (Ky).

RHYTHM, unhurried while outrun into the backstretch while saving ground, found himself behind a wall of horses approaching the end of the backstretch, eased out to find room at the far turn, moved fast while racing wide after entering the stretch and drew off after catching SIR RICHARD LEWIS. SHOT GUN SCOTT, away alertly, showed speed into the backstretch, continued to vie for the lead while between horses around the far turn, then continued on with good courage to gain the place. SIR RICHARD LEWIS, close up into the backstretch, moved through along the inside join the leaders before going six furlongs, dueled for the lead into the stretch and after opening a clear advantage, weakened. BARON DE VAUX raced within easy striking distance to the stretch and weakened. PROFIT KEY, well placed to the far turn, tired. SECRET HELLO failed to be a serious factor. GO AND GO, hustled up outside horses racing to the first turn, raced six wide into the backstretch and was finished entering the stretch. THIRTY SIX RED showed good early foot, dueled for command while racing outside SIR RICHARD LEWIS and SHOT GUN SCOTT to the stretch and gave way. ROWDY REGAL, bothered, racing to the first turn, failed to be a factor. YONDER, bothered at the start, failed to reach serious contention. TEE'S PROSPECT tired badly. RESTLESS CON showed some early foot, was eased back between horses midway along the backstretch and gave way readily. SOLAR SPLENDOR broke to the outside, was checked sharply while getting out between horses at the first turn and stopped badly.

Owners— 1, Phipps O M; 2, Friedberg J S; 3, Baker-Feinbloom-Kaskel; 4, Sharp B; 5, Allen & Mid-America Stable; 6, Lazy Lane Farm Inc; 7, Moyglare Stud; 8, Brophy B G; 9, Thompson P A; 10, Stronach F; 11, Nedlaw Stable; 12, Chambers Jane; 13, Live Oak Plantation.

Trainers— 1, McGaughey Claude III; 2, Bonnafon Eddie; 3, Lukas D Wayne; 4, Peoples Charles; 5, Lukas D Wayne; 6, Brothers Frank L; 7, Weld Dermot K; 8, Zito Nicholas P; 9, Stirling Kent H; 10, Penna Angel; 11, Thompson J Willard; 12, Offield Daniel; 13, Kelly Patrick J.

Scratched—Le Prince (20Jly90 ^{1}Bel^{1}).

EIGHTH RACE
Saratoga
AUGUST 17, 1991

1 ¼ MILES. (2.00) 122nd Running THE TRAVERS (Grade I). Purse $1,000,000. 3–year–olds. By subscription of $1,500 each, which should accompany the nomination; $3,000 to pass the entry box; $7,500 to start. The purse to be divided 60% to the winner, 22% to second, 12% to third and 6% to fourth. 126 lbs. Starters to be named at the closing time of entries. The winner shall have its name inscribed on the Man o'War Cup and a gold plated replica will be presented to the winning owner. Trophies will also be presented to the winning trainer and jockey. Closed Wendesday, July 31 with 16 nominations.
Value of race $1,000,000; value to winner $600,000; second $220,000; third $120,000; fourth $60,000. Mutuel pool $1,478,941. Exacta Pool $1,020,965 Triple Pool $646,797

Last Raced	Horse	M/Eqt.A.Wt	PP	¼	½	¾	1	Str	Fin	Jockey	Odds $1
27Jly91 ^{10}Mth^{2}	Corporate Report	b 3 126	4	1^{1}	1^{1}	$1^{1/2}$	1^{hd}	$1^{1/2}$	1^{nk}	McCarron C J	7.30
27Jly91 ^{10}Mth^{3}	Hansel	3 126	2	2^{1}	$2^{1 1/2}$	2^{2}	$2^{1 1/2}$	2^{2}	$2^{2 1/2}$	Bailey J D	1.90
28Jly91 ^{8}Sar^{1}	Fly So Free	3 126	3	3^{3}	3^{9}	3^{6}	3^{1}	$3^{2 1/2}$	3^{3}	Santos J A	4.10
28Jly91 ^{8}Sar^{3}	Strike the Gold	3 126	5	6	6	$4^{1/2}$	4^{1}	$4^{1/2}$	$4^{1 1/2}$	Cordero A Jr	1.70
27Jly91 ^{10}Mth^{1}	Lost Mountain	b 3 126	6	5^{2}	$5^{1 1/2}$	6	5^{3}	5^{14}	5	Perret C	6.30
28Jly91 ^{8}Sar^{5}	Tong Po	3 126	1	$4^{1 1/2}$	4^{1}	$5^{1/2}$	6	6	—	Antley C W	17.60

Tong Po, Eased.

OFF AT 5:24 Start good. Won driving. Time, :23^{3}, :47^{2}, 1:11^{2}, 1:36 , 2:01^{1} Track fast.

$2 Mutuel Prices:

4–(D)–CORPORATE REPORT	16.60	5.60	4.20
2–(B)–HANSEL		4.20	3.80
3–(C)–FLY SO FREE			4.60

$2 EXACTA 4–2 PAID $61.60 TRIPLE 4–2–3 PAID $271.00

Ch. c, (Apr), by Private Account—Ten Cents a Kiss, by Key to the Mint. Trainer Lukas D Wayne. Bred by Equigroup Thoroughbreds (Ky).

CORPORATE REPORT, took charge soon after the start, was rated on the lead while racing three wide on the first turn, set the pace while continuing off the rail along the backstretch, angled to the inside while being asked for run on the far turn, dug in when challenged by HANSEL midway on the turn, battled gamely inside that one through the lane and prevailed under strong right hand encouragement. HANSEL attempted to drift out while racing close up approaching the first turn, stalked the pace from outside along the backstretch, drew on even terms with CORPORATE REPORT leaving the five-sixteenths pole, dueled heads apart with that one into midstretch then hung slightly in the final twenty yards. HANSEL pulled up in distress after the finish and was vanned off. FLY SO FREE, never far back, angled inside the leaders on the first turn, was taken to the outside while racing in good position along the backstretch, saved ground on the far turn, angled to the outside when asked for run approaching the stretch but was no match for the top two while finishing willing to gain a share. STRIKE THE GOLD, outrun early, gradually worked his way forward while four wide along the backstretch, steadily gained while saving ground on the far turn, launched a rally under pressure leaving the three-eighths pole, moved within striking distance from outside at the top of the stretch and lacked a strong closing bid. LOST MOUNTAIN, far back for six furlongs, rallied mildly along the inside on the turn but couldn't sustain his bid. TONG PO was never a factor and was eased late when hopelessly beaten.

Owners— 1, Young William T; 2, Lazy Lane Farms Inc; 3, Valando Thomas; 4, B C C Gold Stable; 5, Loblolly Stable; 6, Quinichett Lorraine.

Trainers— 1, Lukas D Wayne; 2, Brothers Frank L; 3, Schulhofer Flint S; 4, Zito Nicholas P; 5, Bohannan Thomas; 6, Blusiewicz Leon J.

SEVENTH RACE
Saratoga
AUGUST 22, 1992

1 ¼ MILES. (2.00) 123rd Running THE TRAVERS (Grade I). Purse $1,000,000 Guaranteed. 3-year-olds. By subscription of $1,500 each which should accompany the nomination; $3,000 to pass the entry box, $7,500 to start. The purse to be divided 60% to the winner, 22% to second, 12% to third, and 6% to fourth. Weight, 126 lbs. Starters to be named at the closing time of entries. The winner shall have its name inscribed on the Man o'War Cup and a gold plated replica will be presented to the winning owner. Trophies will also be presented to the winning trainer and jockey. Closed Wednesday, August 5 with 22 nominations.

Value of race $1,000,000; value to winner $600,000; second $220,000; third $120,000; fourth $60,000. Mutuel pool $1,429,699. Exacta Pool $1,183,044 Triple Pool $1,015,519

Last Raced	Horse	M/Eqt.	A.Wt	PP	¼	½	¾	1	Str	Fin	Jockey	Odds $1
2Aug92 8Sar1	Thunder Rumble		3 126	10	4hd	5hd	5hd	41	11½	14½	McCauley W H	7.60
2Aug92 8Sar3	Devil His Due		3 126	7	92½	91½	94	7½	31½	24½	Maple E	5.40
2Aug92 10Mth9	Dance Floor		3 126	8	61½	73	7½	51	41½	3nk	Antley C W	23.60
2Aug92 8Sar2	Dixie Brass		3 126	1	11½	12	11	1½	21½	45	Pezua J M	3.90
10Aug92 8Sar1	Tank's Number		3 126	3	5hd	6½	3hd	6½	61	5¾	Bailey J D	25.10
2Aug92 8Sar4	Furiously		3 126	6	72	4½	41	2½	5½	61½	Smith M E	6.90
2Aug92 10Mth5	Lee n Otto		3 126	9	81½	82½	82½	82	71	78	Migliore R	81.60
26Jly92 8FE2	Alydeed		3 126	5	3½	31	2½	3hd	88	83	Perret C	1.70
8Aug92 9Aks1	Hold Old Blue	b	3 126	4	21	2hd	63	98	91	94¼	Day P	26.80
25Jly92 8Hol1	Bien Bien	b	3 126	2	10	10	10	10	10	10	McCarron C J	8.00

OFF AT 5:09 Start good for all but BIEN BIEN, Won driving. Time, :23 , :46^4, 1:10^3, 1:35^2, 2:00^4 Track fast.

$2 Mutuel Prices:

10-(J)-THUNDER RUMBLE	17.20	7.80	5.40
7-(G)-DEVIL HIS DUE		6.20	4.80
8-(H)-DANCE FLOOR			6.80

$2 EXACTA 10-7 PAID $105.00 $2 TRIPLE 10-7-8 PAID $1,973.00

Dk. b. or br. c, (Mar), by Thunder Puddles—Lyphette, by Lyphard. Trainer O'Connell Richard. Bred by Widmer Konrad (NY).

THUNDER RUMBLE, moved up steadily from outside to contest the pace while four wide approaching the first turn, bumped with DANCE FLOOR while angling in a bit leaving the first turn, tucked in behind the leaders between horses along the backstretch, waited patiently while gaining a bit midway on the turn, was taken to the outside on the turn, circled four wide to challenge at the top of the stretch, accelerated to the front opening a clear advantage in midstretch then steadily increased his margin under strong right hand encouragement. DEVIL HIS DUE, raced far back while saving ground for six furlongs, closed a lengthy gap while slightly off the rail on the turn, launched a rally between horses in upper stretch, angled out slightly in midstretch then finished willingly to clearly best the others. DANCE FLOOR, in hand early, was bumped soundly while sandwiched between horses along the backstretch, swung to the outside midway on the turn, circled five wide into the stretch then lacked a strong closing bid. DIXIE BRASS was sent immediately to the front at the start, opened a clear advantage while saving ground on the first turn, widened his margin a bit while setting a brisk pacer along the backstretch, continued on the front maintaining a narrow advantage on the turn, relinquished the lead in upper stretch then gradually tired thereafter. FURIOUSLY, unhurried early, moved up steadily while four wide along the backstretch, gradually cut into the leaders margin while four wide on the far turn, made a run between horses to challenge approaching the quarter pole then flattened out. TANK'S NUMBER, bumped with DANCE FLOOR while in tight along the rail on the first turn, raced in close contention while saving ground for seven furlong then lacked a further response. LEE N OTTO was never a factor while four wide. ALYDEED raced in close contention between horses along the backstretch, remained a factor while saving ground on the turn then gave way at the top of the stretch. HOLD OLD BLUE was used up chasing DIXIE BRASS for five furlongs. BIEN BIEN, stumbled badly at the start and was never close thereafter.

Owners— 1, Braeburn Farm; 2, Lion Crest Stable; 3, Oaktown Stable; 4, Watral Michael; 5, Flying Zee Stables; 6, Mill House; 7, Epstein Bernard; 8, Kinghaven Farms; 9, Tafel James B; 10, Toffan John.

Trainers— 1, O'Connell Richard; 2, Jerkens H Allen; 3, Lukas D Wayne; 4, Brida Dennis J; 5, Martin Carlos F; 6, McGaughey Claude III; 7, Wismer Glenn; 8, Attfield Roger; 9, Nafzger Carl A; 10, Gonzalez Juan.

SEVENTH RACE
Saratoga
AUGUST 21, 1993

1 ¼ MILES. (2.00) 124th Running THE TRAVERS (Grade I). Purse $1,000,000. 3-year-olds. By subscription of $1,500 each which should accompany the nomination; $3,000 to pass the entry box; $7,500 to start. The purse to be divided 60% to the winner, 22% to second, 12% to third and 6% to fourth. Weight: 126 lbs. Starters to be named at the closing time of entries. The winner shall have its name decribed on the Man O' War Cup and a gold plated replica will be presented to the winning owner. Trophies will be presented to the winning trainer and jockey. Nominations closed Wednesday, August 4, 1993, with 15 nominations.

Value of race $1,000,000; value to winner $600,000; second $220,000; third $120,000; fourth $60,000. Mutuel pool $1,525,453. Exacta Pool $1,398,824 Triple Pool $1,131,887

Last Raced	Horse	M/Eqt.	A.Wt	PP	¼	½	¾	1	Str	Fin	Jockey	Odds $1
1Aug93 8Sar4	Sea Hero		3 126	7	81½	82	82	4hd	1½	12	Bailey J D	6.70
1Aug93 11Mth1	Kissin Kris	b	3 126	2	91½	91	9½	9½	51½	21	Santos J A	2.60
1Aug93 8Sar1	Miner's Mark		3 126	8	72½	73½	72	3hd	4hd	3hd	McCarron C J	3.80
1Aug93 8Sar3	Colonial Affair	b	3 126	10	6hd	5½	51	21	31½	4hd	Krone J A	3.70
24Jly93 2Hol1	Devoted Brass	b	3 126	5	41	41½	31½	1hd	2hd	56½	Pincay L Jr	9.40
13Aug93 6Sar2	Wallenda		3 126	9	5½	61	6hd	8hd	74	6nk	McCauley W H	a-7.70
1Aug93 11Mth4	Cherokee Run		3 126	1	31	31	4hd	71½	61	75	Day P	a-7.70
1Aug93 8Sar5	Wild Gale		3 126	4	11	11	11	11	8½	84¾	Davis R G	20.30
3Jly93 8Bel3	Silver of Silver		3 126	6	101½	102½	104	101	103	9nk	Vasquez J	22.50
31Jly93 6Bir1	Foxtrail		3 126	11	2½	1½	21	5½	91½	102½	Smith M E	15.70
15May93 10Pim3	El Bakan		3 126	3	1½	22	1hd	6hd	11	11	Perret C	35.30

a-Coupled: Wallenda and Cherokee Run.

OFF AT 5:10 Start good. Won driving. Time, :23 , :47 , 1:11^3, 1:37 , 2:01^4 Track fast.

$2 Mutuel Prices:

7-(G)-SEA HERO	15.40	6.80	5.20
2-(B)-KISSIN KRIS		4.20	3.20
8-(H)-MINER'S MARK			4.00

$2 EXACTA 7-2 PAID $83.80 $2 TRIPLE 7-2-8 PAID $437.00

B. c, (Mar), by Polish Navy—Glowing Tribute, by Graustark. Trainer Miller MacKenzie. Bred by Mellon Paul (Va).

SEA HERO broke sharply then was eased back in the early stages, was unhurried while racing three wide along the backstretch, launched a rally between horses on the far turn, swung four wide while steadily gaining approaching the quarter pole, brushed with MINER'S MARK in upper stretch, accelerated to the front nearing the furlong marker then drew clear under strong handling. KISSIN KRIS outrun for six furlongs, while slightly off the rail, continued well back while angling out on the turn, circled six wide into the stretch, then finished strongly in the middle of the track to gain the place. MINER'S MARK broke bit slowly, moved up between horses entering the first turn, was reserved along the backstretch while between horses, waited briefly for room while blocked behind the leaders midway on the turn, angled out to brush with the winner leaving the quarter pole, then finished willingly to gain a share. COLONIAL AFFAIR settled in midpack while four wide through the early stages, made steady progress while continuing wide on the far turn, made a run from outside to gain a brief lead at the five-sixteenths pole, battled heads apart outside DEVOTED BRASS into midstretch then weakened in the final eighth. DEVOTED BRASS rated in good position for six furlongs, rallied between horses to challenge on the turn, surged to the front approaching the quarter pole, remained a factor into midstretch, then gradually tired thereafter. WALLENDA raced within striking distance while saving ground to the far turn, angled out midway on the turn, then lacked the needed response when called upon. CHEROKEE RUN raced in close contention along the inside for seven furlongs, split horses on the turn then lacked a strong closing response. WILD GALE never reached contention. SILVER OF SILVER was never a factor. EL BAKAN and FOXTRAIL alternated for the lead for seven furlongs and tired from their early efforts.

Owners— 1, Rokeby Stable; 2, Franks John; 3, Phipps Ogden; 4, Centennial Farms; 5, Jordens Don W; 6, Dogwood Stable; 7, Robinson Jill E; 8, Little Fish Stable; 9, Chevalier Stable; 10, Bennett Linda A; 11, Perez Robert.

Trainers— 1, Miller MacKenzie; 2, Bell David R; 3, McGaughey Claude III; 4, Schulhofer Flint S; 5, Threewitt Noble; 6, Alexander Frank A; 7, Alexander Frank A; 8, Doyle Michael J; 9, Shapoff Stanley R; 10, Robideaux Larry R Jr; 11, Callejas Alfredo.

SEVENTH RACE
Saratoga
AUGUST 20, 1994

1¼ MILES. (2) 125th Running of THE TRAVERS. Purse $750,000. Grade I. 3-year-olds. By subscription of $750 each which should accompany the nomination; $3,500 to pass the entry box, $4,000 to start. The purse to be divided 60% to the winner, 22% to second, 12% to third and 6% to fourth. Weight, 126 lbs. Starters to be named at the closing time of entries. The winner shall have its name inscribed on the Man o'War Cup and a gold plated replica will be presented to the winning owner. Trophies will also be presented to the winning trainer and jockey. Closed Wednesday, August 3, with 16 nominations.

Value of Race: $750,000 Winner $450,000; second $165,000; third $90,000; fourth $45,000. Mutuel Pool $1,684,935.00

Last Raced	Horse	M/Eqt.	A.Wt	PP	¼	½	¾	1	Str	Fin	Jockey	Odds $1
31Jly94 10Mth1	Holy Bull		3 126	1	21½	25	13½	14	11½	1nk	Smith M E	0.80
31Jly94 10Mth3	Concern	b	3 126	3	5	5	5	2½	28	217	Bailey J D	5.50
31Jly94 8Sar2	Tabasco Cat	b	3 126	2	33	31½	412	416	3½	31	Day P	a-1.60
31Jly94 8Sar1	Unaccounted For		3 126	4	412	416	3½	31	4	4	Santos J A	6.00
28Jly94 9Sar5	Commanche Trail		3 126	5	1hd	1hd	2hd	5	—	—	Velazquez J R	a-1.60

Commanche Trail: Eased

a-Coupled: Tabasco Cat and Commanche Trail.

OFF AT 5:04 Start Good. Won driving. Time, :22^4, :46^1, 1:10^2, 1:35^4, 2:02 Track wet fast.

$2 Mutuel Prices:

2-(A)-HOLY BULL	3.60	3.00	—
3-(C)-CONCERN		3.40	—
1-(B)-TABASCO CAT (a-entry)		—	—

No Show or Exacta Wagering

Gr. c, (Jan), by Great Above–Sharon Brown, by Al Hattab. Trainer Croll Warren A Jr. Bred by Pelican Stable (Fla).

HOLY BULL away alertly, relinquished the lead to COMMANCHE TRAIL after going a sixteenth of a mile, was rated just to the inside of that one into the backstretch, shook off COMMANCHE TRAIL opening a clear advantage at the five-eighths pole, maintained a comfortable lead to the top of the stretch, dug in when challenged by CONCERN in midstretch, turned back that one under strong left hand encouragement. CONCERN lost contact with the field in the early stages, raced far back for six furlongs while saving ground, rapidly closed the gap between horses on the turn, drifted in under right hand urging while making a run to challenge inside the furlong marker but couldn't get by the winner while drifting out in the late stages. TABASCO CAT settled in good position while saving ground along the backstretch, dropped back on the turn then lacked the needed response while under steady right hand pressure through the stretch. UNACCOUNTED FOR reserved for five furlongs, closed the gap a bit while moving alongside TABASCO CAT on the far turn then tired in the drive. COMMANCHE TRAIL was sent after HOLY BULL soon after the start, held a narrow lead while just outside the winner for a half mile, dropped back considerably while tiring on the far turn and was eased in the stretch.

Owners— 1, Croll Warren A Jr; 2, Meyerhoff Robert E; 3, Reynolds David P & Young William T; 4, Morven Stud; 5, Young William T

Trainers— 1, Croll Warren A Jr; 2, Small Richard W; 3, Lukas D Wayne; 4, Schulhofer Flint S; 5, Lukas D Wayne

Scratched— Copper Mount (4Aug94 9SAR1)

$2 Pick-3 (7-2-2) Paid $121.00; Pick-3 Pool $381,740.

EIGHTH RACE
Saratoga
AUGUST 19, 1995

1¼ MILES. (2:00) 126th Running of THE TRAVERS. Purse $750,000. Grade I. 3-year-olds. By subscription of $750 each, which should accompany the nomination, $3,500 to pass the entry box, $4,000 to start. The purse to be divided 60% to the winner, 20% to second, 11% to third, 6% to fourth and 3% to fifth. Weight, 126 lbs. Starters to be named at the closing time of entries. The winner shall have its name inscribed on the Man O'War Cup and a gold plated replica will be presented to the winning owner. Trophies will be presented to the winning trainer and jockey. Closed Saturday, August 5, with 16 nominations.

Value of Race: $750,000 Winner $450,000; second $150,000; third $82,500; fourth $45,000; fifth $22,500. Mutuel Pool $1,866,034.00 Exacta Pool $1,486,748.00 Triple Pool $1,122,281.00

Last Raced	Horse	M/Eqt.	A.Wt	PP	¼	½	¾	1	Str	Fin	Jockey	Odds $1
23Jly95 8Hol1	Thunder Gulch	b	3 126	5	41	43½	42	1hd	1½	14½	Stevens G L	0.75
30Jly95 11Mth2	Pyramid Peak		3 126	2	1hd	2½	1½	21½	22	22	McCauley W H	4.10
30Jly95 8Sar2	Malthus		3 126	3	7	7	7	51½	3½	32½	Chavez J F	25.00
30Jly95 8Sar1	Composer		3 126	1	5½	51½	56	32½	44	415	Bailey J D	4.10
30Jly95 8Sar5	Star Standard		3 126	6	2½	1hd	31	4½	51½	52	Day P	8.50
30Jly95 11Mth3	Citadeed		3 126	7	31½	31½	2½	6½	6hd	66	Maple E	13.60
5Aug95 6Sar1	Rank And File		3 126	4	62	63	61½	7	7	7	Luzzi M J	56.00

OFF AT 4:41 Start Good. Won driving. Time, :23^2, :47^1, 1:11^2, 1:37^1, 2:03^3 Track fast.

$2 Mutuel Prices:

5-THUNDER GULCH	3.50	2.70	2.10
2-PYRAMID PEAK		3.60	2.80
3-MALTHUS			3.30

$2 EXACTA 5-2 PAID $11.20 $2 TRIPLE 5-2-3 PAID $101.50

Ch. c, (May), by Gulch–Line of Thunder, by Storm Bird. Trainer Lukas D Wayne. Bred by Brant Peter M (Ky).

THUNDER GULCH broke in the air at the start, recovering quickly moved up from outside to settle just off the pace on the first turn, was kept just behind the leaders while seven wide along the backstretch, angled in a bit while launching his bid on the far turn, drew alongside PYRAMID PEAK to challenge on the turn, surged to the front at the quarter pole, battled heads apart from outside into midstretch, shook off PYRAMID PEAK under brisk left hand urging inside the furlong marker, switched to the right hand whip while drifting out briefly in deep stretch, then drew off with authority. PYRAMID PEAK rushed up along the rail to contest the early pace, drifted out carrying out STAR STANDARD on the first turn and into the backstretch, alternated for the lead inside STAR STANDARD while racing in the four path down the backstretch, fought gamely into midstretch but couldn't match strides with the winner in the final eighth. MALTHUS raced far back while trailing for seven furlongs, closed the gap a bit while saving ground on the turn, made a run along the inside to threaten in midstretch but was no match for the top two. COMPOSER unhurried for six furlongs while saving ground, split horses while gaining on the turn, angled to the outside of THUNDER GULCH at the top of the stretch, then lacked a strong closing response. STAR STANDARD was carried out by PYRAMID PEAK while battling heads apart on the first turn, alternated for the lead while five wide on the backstretch, checked slightly and angled to the inside on the far turn, then gradually tired thereafter. CITADEED stalked the early pace while six wide, made a brief run to challenge on the far turn, then gave way abruptly. RANK AND FILE never reached contention. STAR STANDARD wore mud caulks.

Owners— 1, Tabor Michael; 2, Oxley John C; 3, Perez Robert; 4, Dekwiatkowski Henryk; 5, Condren W J & Cornacchia J M; 6, Allan Ivan; 7, Am W D Stable & Caputo John

Trainers— 1, Lukas D Wayne; 2, Ward John T Jr; 3, Callejas Alfredo; 4, Mott William I; 5, Zito Nicholas P; 6, Violette Richard A Jr; 7, Schettino Dominick A

SEVENTH RACE
Saratoga
AUGUST 24, 1996

1¼ MILES. (2.00) 127th Running of THE TRAVERS. Purse $750,000 (plus up to $39,000 NYSBFOA). Grade I. 3-year-olds. By subscription of $750 each, which should accompany the nomination. $3,750 to enter and $3,750 additional to start. $450,000 to the owner of the winner, $150,000 to second, $82,500 to third, $45,000 to fourth and $22,500 to fifth. Weight, 126 lbs. In the event The Travers overfills, preference will be given by condition eligibility, beginning with grade I stakes winners, grade II stakes winners, grade III stakes winners, listed stakes winners, stakes winners, restricted stakes winners and highest allowance conditions. Starters to be named at the closing time of entries. Trophies will be presented to the winning owner, trainer and jockey. Closed Saturday, August 10 with 9 nominations.

Value of Race: $750,000 Winner $450,000; second $150,000; third $82,500; fourth $45,000; fifth $22,500. Mutuel Pool $1,675,525.00 Exacta Pool $1,327,422.00 Trifecta Pool $817,018.00

Last Raced	Horse	M/Eqt.	A.	Wt	PP	¼	½	¾	1	Str	Fin	Jockey	Odds $1
4Aug96 ^{8}Sar^{2}	Will's Way		3	126	4	$5^{3\frac{1}{2}}$	5^{4}	3^{1}	2^{1}	1^{hd}	$1^{\frac{3}{4}}$	Chavez J F	7.30
4Aug96 ^{8}Sar^{1}	Louis Quatorze	L	3	126	1	1^{hd}	1½	1^{hd}	1^{hd}	$2^{1\frac{1}{2}}$	2^{1}	Day P	2.85
4Aug96 ^{10}Mth^{1}	Skip Away	Lb	3	126	3	$4^{1\frac{1}{2}}$	3^{hd}	$4^{1\frac{1}{2}}$	3½	3^{2}	$3^{3\frac{1}{2}}$	Santos J A	1.45
4Aug96 ^{8}Sar^{4}	Editor's Note	L	3	126	2	6^{1}	6^{1}	7	5^{6}	5^{24}	4no	Smith M E	3.30
4Aug96 ^{8}Sar^{3}	Secreto de Estado		3	126	6	7	7	6½	$4^{1\frac{1}{2}}$	4^{hd}	5	Migliore R	a-31.00
4Aug96 ^{8}Sar^{7}	Prince Heaven	L	3	126	5	$2^{1\frac{1}{2}}$	$2^{1\frac{1}{2}}$	2^{1}	6^{16}	6	—	Velasquez Cornelio	a-31.00
4Aug96 ^{10}Mth^{2}	Dr. Caton	L	3	126	7	3^{hd}	4^{1}	5½	7	—	—	Bailey J D	6.30

Prince Heaven:Eased; Dr. Caton:Eased

a-Coupled: Secreto de Estado and Prince Heaven.

OFF AT 3:37 Start Good. Won driving. Time, :23, :46^{1}, 1:10^{3}, 1:36^{1}, 2:02^{2} Track fast.

$2 Mutuel Prices:

5-WILL'S WAY	16.60	6.70	3.30
2-LOUIS QUATORZE		4.70	2.80
4-SKIP AWAY			2.40

$2 EXACTA 5-2 PAID $53.00 $2 TRIFECTA 5-2-4 PAID $130.00

B. c, (Apr), by Easy Goer-Willamae, by Tentam. Trainer Bond Harold James. Bred by Quinichett Robert (Ky).

WILL'S WAY unhurried early, was rated in the middle of the pack while three wide along the backstretch, launched a rally from outside on the far turn, rapidly closed the gap to challenge approaching the quarter pole, battled heads apart outside LOUIS QUATORZE into midstretch then edged away from that one under strong right hand encouragement. LOUIS QUATORZE took the lead along the inside on the first turn, dueled heads apart inside PRINCE HEAVEN to the far turn, shook loose midway on the turn, dug in when challenged at the top of the stretch, fought gamely into midstretch but couldn't match strides with the winner through the final eighth. SKIP AWAY settled just off the pace while saving ground, was caught in tight quarters along the rail approaching the three-quarters pole, moved off the rail a bit nearing the far turn, angled out for room on the turn, circled four wide while moving into contention at the top of the stretch but couldn't gain on the top two through the lane. EDITOR'S NOTE broke a bit sluggishly, raced well back for five furlongs, trailed leaving the backstretch, circled five wide while gaining considerably to reach contention approaching the stretch, but couldn't sustain his bid. SECRETO DE ESTADO outrun for six furlongs while saving ground, rallied along the rail to threaten briefly nearing the quarter pole, flattened out. PRINCE HEAVEN rushed up from outside to contest the early pace, dueled heads apart to the far turn then gave way and was eased in the stretch. DR. CATON raced just behind the dueling leaders for five furlongs then stopped abruptly on the far turn and was eased in the stretch.

Owners— 1, Clifton William Jr & Rudlein Stable; 2, Condren & Cornacchia & Hofmann; 3, Hine Carolyn H; 4, Overbrook Farm; 5, Perez Robert; 6, Perez Robert; 7, Lewis Beverly J & Robert B

Trainers—1, Bond Harold James; 2, Zito Nicholas P; 3, Hine Hubert; 4, Lukas D Wayne; 5, Callejas Alfredo; 6, Callejas Alfredo; 7, Lukas D Wayne

NINTH RACE
Saratoga
AUGUST 23, 1997

1¼ MILES. (2.00) 128th Running of THE TRAVERS. Purse $750,000 (plus up to $39,000 NYSBFOA). Grade I. 3-year-olds. By subscription of $750 each, which should accompany the nomination. $3,750 to enter and $3,750 additional to start. $450,000 to the owner of the winner, $150,000 to second, $82,500 to third, $45,000 to fourth and $22,500 to fifth. Weight, 126 lbs. In the event the Travers overfills, preference will be given by condition eligibility, beginning with Grade I stakes winners, Grade II stakes winners, Grade III stakes winners, listed stakes winners, stakes winners, restricted stakes winners and highest earnings. Starters to be named at the closing time of entries. Trophies will be presented to the winning owner, trainer and jockey. Closed Saturday, August 9 with 19 nominations.

Value of Race: $750,000 Winner $450,000; second $150,000; third $82,500; fourth $45,000; fifth $22,500. Mutuel Pool $2,248,471.00 Exacta Pool $1,543,316.00 Trifecta Pool $1,234,621.00

Last Raced	Horse	M/Eqt.	A.	Wt	PP	¼	½	¾	1	Str	Fin	Jockey	Odds $1
20Jly97 ^{4}Hol^{2}	Deputy Commander	L	3	126	4	$3^{1\frac{1}{2}}$	3^{2}	$3^{1\frac{1}{2}}$	1½	1½	1no	McCarron C J	4.00
3Aug97 ^{8}Sar^{4}	Behrens	Lf	3	126	2	$6^{2\frac{1}{2}}$	4^{hd}	4^{hd}	3^{hd}	2^{1}	2^{7}	Bailey J D	2.45
3Aug97 ^{8}Sar^{1}	Awesome Again	L	3	126	6	5^{hd}	5½	5^{1}	$4^{3\frac{1}{2}}$	3^{3}	3^{2}	Smith M E	1.45
10Aug97 ^{7}RP^{2}	Blazing Sword	Lf	3	126	1	4½	$6^{4\frac{1}{2}}$	6^{4}	5½	4½	4^{5}	Boulanger G	10.60
27Jly97 ^{9}FE^{1}	Cryptocloser	L	3	126	7	$7^{1\frac{1}{2}}$	$7^{3\frac{1}{2}}$	7^{8}	6½	5^{2}	5^{3}	Antley C W	8.40
3Aug97 ^{8}Mth^{6}	Twin Spires	b	3	126	3	1½	2½	2½	7^{8}	$7^{2\frac{1}{2}}$	6^{nk}	Bravo J	68.50
3Aug97 ^{8}Sar^{3}	Affirmed Success	L	3	126	5	2^{2}	1^{hd}	1^{hd}	2½	6^{3}	7^{3}	Chavez J F	14.00
12Aug97 ^{7}Del^{7}	Affairwithpeaches	Lb	3	126	8	8	8	8	8	8	8	Migliore R	71.50

OFF AT 5:12 Start Good. Won driving. Time, :23^{1}, :47^{1}, 1:11^{1}, 1:36^{4}, 2:04 Track wet fast.

$2 Mutuel Prices:

4-DEPUTY COMMANDER	10.00	4.90	3.20
2-BEHRENS		4.30	2.90
6-AWESOME AGAIN			2.50

$2 EXACTA 4-2 PAID $36.20 $2 TRIFECTA 4-2-6 PAID $75.50

Dk. b. or br. c, (Apr), by Deputy Minister-Anka Germania*Ire, by Malinowski. Trainer Dollase Wallace. Bred by Crystal Springs Farm & Moore Robert & Allred E C (Ky).

DEPUTY COMMANDER settled just behind the early leaders leaving the first turn, moved up from outside along the backstretch, edged a bit closer on the far turn, accelerated to the front approaching the quarter pole, opened a clear advantage in upper stretch, dug in when challenged in midstretch, battled heads apart under strong left hand urging into deep stretch and prevailed in a hard drive. BEHRENS was eased back a bit in the early stages, improved his position while between horses midway down the backstretch, steadily closed the gap while just inside AWESOME AGAIN on the final turn, made a run to challenge leaving the furlong marker, fought gamely into deep stretch and just missed in a tight finish. AWESOME AGAIN was carried a bit wide on the first turn, raced heads apart outside BEHRENS to the final turn, lodged a brief bid while four wide entering the stretch but couldn't sustain his rally. BLAZING SWORD, away alertly, was unhurried for six furlongs while saving ground, moved up a bit from outside on the turn but lacked a strong closing response. CRYPTOCLOSER raced far back for seven furlongs, circled five wide on the turn then flattened out in the stretch. TWIN SPIRES was hustled up to gain the early advantage, dueled along the inside for six furlongs, fell back midway on the turn and steadily tired thereafter. AFFIRMED SUCCESS moved up between horses to contest the early pace, set the pace under pressure along the backstretch, relinquished the lead to the winner at the quarter pole then tired in the drive. AFFAIRWITHPEACHES never reached contention.

Owners— 1, Horizon St & Jarvis & Mandysland Fm; 2, Clifton William Jr & Rudlein Stable; 3, Stronach Frank H; 4, Campbell Gilbert G; 5, Mack Earle I & Sorokolit William Jr; 6, Lewis Beverly J & Robert B; 7, Fried Albert A Jr; 8, Kleemann Sandi L

Trainers—1, Dollase Wallace; 2, Bond Harold James; 3, Hofmans David; 4, O'Connell Kathleen; 5, Frostad Mark; 6, Lukas D Wayne; 7, Schosberg Richard; 8, Marino Phil

NINTH RACE
Saratoga
AUGUST 29, 1998

1¼ MILES. (2.00) 129th Running of THE TRAVERS. Grade I. Purse $750,000 (plus up to $65,500 NYSBFOA.) 3-year-olds. By subscription of $750 each, which should accompany the nomination, $3,500 to enter and $4,000 to start. The purse to be divided 60% to the owner of the winner, 20% to second, 11% to third, 6% to fourth and 3% to fifth. Weight, 126 lbs. Starters to be named at the closing time of entries. In the event the Travers overfills, preference will be given by condition eligibility beginning with graded stakes winners, then stakes winners. Ties broken by gross lifetime earnings. Trophies will be presented to the winning owner, trainer and jockey. Closed Saturday, August 15.

Value of Race: $750,000 Winner $450,000; second $150,000; third $82,500; fourth $45,000; fifth $22,500. Mutuel Pool $2,107,466.0 Exacta Pool $1,530,734.0 Trifecta Pool $1,147,323.0

Last Raced	Horse	M/Eqt.	A.	Wt	PP	¼	½	¾	1	Str	Fin	Jockey	Odds $1
9Aug98 ^{11}Mth^{1}	Coronado's Quest	L	3	126	3	2^{hd}	3^{1}	3^{1}	$1^{1\frac{1}{2}}$	$1^{1\frac{1}{2}}$	1no	Smith M E	1.45
9Aug98 ^{11}Mth^{2}	Victory Gallop	L	3	126	7	5½	5^{2}	5^{5}	3^{2}	3^{2}	2no	Solis A	1.20
9Aug98 ^{8}Sar^{3}	Raffie's Majesty	L	3	126	6	7	7	7	4½	4^{2}	3^{5}	Chavez J F	11.50
9Aug98 ^{8}Sar^{6}	Archers Bay		3	126	4	$6^{3\frac{1}{2}}$	6^{3}	6^{hd}	6½	5^{1}	4^{nk}	Day P	17.50
9Aug98 ^{11}Mth^{3}	Grand Slam	L	3	126	1	3^{1}	2½	2½	2½	2^{hd}	$5^{2\frac{1}{4}}$	Bailey J D	11.60
9Aug98 ^{8}Sar^{2}	Deputy Diamond		3	126	5	4^{hd}	4½	4^{1}	5^{1}	6^{10}	6^{27}	Santos J A	10.50
1Aug98 ^{4}Sar^{1}	Dice Dancer	L	3	126	2	1½	1½	1^{hd}	7	7	7	Samyn J L	33.00

OFF AT 5:12 Start Good. Won driving. Time, :24^{3}, :48^{4}, 1:13, 1:37^{2}, 2:03^{2} Track fast.

$2 Mutuel Prices:

4-CORONADO'S QUEST	4.90	3.00	2.70
1-VICTORY GALLOP		2.60	2.20
7-RAFFIE'S MAJESTY			3.10

$2 EXACTA 4-1 PAID $8.80 $2 TRIFECTA 4-1-7 PAID $44.00

Ch. c, (Feb), by Forty Niner-Laughing Look, by Damascus. Trainer McGaughey Claude III. Bred by Janney Stuart S III (Ky).

CORONADO'S QUEST, away in good order and with the pace while three wide into the first turn, attended the pace from the outside, moved three wide to take control leaving the backstretch, settled into the stretch with a clear lead, dug in gamely when put to the test in deep stretch and held on in a rousing finish. VICTORY GALLOP broke to the inside, bumping RAFFIE'S MAJESTY then settled into stride in close attendance from the outside, advanced outside on the second turn and finished fast, just missing. RAFFIE'S MAJESTY, bumped at the start and unhurried while outrun early, rallied four wide on the second turn and finished with a rush from the far outside. ARCHERS BAY, bumped after the start and rated along inside, saved ground into the stretch and finished with good interest, GRAND SLAM prompted the pace from between rivals and tired in the stretch. DEPUTY DIAMOND, bumped and pinched back at the start, raced along the inside just behind the leaders, was steadied slightly on the second turn and lacked a solid closing kick. DICE DANCER showed in front after the start, made the pace for three quarters then tired badly in the stretch run.

Owners— 1, Janney III Stuart S; 2, Prestonwood Farm Inc; 3, Prieger Henry H; 4, Melnyk Eugene N; 5, Baker Robert C; 6, Centennial Farms; 7, Hobeau Farm

Trainers—1, McGaughey Claude III; 2, Walden W Elliott; 3, Bond Harold James; 4, Pletcher Todd A; 5, Lukas D Wayne; 6, Schulhofer Flint S; 7, Jerkens H Allen

Scratched— Sheila's Flag (18Jly98 ^{9}PHA^{5})

NINTH RACE
Saratoga
AUGUST 28, 1999

1¼ MILES. (2.00) TRAVERS S. Grade I. Purse $1,000,000 (Up To $72,000 NYSBFOA) FOR THREE-YEAR-OLDS. By subscription of $1,000 each, which should accompany the nomination; $5,000 to pass the entry box and $5,000 to start. The purse to be divided 60% to the winner, 20% to second, 11% to third, 6% to fourth and 3% to fifth. 126 lbs.

Value of Race: $1,000,000 Winner $600,000; second $200,000; third $110,000; fourth $60,000; fifth $30,000. Mutuel Pool $2,791,218.00 Exacta Pool $1,848,067.00 Trifecta Pool $1,449,591.00

Last Raced	Horse	M/Eqt.	A.	Wt	PP	¼	½	¾	1	Str	Fin	Jockey	Odds $1
8Aug99 ^{8}Sar^{2}	Lemon Drop Kid	L	3	126	6	5½	3^{hd}	3^{hd}	2½	1^{hd}	1¾	Santos J A	3.65
8Aug99 ^{8}Sar^{6}	Vision and Verse	L b	3	126	8	2½	2^{1}	2½	1^{hd}	2^{2}	$2^{1\frac{3}{4}}$	Sellers S J	14.90
8Aug99 ^{11}Mth^{1}	Menifee	L	3	126	1	6^{hd}	$7^{5\frac{1}{2}}$	$7^{3\frac{1}{2}}$	$6^{2\frac{1}{2}}$	3^{1}	$3^{1\frac{3}{4}}$	Day P	1.60
8Aug99 ^{8}Sar^{1}	Ecton Park	L b	3	126	5	4^{hd}	4^{hd}	5^{1}	4^{hd}	4^{2}	$4^{6\frac{3}{4}}$	Solis A	7.50
8Aug99 ^{8}Sar^{4}	Best of Luck	bf	3	126	2	8	8	8	8	6½	5¾	Samyn J L	19.80
8Aug99 ^{8}Sar^{3}	Badger Gold	L	3	126	3	3^{hd}	5^{1}	4^{hd}	$7^{2\frac{1}{2}}$	$7^{1\frac{1}{2}}$	6½	Velazquez J R	54.00
8Aug99 ^{11}Mth^{2}	Cat Thief	L b	3	126	4	1½	1^{hd}	1^{hd}	3^{hd}	$5^{2\frac{1}{2}}$	$7^{1\frac{3}{4}}$	Smith M E	4.60
8Aug99 ^{11}Mth^{4}	Unbridled Jet	L	3	126	7	7^{6}	6^{hd}	6^{hd}	5½	8	8	Bailey J D	5.30

OFF AT 5:13 Start Good For All But. Won . Track fast.

TIME :24, :48^{1}, 1:12^{2}, 1:36^{4}, 2:02 (:24.08, :48.38, 1:12.50, 1:36.97, 2:02.19)

$2 Mutuel Prices:

6 – LEMON DROP KID	9.30	5.80	3.20
8 – VISION AND VERSE		11.80	4.90
1 – MENIFEE			2.50

$2 EXACTA 6-8 PAID $96.00 $2 TRIFECTA 6-8-1 PAID $289.00

B. c, (May), by Kingmambo – Charming Lassie , by Seattle Slew . Trainer Schulhofer Flint S. Bred by W S Farish & W S Kilroy (Ky).

LEMON DROP KID, away well and close up three wide while well in hand, raced just outside of the front runners on the backstretch, advanced three wide on the second turn, dug in resolutely when set down turning for home and bested VISION AND VERSE after a long struggle. VISION AND VERSE moved up quickly to prompt the pace, gained a short lead approaching the stretch and fought it out gamely along the inside through the stretch. MENIFEE, taken in hand after the start and checked while a bit rank along the inside early on, raced behind horses along the backstretch and into the turn, advanced inside on the second turn, came wide in upper stretch and finished gamely from the outside. ECTON PARK, rated along between rivals, rallied four wide approaching the stretch and stayed on well outside. BEST OF LUCK, outrun early, was hustled along on the backstretch, picked it up a bit on the second turn, came wide into the stretch but could not gain in the drive. BADGER GOLD, rated along inside, saved ground on both turns but had no response when roused. CAT THIEF quickly showed in front, set the pace along the inside and tired in the stretch. UNBRIDLED JET raced wide, drifted into the stretch and tired.

Owners– 1, Vance Jeanne G; 2, Lunsford Bruce; 3, Stone James H and Hancock III Arthur B; 4, Stanley Mark H; 5, Bohemia Stable; 6, Flying Zee Stable; 7, Overbrook Farm; 8, Double H Stable

Trainers– 1, Schulhofer Flint S; 2, Mott William I; 3, Walden W Elliott; 4, Walden W Elliott; 5, Jerkens H Allen; 6, Serpe Philip M; 7, Lukas D Wayne; 8, Mott William I

$2 Pick Three (10-5-6) Paid $216.00 ; Pick Three Pool $313,943 .

NINTH RACE
Saratoga
AUGUST 26, 2000

1¼ MILES. (2.00) TRAVERS S. Grade I. Purse $1,000,000 (Up To $72,000 NYSBFOA) For three year olds. By subscription of $1,000 each, which should accompany the nomination; $5,000 to pass the entry box and $5,000 to start. The purse to be divided 60% to the winner, 20% to second, 11% to third, 6% to fourth and 3% to fifth. 126 lbs. Trophies will be presented to the winning owner, trainer and jockey. Closed Saturday August 12, with 18 Nominations.

Value of Race: $1,000,000 Winner $600,000; second $200,000; third $110,000; fourth $60,000; fifth $30,000. Mutuel Pool $2,475,063.00 Exacta Pool $1,607,822.00 Trifecta Pool $1,256,265.00 Superfecta Pool $242,597.00

Last Raced	Horse	M/Eqt.	A.	Wt	PP	¼	½	¾	1	Str	Fin	Jockey	Odds $1
5Aug00 ^{8}Sar^{3}	Unshaded	L f	3	126	6	$6\frac{1}{2}$	6^{5}	6^{6}	2^{1}	$2^{2\frac{1}{2}}$	1^{hd}	Sellers S J	3.45
5Aug00 ^{8}Sar^{7}	Albert the Great	L	3	126	9	$2\frac{1}{2}$	$2\frac{1}{2}$	1^{hd}	1^{hd}	$1\frac{1}{2}$	$2^{6\frac{1}{2}}$	Chavez J F	7.90
6Aug00 ^{11}Mth^{8}	Commendable	L b	3	126	3	$1\frac{1}{2}$	$1\frac{1}{2}$	$3\frac{1}{2}$	3^{hd}	3^{hd}	$3^{2\frac{3}{4}}$	Day P	9.20
6Aug00 ^{11}Mth^{1}	Dixie Union	L	3	126	7	3^{2}	$3^{1\frac{1}{2}}$	2^{hd}	$4^{1\frac{1}{2}}$	$4^{3\frac{1}{2}}$	4^{nk}	Solis A	2.55
6Aug00 ^{11}Mth^{6}	Impeachment	L	3	126	8	9	9	9	9	7^{hd}	5^{hd}	Migliore R	17.60
5Aug00 ^{8}Sar^{4}	Postponed	L	3	126	5	7^{2}	7^{2}	$7^{2\frac{1}{2}}$	$7^{2\frac{1}{2}}$	5^{2}	$6^{1\frac{1}{2}}$	Prado E S	20.70
6Aug00 ^{11}Mth^{3}	Milwaukee Brew	L	3	126	4	$4^{1\frac{1}{2}}$	4^{hd}	$5^{1\frac{1}{2}}$	$6^{1\frac{1}{2}}$	$6\frac{1}{2}$	$7\frac{3}{4}$	Bailey J D	4.00
27Jly00 ^{3}Sar^{2}	Country Coast	L b	3	126	1	$8^{1\frac{1}{2}}$	$8^{3\frac{1}{2}}$	$8^{4\frac{1}{2}}$	8^{2}	9	$8^{1\frac{1}{2}}$	St Julien M	69.50
5Aug00 ^{8}Sar^{2}	Curule	L	3	126	2	$5^{1\frac{1}{2}}$	$5^{2\frac{1}{2}}$	4^{1}	5^{2}	$8\frac{1}{2}$	9	Smith M E	5.50

OFF AT 5:15 Start Good. Won driving. Track fast.

TIME :24^{1}, :48^{2}, 1:12^{3}, 1:37^{3}, 2:02^{2} (:24.20, :48.43, 1:12.74, 1:37.66, 2:02.59)

$2 Mutuel Prices:			
6 – UNSHADED	8.90	5.30	3.60
9 – ALBERT THE GREAT		8.90	5.60
3 – COMMENDABLE			5.30

$2 EXACTA 6–9 PAID $103.00 $2 TRIFECTA 6–9–3 PAID $698.00
$2 SUPERFECTA 6–9–3–7 PAID $4,043.00

B. g, (Apr), by Unbridled – Shade the Flame, by Caucasus. Trainer Nafzger Carl A. Bred by Shawnna Sorenson (Ky).

UNSHADED was pinched back slightly at the start, raced well back while unhurried for five furlongs, rapidly gained leaving the far turn, split horses to reach contention nearing the quarter pole, moved outside the leader to threaten at the top of the stretch then, gained gradually under left hand urging through the lane and wore down ALBERT THE GREAT in the final seventy yards. ALBERT THE GREAT was carried five wide going into the first turn, forced the pace from outside along the backstretch, surged to the front gaining a slim lead on the far turn, dug in when challenged at the top of the stretch, fought gamely along the inside into deep stretch and yielded grudgingly. COMMENDABLE rushed up to gain the early advantage, went four wide going into the first turn, set the pace while racing out from the rail along the backstretch, relinquished the lead nearing the half mile pole, remained a factor into upper stretch then weakened from his early efforts. DIXIE UNION steadied in tight between horses in the early stages, angled to the inside on the first turn, raced just off the pace while saving ground for seven furlongs, made a run to challenge on the far turn, battled along the inside to the top of the stretch and lacked a strong closing bid. IMPEACHMENT trailed to the turn while racing wide, continued wide advancing into the stretch and failed to threaten while improving his position. POSTPONED outrun early, never reached contention. MILWAUKEE BREW was rated just off the pace while five wide for six furlongs, continued wide on the turn then steadily tired thereafter. COUNTRY COAST raced well back early, drifted out in upper stretch then failed to menace while continuing to drift out through the lane. CURULE raced up close while in hand for five furlongs, lodged a mild bid while five wide on the turn then flattened out.

Owners– 1, Jim Tafel LLC; 2, Farmer Tracy; 3, Lewis Robert B and Beverly J; 4, Diamond A Racing Corporation; 5, Dogwood Stable; 6, Vance Jeanne G; 7, Stronach Stables; 8, Oxford Stables; 9, Godolphin Racing LLC

Trainers– 1, Nafzger Carl A; 2, Zito Nicholas P; 3, Lukas D Wayne; 4, Mandella Richard; 5, Pletcher Todd A; 6, Schulhofer Flint S; 7, Attard Tino; 8, Amoss Thomas; 9, bin Suroor Saeed

$2 Pick Three (1–4–3) Paid $49.40 ; Pick Three Pool $309,218 .

TENTH RACE
Saratoga
AUGUST 25, 2001

1¼ MILES. (2.00) TRAVERS S. Grade I. Purse $1,000,000 (Up to $72,000 NYSBFOA)FOR THREE YEAR OLDS. By subscription of $1,000 each, which should accompany the nomination; $5,000 to pass the entry box, $5,000 to start. The purse to be divided 60% to the winner, 20% to second, 11% to third, 6% to fourth and 3% to fifth. 126 lbs. Trophies will be presented to the winning owner, trainer and jockey. Closed Saturday, August 11, 2001 with 19 Nominations.

Value of Race: $1,000,000 Winner $600,000; second $200,000; third $110,000; fourth $60,000; fifth $30,000. Mutuel Pool $2,879,751.00 Exacta Pool $1,981,299.00 Trifecta Pool $1,668,138.00 Superfecta Pool $353,090.00

Last Raced	Horse	M/Eqt.	A.	Wt	PP	¼	½	¾	1	Str	Fin	Jockey	Odds $1
5Aug01 ^{11}Mth^{1}	Point Given	L br	3	126	7	$5\frac{1}{2}$	$3\frac{1}{2}$	3^{1}	2^{2}	1^{hd}	$1^{3\frac{1}{2}}$	Stevens G L	0.65
8Jly01 ^{8}Bel^{1}	E Dubai	L	3	126	6	$2\frac{1}{2}$	2^{1}	$2\frac{1}{2}$	$1\frac{1}{2}$	2^{5}	$2^{1\frac{1}{4}}$	Bailey J D	4.40
9Jun01 ^{10}Bel^{4}	Dollar Bill	L b	3	126	8	$7\frac{1}{2}$	$6\frac{1}{2}$	5^{hd}	5^{3}	3^{hd}	$3\frac{3}{4}$	Chavez J F	10.10
4Aug01 ^{9}Sar^{4}	A P Valentine	L	3	126	1	3^{hd}	$4^{1\frac{1}{2}}$	$4^{2\frac{1}{2}}$	3^{hd}	4^{hd}	$4^{2\frac{1}{4}}$	Velazquez J R	9.30
4Aug01 ^{9}Sar^{2}	Free of Love	L	3	126	3	$1\frac{1}{2}$	$1\frac{1}{2}$	1^{hd}	$4\frac{1}{2}$	5^{7}	$5^{7\frac{1}{4}}$	Day P	33.00
4Aug01 ^{9}Sar^{1}	Scorpion	L	3	126	5	$4\frac{1}{2}$	$5\frac{1}{2}$	$7\frac{1}{2}$	$6\frac{1}{2}$	$6^{3\frac{1}{2}}$	$6^{1\frac{1}{2}}$	Guidry M	12.30
30Jly01 ^{9}Sar^{1}	Volponi	L b	3	126	2	$8\frac{1}{2}$	8^{6}	8^{8}	$7^{3\frac{1}{2}}$	$7\frac{1}{2}$	7^{2}	Migliore R	13.70
11Aug01 ^{5}Sar^{3}	Hadrian's Wall	L	3	126	9	9	9	9	8^{3}	8^{10}	$8^{26\frac{1}{2}}$	Davis R G	102.75
22Jly01 ^{6}Del^{3}	Harrisand-FR	L	3	126	4	$6^{1\frac{1}{2}}$	$7^{2\frac{1}{2}}$	$6^{1\frac{1}{2}}$	9	9	9	Prado E S	53.75

OFF AT 5:46 Start Good. Won driving. Track fast.

TIME :23^{3}, :47^{3}, 1:11^{1}, 1:35^{4}, 2:01^{2} (:23.73, :47.70, 1:11.37, 1:35.82, 2:01.40)

$2 Mutuel Prices:			
7 – POINT GIVEN	3.30	2.80	2.30
6 – E DUBAI		4.10	3.40
8 – DOLLAR BILL			3.60

$2 EXACTA 7–6 PAID $12.20 $2 TRIFECTA 7–6–8 PAID $62.50
$2 SUPERFECTA 7–6–8–1 PAID $119.50

Ch. c, (Mar), by Thunder Gulch – Turko's Turn, by Turkoman. Trainer Baffert Bob. Bred by The Thoroughbred Corporation (Ky).

POINT GIVEN broke a bit slowly but raced close up while three wide, advanced three wide leaving the backstretch, responded when set down for the drive, drew clear from E DUBAI inside the eighth pole and was clear under the wire, driving. E DUBAI raced with the pace from the outside while in hand, took over from pacesetter FREE OF LOVE entering the second turn, responded when joined from the outside by the winner turning for home and dug in gamely but could not stay with that rival in the final furlong. DOLLAR BILL was unhurried outside early on, was put to the whip nearing the second turn, advanced wide approaching the stretch and stayed on stubbornly to the finish. A P VALENTINE raced close up inside, was roused on the backstretch, angled out and came wide approaching the stretch and stayed on well. FREE OF LOVE quickly showed in front, set the pace for three quarters and faded along the inside. SCORPION chased the pace while between rivals, had no response when roused and tired in the stretch. VOLPONI came away a step slowly, was rated along early, raced wide and had no response when roused. HADRIAN'S WALL dropped back early, raced inside and had no response when roused. HARRISAND (FR) was rated inside, had no response when put to the whip on the backstretch and tired.

Owners– 1, The Thoroughbred Corporation; 2, Godolphin Racing LLC; 3, Gary and Mary West Stables Inc; 4, OI Memorial Stable; 5, Aprilante Anthony J and Evans Ralph M; 6, Baker Robert C Cornstein David and Mack William L; 7, Amherst Stable and Spruce Pond Stable; 8, Gilbert Ross S; 9, Gann Edmund A

Trainers– 1, Baffert Bob; 2, bin Suroor Saeed; 3, Stewart Dallas; 4, Zito Nicholas P; 5, Violette Richard A Jr; 6, Lukas D Wayne; 7, Johnson Philip G; 8, Hennig Mark; 9, Frankel Robert

TENTH RACE
Saratoga
AUGUST 24, 2002

1¼ MILES. (2.00) TRAVERS S. Grade I. Purse $1,000,000 (Up to $72,000 NYSBFOA) FOR THREE YEAR OLDS. By subscription of $1,000 each, which should accompany the nomination; $5,000 to pass the entry box, $5,000 to start. The purse to be divided 60% to the winner, 20% to second, 11% to third, 6% to fourth and 3%to fifth. 126 lbs. Trophies will be presented to the winning owner, trainer and jockey. Closed Saturday, August 10, 2002 with 20 Nominations.

Value of Race: $1,000,000 Winner $600,000; second $200,000; third $110,000; fourth $60,000; fifth $30,000. Mutuel Pool $2,193,323.00 Exacta Pool $1,655,801.00 Trifecta Pool $1,359,925.00 Superfecta Pool $369,724.00

Last Raced	Horse	M/Eqt.	A.	Wt	PP	¼	½	¾	1	Str	Fin	Jockey	Odds $1
4Aug02 ^{9}Sar^{1}	Medaglia d'Oro	L	3	126	5	$2\frac{1}{2}$	$2\frac{1}{2}$	$1\frac{1}{2}$	$1^{1\frac{1}{2}}$	1^{1}	$1\frac{1}{2}$	Bailey J D	0.75
6Apr02 ^{8}Spt^{2}	Repent	L b	3	126	4	6^{2}	6^{2}	$6\frac{1}{2}$	$3^{1\frac{1}{2}}$	2^{5}	$2^{7\frac{1}{2}}$	Prado E S	3.85
4Aug02 ^{9}Sar^{6}	Nothing Flat	L	3	126	8	9	9	9	$8\frac{1}{2}$	$6^{2\frac{1}{2}}$	$3\frac{3}{4}$	Santos J A	31.25
4Aug02 ^{11}Mth^{3}	Like a Hero	L	3	126	3	8^{6}	8^{6}	8^{6}	$6\frac{1}{2}$	3^{1}	4^{nk}	Pincay L Jr	8.70
24Jly02 ^{7}Sar^{1}	Puzzlement		3	126	9	$7^{1\frac{1}{2}}$	$7^{2\frac{1}{2}}$	5^{hd}	4^{4}	$5\frac{1}{2}$	$5^{5\frac{1}{2}}$	Samyn J L	7.30
4Aug02 ^{9}Sar^{8}	Quest	L	3	126	2	$4^{2\frac{1}{2}}$	4^{6}	$3^{1\frac{1}{2}}$	$2\frac{1}{2}$	4^{hd}	6^{3}	Castellano J J	26.00
4Aug02 ^{9}Sar^{2}	Gold Dollar	L b	3	126	6	$5^{2\frac{1}{2}}$	$5^{2\frac{1}{2}}$	7^{5}	$5\frac{1}{2}$	7^{15}	$7^{19\frac{3}{4}}$	Chavez J F	27.00
28Jly02 ^{7}Sar^{1}	Saint Marden	L	3	126	7	$3\frac{1}{2}$	3^{2}	4^{3}	7^{1}	8^{8}	$8^{19\frac{1}{2}}$	Smith M E	21.50
27Jly02 ^{6}Sar^{4}	Shah Jehan	L b	3	126	1	$1\frac{1}{2}$	1^{hd}	2^{hd}	9	9	9	Velazquez J R	36.75

OFF AT 5:57 Start Good. Won driving. Track sloppy.

TIME :23, :46^{4}, 1:11^{2}, 1:37, 2:02^{2} (:23.14, :46.82, 1:11.53, 1:37.08, 2:02.53)

$2 Mutuel Prices:			
5 – MEDAGLIA D'ORO	3.50	2.60	2.40
4 – REPENT		3.40	3.10
8 – NOTHING FLAT			6.00

$2 EXACTA 5–4 PAID $12.60 $2 TRIFECTA 5–4–8 PAID $130.00
$2 SUPERFECTA 5–4–8–3 PAID $398.50

Dk. b or br. c, (Apr), by El Prado-Ire – Cappucino Bay, by Bailjumper. Trainer Frankel Robert. Bred by Albert Bell & Joyce Bell (Ky).

MEDAGLIA D'ORO came away running, pressed the pace while between rivals, drew clear approaching the stretch, took a clear lead past the eighth pole, dug in determinedly when joined by REPENT in deep stretch and held off that rival under a steady drive. REPENT was outrun along the inside early, advanced inside on the second turn, came wide into the stretch and finished gamely outside but could not get by the winner. NOTHING FLAT dropped back along the inside early, picked it up when asked on the second turn, rallied four wide, angled to the inside in upper stretch and offered a mild rally while no real threat to the top two. LIKE A HERO was unhurried along the inside early, angled out and rallied four wide approaching the stretch but had little left for the drive. PUZZLEMENT was outrun early while wide, put in a four wide run on the second turn but could not sustain that bid. QUEST was hustled up inside, chased the pace, put in a three wide move leaving the backstretch and tired in the drive. GOLD DOLLAR was hustled along inside and had no response when roused. SAINT MARDEN raced close up while four wide for the opening three quarters and tired. SHAH JEHAN was hustled to the front, set the pace along the inside and tired on the second turn.

Owners– 1, Gann Edmund A; 2, Select Stable; 3, Condren William J and Sherman Michael H; 4, Columbine Stable; 5, Shields Joseph V Jr; 6, Hancock III Arthur B and Healy Gerald F; 7, Overbrook Farm; 8, Schwartz Martin S and Drazin Dennis; 9, Tabor Michael B and Magnier Mrs John

Trainers– 1, Frankel Robert; 2, McPeek Kenneth G; 3, Zito Nicholas P; 4, Greely C Beau; 5, Jerkens H Allen; 6, Zito Nicholas P; 7, Lukas D Wayne; 8, Matz Michael R; 9, Lukas D Wayne

$2 Pick Three (6–9–5) Paid $52.50 ; Pick Three Pool $257,609 .
$2 Pick Four (2–6–9–5) Paid $135.00 ; Pick Four Pool $1,369,444 .

ELEVENTH RACE
Saratoga
AUGUST 23, 2003

1¼ MILES. (2.00) TRAVERS S. Grade I. Purse $1,000,000 (Up to $72,000 NYSBFOA) FOR THREE YEAR OLDS. By subscription of $1,000 each, which should accompany the nomination; $5,000 to pass the entry box, $5,000 to start. 126 lbs. Closed Saturday, August 9th, 2003 with 18 Nominations.

Value of Race: $1,000,000 Winner $600,000; second $200,000; third $110,000; fourth $60,000; fifth $30,000. Mutuel Pool $3,246,367.00 Exacta Pool $1,860,759.00 Trifecta Pool $1,295,476.00

Last Raced	Horse	M/Eqt.	A.	Wt	PP	¼	½	¾	1	Str	Fin	Jockey	Odds $1
13Jly03 ^{6}Hol^{2}	Ten Most Wanted	L b	3	126	4	$5^{4\frac{1}{2}}$	$4^{5\frac{1}{2}}$	4^{8}	1^{hd}	$1\frac{1}{2}$	$1^{4\frac{1}{2}}$	Day P	2.75
3Aug03 ^{11}Mth^{1}	Peace Rules	L	3	126	3	2^{2}	$2^{4\frac{1}{2}}$	$2^{1\frac{1}{2}}$	$2\frac{1}{2}$	$2^{5\frac{1}{2}}$	2^{10}	Bailey J D	2.30
3Aug03 ^{9}Sar^{1}	Strong Hope	L	3	126	2	1^{hd}	1^{hd}	$1\frac{1}{2}$	3^{6}	3^{5}	$3\frac{3}{4}$	Velazquez J R	4.40
3Aug03 ^{11}Mth^{4}	Wild and Wicked	L	3	126	5	6	6	6	6	4^{hd}	$4^{3\frac{1}{4}}$	Sellers S J	16.90
3Aug03 ^{9}Sar^{3}	Congrats	L b	3	126	1	$4\frac{1}{2}$	5^{7}	$5^{5\frac{1}{2}}$	$5^{2\frac{1}{2}}$	$5^{2\frac{1}{2}}$	5^{2}	Luzzi M J	13.20
3Aug03 ^{11}Mth^{2}	Sky Mesa	L	3	126	6	$3\frac{1}{2}$	$3\frac{1}{2}$	3^{hd}	4^{hd}	6	6	Prado E S	2.50

OFF AT 6:28 Start Good. Won driving. Track fast.

TIME :23^{2}, :46^{1}, 1:09^{4}, 1:35^{2}, 2:02 (:23.55, :46.36, 1:09.98, 1:35.46, 2:02.14)

$2 Mutuel Prices:			
4 – TEN MOST WANTED	7.50	3.40	2.80
1 – PEACE RULES		3.80	2.80
3 – STRONG HOPE			3.10

$2 EXACTA 4–1 PAID $27.00 $2 TRIFECTA 4–1–3 PAID $76.00

Dk. b or br. c, (Feb), by Deputy Commander – Wanted Again, by Criminal Type. Trainer Dollase Wallace. Bred by Jim H Plemmons (Ky).

TEN MOST WANTED broke inward brushing with PEACE RULES at the start, bumped with CONGRATS going info the first turn, settled in good position entering the backstretch, raced in hand while tucked in behind the leaders for six furlongs, angled out leaving the three-eighths pole, closed the gap to challenge on the turn, drew on even terms with PEACE RULES in upper stretch, surged to the front approaching the furlong marker then drew off under a vigorous hand ride. PEACE RULES rushed up from outside to contest the early, dueled through brisk fractions along the backstretch, fought heads apart along the rail to the top of the stretch, hung in gamely into midstretch, but couldn't stay with the winner through the final eighth. STRONG HOPE moved up along the rail to gain a slim early advantage, set the pace under pressure along the inside to the turn, dropped back leaving the quarter pole and gradually tired thereafter. WILD AND WICKED trailed to the top of the stretch and failed to threaten while improving his position. CONGRATS steadied after bumping with the winner and hitting the rail on the first turn and failed to seriously threaten thereafter. SKY MESA broke awkwardly, moved quickly into contention while three wide on the first turn, raced just outside the leaders along the backstretch, was put to the whip nearing the far turn, then gave way after going seven furlongs.

Owners– 1, Chisholm James Jarvis Michael Reddam J Paul et al; 2, Gann Edmund A; 3, Melnyk Eugene and Laura; 4, Randal Mr and Mrs R David; 5, Claiborne Farm and Dilschneider Adele B; 6, Oxley John C

Trainers– 1, Dollase Wallace; 2, Frankel Robert; 3, Pletcher Todd A; 4, McPeek Kenneth G; 5, McGaughey III Claude R; 6, Ward John T Jr

Scratched– Empire Maker (03Aug03 ^{9}Sar^{2}) , Funny Cide (03Aug03 ^{11}Mth^{3})

$2 Pick Three (5–2–4) Paid $303.50 ; Pick Three Pool $371,739 .
$2 Pick Four (3–5–2–4) Paid $3,606.00 ; Pick Four Pool $1,488,479 .
$2 Pick Six (6–12–3–5–2–4) 6 Correct Paid $128,675.00 ; Pick Six Pool $541,466 .
$2 Pick Six (6–12–3–5–2–4) 5 Correct Paid $914.00 .

ELEVENTH RACE
Saratoga
AUGUST 28, 2004

1¼ MILES. (2.00) 135TH RUNNING OF THE TRAVERS. Grade I. Purse $1,000,000 (UP TO $70,000 NYSBFOA) FOR THREE YEAR OLDS. By subscription of $1,000 each, which should accompany the nomination; $5,000 to pass the entry box, $5,000 to start. The purse to be divided 60% to the winner, 20% to second, 10% to third, 5% to fourth, 3% tofifth and 2% divided equally among remaining finishers. 126 lbs. Trophies will be presented to the winning owner, trainer and jockey. Closed Saturday, August 14, 2004 with 12 Nominations.

Value of Race: $1,000,000 Winner $600,000; second $200,000; third $100,000; fourth $50,000; fifth $30,000; sixth $10,000; seventh $10,000. Mutuel Pool $2,167,135.00 Exacta Pool $1,280,324.00 Trifecta Pool $1,003,804.00

Last Raced	Horse	M/Eqt.	A.	Wt	PP	¼	½	¾	1	Str	Fin	Jockey	Odds $1
5Jun04 ^{11}Bel^{1}	Birdstone	L	3	126	5	$6^{4½}$	$5^{½}$	$4^{2½}$	$2^{1½}$	$1^{1½}$	$1^{2½}$	Prado E S	4.80
8Aug04 ^{9}Sar^{2}	The Cliff's Edge	L	3	126	6	7	7	$5^{4½}$	$3^{½}$	2^{hd}	$2^{3½}$	Sellers S J	3.15
8Aug04 ^{9}Sar^{4}	Eddington	L b	3	126	1	$3^{1½}$	$3^{2½}$	3^{hd}	4^{hd}	4^{6}	3^{nk}	Migliore R	9.70
8Aug04 ^{9}Sar^{1}	Purge	L	3	126	3	$2^{½}$	2^{1}	2^{1}	1^{hd}	$3^{2½}$	4^{5}	Velazquez J R	4.00
7Aug04 ^{8}Mnr^{1}	Sir Shackleton	L	3	126	4	4^{hd}	$6^{½}$	$6^{½}$	$6^{½}$	5^{5}	$5^{5½}$	Bejarano R	7.20
10Jly04 ^{7}Hol^{2}	Suave	L b	3	126	7	$5^{½}$	$4^{½}$	7	7	$6^{1½}$	$6^{5¼}$	Day P	14.20
8Aug04 ^{13}Mth^{1}	Lion Heart		3	126	2	$1^{1½}$	$1^{1½}$	1^{hd}	$5^{3½}$	7	7	Bravo J	2.60

OFF AT 6:22 Start Good. Won driving. Track fast.

TIME :24^{2}, :49, 1:12^{4}, 1:37, 2:02^{2} (:24.48, :49.15, 1:12.82, 1:37.15, 2:02.45)

$2 Mutuel Prices:

5 – BIRDSTONE	11.60	5.70	4.00
6 – THE CLIFF'S EDGE		3.90	3.00
1 – EDDINGTON			4.30

$2 EXACTA 5–6 PAID $46.40 $2 TRIFECTA 5–6–1 PAID $277.50

B. c, (May), by Grindstone – Dear Birdie , by Storm Bird . Trainer Zito Nicholas P. Bred by Marylou Whitney Stables (Ky).

BIRDSTONE was unhurried in the early stages, angled to the rail approaching the first turn, saved ground entering the backstretch, gradually closed the gap midway down the backstretch, angled out nearing the far turn, moved up three wide to challenge at the quarter pole, took charge in upper stretch, shook off LION HEART to get clear in midstretch then turned back THE CLIFF'S EDGE under steady left hand encouragement. THE CLIFF'S EDGE was outrun in the early stages, trailed for nearly a half, rapidly gained while four wide nearing the far turn, closed the gap from outside leaving the quarter pole, made a run to threaten in midstretch but was no match for the winner. EDDINGTON was taken in hand in the early stages, was rated just behind the leaders along the backstretch, moved out briefly on the turn, angled back to the rail in upper stretch then lacked a strong closing response. PURGE moved up from outside in the early stages, stalked the pace from outside along the backstretch, took up chase after LION HEART midway on the turn, surged to the front nearing the quarter pole, battled into upper stretch and weakened in the final eighth. SIR SHACKLETON was rated along the inside in the early stages, moved between horses along the backstretch, dropped back on the far turn and steadily tired thereafter. SUAVE raced in the middle of the pack while four wide along the backstretch, trailed on the far turn and was never close thereafter. LION HEART rushed up to gain the early advantage, set a moderate pace along the inside to the turn, relinquished the lead nearing the top of the stretch then gave way.

Owners– 1, Marylou Whitney Stables; 2, LaPenta Robert V; 3, Willmott Stables Inc; 4, Starlight Stable LLC Saylor Paul and Martin Johns; 5, Farmer Tracy; 6, Jay Em Ess Stable; 7, Tabor Michael B and Smith Derrick

Trainers– 1, Zito Nicholas P; 2, Zito Nicholas P; 3, Hennig Mark; 4, Pletcher Todd A; 5, Zito Nicholas P; 6, McGee Paul J; 7, Biancone Patrick L

$2 Pick Three (2–3–5) Paid $314.00 ; Pick Three Pool $325,624 .
$2 Pick Four (3–2–3–5) Paid $1,314.00 ; Pick Four Pool $1,479,908 .
$2 Pick Six (9–3–2–3–5–ALL) 6 Correct Paid $1,991.00 ; Pick Six Pool $263,567 .
$2 Pick Six (9–3–2–3–5–ALL) 5 Correct Paid $16.00 .
$2 Daily Double (3–5) Paid $93.00 ; Daily Double Pool $232,322 .
$2 Consolation Pick 3 (3–5–ALL (RACES 10–12)) Paid $90.50 ; Consolation Pick 3 Pool $267,405 .
$2 Consolation Daily Double (5–ALL (RACES 11& 12)) Paid $12.60 ; Consolation Daily Double Pool $421,247 .

Saratoga Attendance: 48,894 Mutuel Pool: $7,391,420.00 ITW Mutuel Pool: $7,027,672.00 ISW Mutuel Pool: $18,653,928.00

ELEVENTH RACE
Saratoga
AUGUST 27, 2005

1¼ MILES. (2.00) 136TH RUNNING OF THE TRAVERS. Grade I. Purse $1,000,000 FOR THREE YEAR OLDS. By subscription of $1,000 each, which should accompany the nomination; $5,000 to pass the entry box, $5,000 to start. The purse to be divided 60% to the winner, 20% to second, 10% to third, 5% to fourth, 3% to fifth and 2% divided equally among remaining finishers. 126 lbs. Trophies will be presented to the winning owner, trainer and jockey. Closed Saturday, August 13, 2005 with 16 Nominations.

Value of Race: $1,000,000 Winner $600,000; second $200,000; third $100,000; fourth $50,000; fifth $30,000; sixth $10,000; seventh $10,000. Mutuel Pool $2,626,345.00 Exacta Pool $1,498,377.00 Trifecta Pool $1,270,319.00

Last Raced	Horse	M/Eqt.	A.	Wt	PP	¼	½	¾	1	Str	Fin	Jockey	Odds $1
30Jly05 ^{9}Sar^{1}	Flower Alley	L b	3	126	7	$2^{½}$	$2^{2½}$	$2^{3½}$	$2^{1½}$	$1^{½}$	$1^{2½}$	Velazquez J R	3.00
7May05 ^{10}CD^{7}	Bellamy Road	L	3	126	1	$1^{2½}$	$1^{½}$	$1^{2½}$	$1^{½}$	$2^{3½}$	$2^{2¾}$	Castellano J J	2.20
7Aug05 ^{12}Mth^{1}	Roman Ruler	L f	3	126	4	$4^{1½}$	$3^{1½}$	$3^{1½}$	$3^{1½}$	$3^{2½}$	$3^{2½}$	Bailey J D	2.15
9Jly05 ^{7}Hol^{5}	Don't Get Mad		3	126	5	6^{6}	5^{hd}	$5^{4½}$	4^{2}	4^{3}	$4^{4¼}$	Prado E S	7.80
30Jly05 ^{9}Sar^{3}	Andromeda's Hero	L b	3	126	2	3^{hd}	4^{5}	4^{3}	$5^{4½}$	$5^{3½}$	$5^{10¼}$	Nakatani C S	15.00
30Jly05 ^{9}Sar^{2}	Reverberate	L b	3	126	6	5^{1}	6^{6}	$6^{3½}$	7	7	$6^{¾}$	Santos J A	15.30
7Aug05 ^{12}Mth^{4}	Chekhov		3	126	3	7	7	7	6^{hd}	6^{2}	7	Stevens G L	17.10

OFF AT 6:33 Start Good. Won driving. Track fast.

TIME :23^{2}, :47^{2}, 1:10^{4}, 1:36^{1}, 2:02^{3} (:23.54, :47.43, 1:10.92, 1:36.38, 2:02.76)

$2 Mutuel Prices:

7 – FLOWER ALLEY	8.00	4.00	2.70
1 – BELLAMY ROAD		4.10	3.00
4 – ROMAN RULER			2.50

$2 EXACTA 7–1 PAID $33.60 $2 TRIFECTA 7–1–4 PAID $53.00

Ch. c, (May), by Distorted Humor – Princess Olivia , by Lycius . Trainer Pletcher Todd A. Bred by George Brunacini & Bona Terra Farms (Ky).

FLOWER ALLEY came away well and took a position to the outside of pacesetter BELLAMY ROAD, stalked that rival for the opening three quarters, was sent after the leader in earnest approaching the stretch, responded to steady left handed pressure and drew clear in the final furlong. BELLAMY ROAD was sent directly to the front, set the pace along the inside, responded when confronted by the winner turning for home, dug in bravely on the rail in the stretch but could not stay with FLOWER ALLEY in the final furlong. ROMAN RULER was taken in hand after the start, was rated along while three wide, advanced three wide on the second turn but had no response when put to the test in upper stretch. DON'T GET MAD was unhurried while outrun along the inside early, put in a good run on the second turn, came wide into the stretch but had little left and faded in the drive. ANDROMEDA'S HERO raced close up along the rail and had no response when roused entering the second turn. REVERBERATE was outrun early, raced three wide and tired after the opening three quarters. CHEKHOV was outrun after a sluggish start, raced inside and had no response when roused.

Owners– 1, Melnyk Racing Stables Inc; 2, Kinsman Stable; 3, Fog City Stable; 4, Hughes B Wayne; 5, LaPenta Robert V; 6, Centennial Farms; 7, Tabor Michael B and Smith Derrick

Trainers– 1, Pletcher Todd A; 2, Zito Nicholas P; 3, Baffert Bob; 4, Ellis Ronald W; 5, Zito Nicholas P; 6, Russo Sal; 7, Biancone Patrick L

$2 Pick Three (2–3–7) Paid $36.80 ; Pick Three Pool $269,734 .
$2 Pick Four (6–2–3–7) Paid $62.50 ; Pick Four Pool $1,659,766 .
$2 Daily Double (3–7) Paid $11.60 ; Daily Double Pool $215,266 .

ELEVENTH RACE
Saratoga
AUGUST 26, 2006

1¼ MILES. (2.00) 137TH RUNNING OF THE TRAVERS. Grade I. Purse $1,000,000 FOR THREE YEAR OLDS. By subscription of $1,000 each, which should accompany the nomination; $5,000 to pass the entry box, $5,000 to start. The purse to be divided 60% to the winner, 20% to second, 10% to third, 5% to fourth, 3% to fifth and 2% divided equally among remaining finishers. 126 lbs. Trophies will be presented to the winning owner, trainer and jockey. Closed Saturday, August 12, 2006 with 16 Nominations.

Value of Race: $1,000,000 Winner $600,000; second $200,000; third $100,000; fourth $50,000; fifth $30,000; sixth $20,000. Mutuel Pool $2,594,322.00 Exacta Pool $1,562,009.00 Trifecta Pool $1,435,637.00

Last Raced	Horse	M/Eqt.	A.	Wt	PP	¼	½	¾	1	Str	Fin	Jockey	Odds $1
29Jly06 ^{9}Sar^{1}	Bernardini	L	3	126	5	$1^{1½}$	$1^{½}$	$1^{½}$	1^{1}	$1^{4½}$	$1^{7½}$	Castellano J J	0.35
6Aug06 ^{12}Mth^{1}	Bluegrass Cat	L f	3	126	6	3^{2}	$2^{2½}$	2^{1}	$2^{3½}$	2^{6}	$2^{6¼}$	Velazquez J R	2.70
29Jly06 ^{9}Sar^{4}	Dr. Pleasure	L	3	126	3	6	5^{hd}	$5^{3½}$	4^{6}	$4^{3½}$	3^{1}	Velasquez C	40.50
29Jly06 ^{3}Sar^{1}	Hesanoldsalt	L b	3	126	1	$4^{1½}$	$4^{2½}$	4^{hd}	$3^{½}$	3^{1}	4^{4}	Coa E M	34.25
15Jly06 ^{13}Tdn^{2}	High Cotton	L	3	126	4	2^{hd}	$3^{½}$	3^{hd}	$5^{1½}$	5^{hd}	$5^{2¼}$	Gomez G K	15.10
29Jly06 ^{9}Sar^{2}	Minister's Bid	L	3	126	2	$5^{½}$	6	6	6	6	6	Prado E S	12.40

OFF AT 6:33 Start Good. Won ridden out. Track fast.

TIME :23^{2}, :48, 1:12^{3}, 1:36^{4}, 2:01^{3} (:23.53, :48.17, 1:12.72, 1:36.83, 2:01.60)

$2 Mutuel Prices:

5 – BERNARDINI	2.70	2.10	2.10
7 – BLUEGRASS CAT		2.50	2.60
3 – DR. PLEASURE			4.70

$2 EXACTA 5–7 PAID $5.00 $2 TRIFECTA 5–7–3 PAID $35.20

B. c, (Mar), by A.P. Indy – Cara Rafaela , by Quiet American . Trainer Albertrani Thomas. Bred by Darley (Ky).

BERNARDINI moved up between horses to take the lead while in hand entering the first turn, set the pace under mild pressure while slightly off the rail along the the backstretch, dug in when challenged by BLUEGRASS CAT midway on the turn, opened a comfortable advantage in upper stretch, extended his lead when tapped once with the left hand whip leaving the furlong marker then drew away under confident handling through the final sixteenth. BLUEGRASS CAT moved up from outside to engage the early leaders, stalked the pace three wide for six furlongs, took a run outside the winner to threaten midway on the turn, lodged another mild bid from outside at the quarter pole but was no match for BERNARDINI while clearly best of the others. DR. PLEASURE checked after being pinched back at the start, was unhurried for six furlongs, moved between horses to launch his bid leaving the far turn, chased the leaders to the top of the stretch and lacked a strong closing bid. HESANOLDSALT stumbled at the start, settled in good position for a half, angled four wide along the backstretch, closed the gap a bit from outside on the far turn, remained a factor to the top of the stretch and steadily tired thereafter. HIGH COTTON raced in close contention along the inside for seven furlongs, swung out on the turn and lacked a further response. MINISTER'S BID fractious in the gate prior to the start, checked while being pinched back at the start then trailed throughout while saving ground.

Owners– 1, Darley Stable; 2, WinStar Farm LLC; 3, Oxley John C; 4, Live Oak Plantation; 5, Peachtree Stable; 6, Oxley John C

Trainers– 1, Albertrani Thomas; 2, Pletcher Todd A; 3, Ward John T Jr; 4, Zito Nicholas P; 5, Pletcher Todd A; 6, Ward John T Jr

Scratched– Kip Deville (15Jul06 ^{9}Cnl^{6})

$2 Pick Three (1–2–5) Paid $7.60 ; Pick Three Pool $351,874 .
$2 Pick Four (7–1–2–5) Paid $58.00 ; Pick Four Pool $1,466,611 .
$2 Pick Six (1–6–7–1–2–5) 6 Correct Paid $515.00 ; Pick Six Pool $329,081 .
$2 Pick Six (1–6–7–1–2–5) 5 Correct Paid $13.60 .
$2 Daily Double (2–5) Paid $5.40 ; Daily Double Pool $209,738 .

NINTH RACE
Saratoga
AUGUST 25, 2007

1¼ MILES. (2.00) 138TH RUNNING OF THE TRAVERS. Grade I. Purse $1,000,000 FOR THREE YEAR OLDS. By subscription of $1,000 each, which should accompany the nomination; $5,000 to pass the entry box, $5,000 to start. The purse to be divided 60% to the winner, 20% to second, 10% to third, 5% to fourth, 3% to fifth and 2% divided equally among remaining finishers. 126 lbs. Trophies will be presented to the winning owner, trainer and jockey. Closed Saturday, August 11, 2007 with 24 Nominations.

Value of Race: $1,000,000 Winner $600,000; second $200,000; third $100,000; fourth $50,000; fifth $30,000; sixth $10,000; seventh $10,000. Mutuel Pool $2,930,849.00 Exacta Pool $1,416,349.00 Trifecta Pool $1,092,653.00 Superfecta Pool $344,510.00 Grand Slam Pool $112,812.00

Last Raced	Horse	M/Eqt.	A.	Wt	PP	¼	½	¾	1	Str	Fin	Jockey	Odds $1
29Jly07 ^{9}Sar^{1}	Street Sense	L f	3	126	4	4^{2}	$3^{½}$	$3^{½}$	$2^{2½}$	1^{hd}	$1^{½}$	Borel C H	0.35
30Jly07 ^{6}Sar^{1}	Grasshopper	L	3	126	5	$2^{2½}$	1^{1}	$1^{½}$	1^{hd}	2^{8}	$2^{10¼}$	Albarado R J	9.60
5Aug07 ^{8}Sar^{4}	Helsinki	L	3	126	1	7	7	7	6^{8}	6^{20}	3^{nk}	Leparoux J R	49.75
29Jly07 ^{9}Sar^{3}	Sightseeing	L b	3	126	7	$6^{5½}$	6^{7}	6^{6}	$5^{2½}$	$3^{½}$	$4^{5½}$	Prado E S	4.60
29Jly07 ^{9}Sar^{2}	C P West	L	3	126	2	1^{hd}	$2^{½}$	$2^{½}$	$4^{½}$	$4^{2½}$	$5^{5¾}$	Velasquez C	8.50
5Aug07 ^{8}Sar^{1}	Loose Leaf	L b	3	126	6	$5^{½}$	4^{hd}	4^{hd}	3^{hd}	$5^{½}$	6	Desormeaux K J	22.20
25Jly07 ^{9}AP^{3}	For You Reppo	L	3	126	3	3^{hd}	$5^{½}$	$5^{½}$	7	7	—	Gomez G K	46.25

OFF AT 5:40 Start Good. Won driving. Track fast.

TIME :23^{3}, :48, 1:12^{2}, 1:36^{4}, 2:02^{3} (:23.68, :48.18, 1:12.43, 1:36.93, 2:02.69)

$2 Mutuel Prices:

4 – STREET SENSE	2.70	2.20	2.10
5 – GRASSHOPPER		4.60	3.80
1 – HELSINKI			7.80

$2 EXACTA 4–5 PAID $13.00 $2 TRIFECTA 4–5–1 PAID $216.00
$2 SUPERFECTA 4–5–1–7 PAID $742.00

Dk. b or br. c, (Feb), by Street Cry-Ire – Bedazzle , by Dixieland Band . Trainer Nafzger Carl A. Bred by James Tafel (Ky).

STREET SENSE moved up from outside going into the first turn, raced in hand while stalking the leaders along the backstretch, launched a bid three wide leaving the far turn, closed the gap from outside while remaining in hand approaching the quarter pole, drew along side GRASSHOPPER to challenge in upper stretch, battled heads apart outside that rival into midstretch, surged to the front under strong right hand urging to take the lead nearing the sixteenth pole then edged away a bit while switched to the left hand whip in the final seventy yards. GRASSHOPPER angled to the rail after taking the lead on the first turn, set the pace under pressure for seven furlongs, dug in when challenged by the winner in upper stretch, battled gamely along the inside into deep stretch before yielding grudgingly. HELSINKI raced far back for six furlongs, advanced inside on the turn, swung wide in upper stretch and lacked a strong closing bid. SIGHTSEEING was unhurried for six furlongs while between horses, split horses while gaining slightly in upper stretch, bumped with LOOSE LEAF and lacked a strong closing response. C P WEST checked slightly and angled outside the pacesetter leaving the first turn, pressed the pace between horses to the far turn and drifted out while tiring in the stretch. LOOSE LEAF stalked four wide along the backstretch, lodged a mild outside bid on the turn, bumped with SIGHTSEEING and stumbled at the three-sixteenths pole then gave way. FOR YOU REPPO saved ground to the turn, gave way and was eased late.

Owners– 1, James B Tafel; 2, Farish William S and Hudson Jr E J; 3, Four Roses Thoroughbreds; 4, Phipps Stable; 5, LaPenta Robert V; 6, Steve Stan Stables; 7, Gessler Jr Carl Samotowka Michael

Trainers– 1, Nafzger Carl A; 2, Howard Neil J; 3, Zito Nicholas P; 4, McGaughey III Claude R; 5, Zito Nicholas P; 6, McPeek Kenneth G; 7, Pitts Helen

$2 Daily Double (3–4) Paid $5.90 ; Daily Double Pool $191,538 .
$2 Grand Slam (6/10–12–1/2/3–1/3/9–4) Paid $28.40 ; Grand Slam Pool $112,812 .

ACKNOWLEDGEMENTS

Although *The History and Art of 25 Travers* represents the work of an author and an artist, it is also a result of the collective efforts of people with a love of Saratoga and one of horse racing's most treasured competitions. In many cases, complete strangers stepped forward to donate their assistance, advice, time, or resources.

Ione, also known as Carole Ione Lewis, the daughter of Spuyten Duyvil co-proprietor Leighla Whipper Ford, searched through her mother's scrapbook to find the engaging photo of the restaurant for the chapter entitled "What's Your Pleasure?".

Other photos arrived from many sources, including the National Sporting Library in Middleburg, Virginia, where Liz Tobey, a director of research, rummaged through archived copies of *The Blood-Horse* magazines, located the Skip Dickstein shots that were needed, and scanned them for the publisher. Similar scanning assistance was provided by Beth McCoy, an art director for *The Blood-Horse* magazine. Sarah Dorroh of the *Thoroughbred Times* came up with several vintage racing shots.

Dickstein, photographer for the Albany *Times Union* newspaper, was the prime contributor of photography. He is a true artist with the camera and a dear friend and co-worker of Greg Montgomery. His shots anchor the text of each chapter in visual reality.

Mike Spain, associate editor of the *Times Union*, made it possible to access a treasure trove of photographic images created by the newspaper's extraordinary group of photographers. Nancy Down, Head Librarian at the Ray and Pat Browne Library for Popular Culture Studies at Bowling Green State University, supplied the NEA Service photos. Rising star photographer Eric Patterson, who donated two exceptional shots of Street Sense, receives a nod for generosity.

Mary Diaz, assistant to Charles Hayward, president of the New York Racing Association, convinced track photographer Adam Coglianese to look for his father Bob's shots from the pre-digital age of 1986 to 1995.

Hayward himself threw his support behind the project. His wife, Betsy Senior, an art gallery owner in New York, was instrumental in guiding us to Rich Rosenbush at the *Daily Racing Form*, where Hayward used to serve as president. Rosenbush, the *Form's* editor-in-chief, made the official Travers charts available.

Jon Forbes, a graduate of the Race Track Industry Program at the University of Arizona, was responsible for the informational sidebars that complement the text. The program's Associate Coordinator Steve Barham identified Forbes as the person to organize the materials.

Additional research was provided by Allan Carter, staff historian of the National Museum of Racing in Saratoga Springs. Victoria Garlanda and Teri Blasko of the Saratoga Room at the Saratoga Springs Public Library were helpful whenever asked.

Another leader in the Saratoga Springs community, Executive Director of the Saratoga Arts Council Joel Reed, deserves thanks for widening the opportunity for everyone to see the Travers posters. John and Janice DeMarco of Lyrical Ballad Bookstore steered us to Reed and also to North Country Books, the publisher.

Cathy Schenk and Phyllis Rogers were accommodating hosts at the Keeneland Library, where facts were checked and memories confirmed by stories that were written during the time when the races were run by contributors of the *Thoroughbred Times*, *The Blood-Horse*, and the *Daily Racing Form*.

Mike Brunker, horse racing editor of MSNBC.com, read through all the chapters, checked them for accuracy, and proved over and again that a writer is only as good as his editor.

Special thanks go out to Rob Igoe, Jr., of North Country Books, who accommodated ideas for making the book as beautiful as possible, and Zach Steffen, his right-hand man, who painstakingly pored over proofs and served as an understanding liaison. The staff at Nancy Did It!, the publisher's book designers, became a guiding force in terms of the book's appearance.

Paula Rosenberg was tireless in her counsel; perfect in her judgment regarding the book's quality and content, and supportive with her encouragement to have deadlines met. There's a small canoe in the right-hand panel of Montgomery's Travers triptych on page 116 which is a bow to Rosenberg's insistence. But, in truth, she's a woman who is deserving of a yacht.

Finally, several people made possible the creation of the Travers posters with their support throughout the length of the period Montgomery has produced them.

Karene Faul, chair of the art department at the College of St. Rose in Albany, New York, patiently instructed Montgomery in the art and science of silk printing and opened her college's facility on weekends and nights to allow him to pursue his art.

Marianne and Dave Barker of Impressions of Saratoga, Vito and Lynn Soavé of Soavé Faire, and Jill Hunegs and Judith Belt-Smith of Designers Studio provided the artist with friendship and places where Saratoga's art lovers and horse lovers could trade. Mary Ellen and Dave Smith have fulfilled poster orders taken online.

Opposite: **The small pieces of metal that form a bit are all it takes for a jockey to control a mighty thoroughbred.** Albany (NY) *Times Union* photograph by Skip Dickstein

REFERENCES

The Blood-Horse
Blood-Horse Publications, Lexington, Kentucky

Daily Racing Form
Daily Racing Form LLC, New York, New York

ESPN.com
ESPN Inc., Bristol, Connecticut

Google.com
Google Inc., Mountainview, California

The New York Times
The New York Times Company, New York, New York

The Record (Bergen County)
North Jersey Media Group, Hackensack, New Jersey

The Saratogian
Journal Register Company, Yardley, Pennsylvania

The Syracuse Post-Standard
Advance Publications, Charlotte, North Carolina

The Thoroughbred Record
Lexington, Kentucky

Thoroughbred Times
Thoroughbred Times Co. Inc., Lexington, Kentucky

The Times Union
Capital Newspapers
Division of The Hearst Corporation, Albany, New York

YouTube.com
Google Inc., Mountainview, California

An exercise rider takes a moment to enjoy the beautiful morning sun at the Oklahoma training track adjacent to the Saratoga Race Course. Albany (NY) *Times Union* photograph by Skip Dickstein

142